THE ONLY
BUSINESS
BOOK
YOU'LL EVER
NEED

Published by CelebrityPress™, Orlando, FL
A division of The Celebrity Branding Agency®

Celebrity Branding® is a registered trademark
Printed in the United States of America.

ISBN: 9780983947035
LCCN: 2011942685

This publication is designed to provide accurate and authoritative information with regard to the subject matter covered. It is sold with the understanding that the publisher is not engaged in rendering legal, accounting, or other professional advice. If legal advice or other expert assistance is required, the services of a competent professional should be sought. The opinions expressed by the authors in this book are not endorsed by CelebrityPress™ and are the sole responsibility of the author rendering the opinion.

Most CelebrityPress™ titles are available at special quantity discounts for bulk purchases for sales promotions, premiums, fundraising, and educational use. Special versions or book excerpts can also be created to fit specific needs.

For more information, please write:

CelebrityPress™,
520 N. Orlando Ave, #2
Winter Park, FL 32789

or call 1.877.261.4930

Visit us online at www.CelebrityPressPublishing.com

THE ONLY
BUSINESS
BOOK
YOU'LL EVER
NEED

Contents

CHAPTER 1

The 12 Keys to Business Success

By Brian Tracy

"Action without planning is the cause of every failure."
~ Peter Drucker

There is a rule that, "Before you do anything, you have to do something else first." The first thing you have to do in business is to plan, plan again, and keep planning until your plans work consistently to get you the results you want. The major reasons for business failure are, first of all, failing to plan in advance, and second of all, failing to revise your plans if they do not work for some reason. *Failing to plan is planning to fail.*

What is the highest paid work in business? Answer: *Thinking!* Thinking is the highest paid work because of a special factor called "consequences."

You can always determine how valuable and important something is by measuring the potential consequences of doing it or not doing it. The potential consequences of having a cup of coffee or chatting with a coworker are virtually zero. It does not matter at all whether you do them or not. But the consequences of planning, of thinking through your actions before you begin, can be enormous. They can make all the difference between success and failure, poverty and wealth, happiness and unhappiness, a life of affluence or a life of despair.

Everything you are or ever will be is the result of your choices and decisions. Your choices and decisions have brought you to where you are today. If you are not happy about your current situation, then you must make new choices and better decisions for the future. There is no other way. The essential ingredient for both choices and decision-making is thinking.

THE 12 KEYS TO BUSINESS SUCCESS

There are 12 critical areas where your ability to think largely determines the success or failure of your business. The greater clarity you have in each of these areas, the better decisions you will make and the better results you will achieve.

1. **Key Purpose:** What is the purpose of a business? Many people think that the purpose of a business is to earn a profit, but they are wrong. The true purpose of a business is to *create and keep a customer.* Profits are the result of creating and keeping a sufficient number of customers in a cost-effective way.

   Fully 50% of your time, efforts and expenses should be focused on creating and keeping customers in some way. The number one reason for business problems is the failure to attract and keep a sufficient number of customers at the prices that you need to charge to make a profit and grow your business.

2. **Key Measure:** The key measure of business success is *customer satisfaction.* The key determinant of growth and profitability, is your ability to satisfy your customers to such a degree that they buy from you rather than from someone else, that they buy again, and that they bring their friends.

   What is the most important sale? It is the second sale! You can acquire customers initially through discounts, special offers and even deception. But it is only when the customer buys for the second time that he proves to you that you have delivered on your promises and satisfied his expectations. The second sale is the true measure of customer satisfaction.

3. **Key Requirement:** The key requirement for wealth building and business success is for you to *add value* in some way. All wealth comes from adding value. All business growth and profitability comes from adding value. Every day, you must be looking for ways to add more and more value to the customer experience.

You can add value in many ways – increasing quality, lowering costs, accelerating delivery, improving customer satisfaction, and satisfying customer needs faster, better or cheaper than your competitors. The ways you can add value are only limited by your imagination.

The one thing that all customers buy, no matter what the product or service, is "improvement." Your goal must be to improve the life or work of your customer in some way, and continue doing so, more and more. By adding value, you create enough value so that you can keep some for yourself. This is called profit.

4. **Key Focus:** The most important person in the business is *the customer.* You must focus on the customer at all times. Customers are fickle, disloyal, changeable, impatient and demanding, just like you. Nonetheless, the customer must be the central focus of everything you do in business.

Sam Walton once said, "We have only one boss, and that is the customer, and he can fire us at any time by simply buying from someone else."

The two great rules for business success are: Rule Number One - The customer is always right; and Rule Number Two – If ever you are in doubt, refer back to Rule Number One.

5. **Key Word:** In life, work and business, you will always be rewarded in direct proportion to the value of your *contribution* to others, as they see it. The focus on outward contribution, to your company, your customers, and your community, is the central requirement for you to become an ever more valuable person, in every area.

Every day you must be looking for ways to increase the value of your contribution. You must be looking for ways to do your job and satisfy your customers better, faster or cheaper.

Everything you learn that you can apply to increase the value of your contribution increases the value of your life and your rewards.

6. **Key Question:** The most important question you ask, to solve any problem, overcome any obstacle or achieve any business goal is the question *"How?"*

Most things that you try in business won't work, at least the first few times. All of business life is a process of trial and error. Over and over, you must ask, "How can we do this? How can we solve this problem? How can we achieve this level of sales and profitability? How can we overcome this obstacle?" Top people always ask the question, *how* and then act on the answers that come to them.

7. **Key Strategy:** In a world of rapid change and continuing, aggressive competition, you must practice ***continuous improvement*** in every area of your business and personal life.

As Pat Riley, the basketball coach, said, "If you're not getting better, you're getting worse."

Never be satisfied. Dedicate yourself to "continuous and never ending improvement" (CANEI). Practice the Japanese method of "Kaizen," which means "continuous betterment."

Continually seek faster, better, cheaper, easier and more efficient ways to generate leads, make sales, produce products and services, deliver them satisfactorily while satisfying your customers so that they come back and buy, continuously. By constantly improving what you are doing, in every area, you will eventually become one of the leading businesses in your industry.

8. **Key Activity:** The heartbeat of your business is ***sales.*** Dunn & Bradstreet analyzed thousands of companies that had gone broke over the years and concluded that the number one reason for business failure was "low sales." When they researched further, they found that the number one reason for business success was "high sales" and all else was commentary.

Morning, noon and night, the best brains, talents and energies of your business must be focused on generating more and better sales from more and better customers. Whenever I have faced a business slowdown or financial problem, my motto has always been, "When in doubt, sell your way out!" This should be your guiding principle as well.

All successful companies have well-organized sales systems, which they continuously improve, every single day. All day long, from the time you start in the morning, you and your whole company must think about and work on sales.

9. Key Number: The most important number in business is *cash flow.* Cash flow is to the business as blood and oxygen is to the brain. You can have every activity working efficiently in your business, but if your cash flow is cut off for any reason, the business can die, sometimes overnight.

As a business owner, you must keep your eye on the cash at all times. Focus on cash flow. Think about cash flow. Ask questions about cash flow. Never allow yourself to run out of cash, no matter what hard decisions you have to make or sacrifices you have to engage in. Cash is king.

10. Key Goal: Every business must have a *growth plan.* Growth must be the goal of all of your business activities. You should have a goal to grow 10%, 20% or even 30% each year. Some companies grow 50% and 100% per year, and not by accident.

The only real growth is profit growth. Profit growth is always measurable in what is called "free cash flow." Above and beyond the total cost and expense of running the business, "free cash flow" is the actual amount of money that the business throws off each month, quarter and year,

You should have a growth plan for the number of new leads you attract, and the number of new customers you acquire from those leads. You should have a growth plan for sales, revenues and profitability. If you do not deliberately plan for continuous growth, you will automatically stagnate and begin to fall behind. Growth is not an accident. It is something that is planned and pursued every single day.

11. Key Quality: The most important quality to assure your success is your level of *determination.* Even though it takes a good deal of courage to start a new business, more than two million people make this leap each year. Thus, initial courage is not enough.

As soon as you start a new business, you immediately begin to experience unexpected problems, setbacks, reversals, obstacles and even temporary failure. When you hit the wall in your business, it will be your level of determination that will see you through.

One of the most important techniques I ever learned was the power of mentally pre-programming yourself in advance of the problem or setback, even when you do not know what it will be. The way you do this is to say to yourself, *"No matter what happens in my business, I will never, never give up."* Repeat this over and over.

By programming your mind with this command, you will be psychologically and emotionally prepared to bounce back and keep on going. But if you have not preprogrammed yourself, you will be in danger of hesitating and even giving up when the going gets rough.

12. **Key Result:** When you apply the first eleven keys to your business life, the result you will enjoy is the ***success and financial independence*** you set out for in the beginning.

Your ultimate goal in business is to reach the point where you have enough money so that you never have to worry about money again. This is called "the number."

How much will you need to acquire before you know that you have enough and that everything else you earn is icing on the cake? For each person, "the number" will be different. What is yours?

STARTING OVER AGAIN TODAY

If you were starting your business over again, and you had to focus all your energy on selling just one or a few products or services, which ones would you choose? Which customers would you dedicate yourself to serving better and better? Which sales and marketing activities yield the best results?

Which people and processes are the most efficient and effective in your business? Where and how can you focus your time and attention to get better business results? These are the key questions in planning. The answers change continually as your business evolves and grows.

Finally, based on your answers to the questions above, what actions should you take immediately to build a more profitable business? What is the first action you should take? When are you going to take it? Who is going to be responsible? Whatever you decide to do, remember that action-orientation is the hallmark of successful entrepreneurs. Once they make a decision they move fast, without procrastination or delay. You must do the same.

About Brian

Brian Tracy is Chairman and CEO of Brian Tracy International, a company specializing in the training and development of individuals and organizations. Brian's goal is to help people achieve their personal and business goals faster and easier than they ever imagined.

Brian Tracy has consulted for more than 1,000 companies and addressed more than 5,000,000 people in 5,000 talks and seminars throughout the US, Canada and 56 other countries worldwide. As a Keynote speaker and seminar leader, he addresses more than 250,000 people each year.

For more information on Brian Tracy programs, go to: www.briantracy.com

CHAPTER 2

NO FLUFF, NO BS: SOCIAL MEDIA STRATEGIES FOR RESULTS

By John Souza

"Social Networking that matters is helping people achieve their goals. Doing it reliably and repeatability, so that, over time, people have an interest in helping you achieve your goals."

- Seth Godin, Seth's Blog

A couple of years ago, a woman received a job offer from corporate giant Cisco. Maybe she wasn't as grateful as she should have been, however... because she quickly sent out the following Tweet:

"Cisco just offered me a job! Now I have to weigh the utility of a fatty pay-check against the daily commute to San Jose and hating the work."

She also wasn't as smart as *she* should have been - because, a little while later, a Cisco associate tweeted back:

"Who is the hiring manager. I'm sure they would love to know that you will hate the work. We here at Cisco are versed in the web."

What's the moral of the story here? Simple. If you think only your

23

friends are paying attention to what you're doing on social media, you're both courting disaster and dismissing incredible opportunities. Social media is not just a fad and it's not just a place for teenagers to talk trash or relatives to share family photos - it's a genuine international cultural shift that affects every aspect of modern life today.

Fact: Social media can bring down politicians. Congressman Anthony Weiner was forced to resign when he accidentally sent out a sexually suggestive picture to everyone following his Twitter feed, rather than just to the woman he was flirting with. Another congressman, Chris Lee, also had to step down after flirting with women on Craigslist.

Fact: Social media can bring down celebrities. Comedian Gilbert Gott-fried, the voice of the annoying duck on all those Aflac commercials, was dropped by the insurance company after he tweeted some tasteless jokes about the tsunami that struck Japan. Charlie Sheen sealed his own fate on the hit sitcom, "Two and a Half Men," when he repeatedly insulted its producer over Twitter.

Fact: Social media *can now take down entire governments*. I'm not exaggerating. Look at what happened in Egypt, Libya and other countries that experienced the so-called "Arab Spring" - those demonstrations and revolutions were organized on Twitter and Facebook. Look at what happened in our own country when coast-to-coast protests against Wall Street seemed to spontaneously break out - again, the Internet enabled those people to communicate and band together, regardless of what you might think of the politics involved.

If you're still saying to yourself, "Well, social media isn't really about business. It's not going to do that much for me." Then you're still really not seeing the big picture any more than that young woman who broadcast her displeasure at the thought of working at Cisco over Twitter, did.

Facebook at this moment has over 800 million members in its community. Only two countries have more residents than that - China and India. How could it be possible that that many people are participating - and that none of them are either current or potential users of your business? Short answer - it's not. Even LinkedIn now has over 150 million members - and those are all businesspeople, with the majority residing in the U.S.A.

Here's probably the most relevant figure to you: Over 88% of all entrepreneurs and career professionals are now using social media in one form or another. You may not like it, you may not want to participate in it, but the truth is social media is here to stay.

The good news is the majority of business users have no idea of how to use it effectively to build their client list and grow their companies. That means if you're ready make an intelligent investment in social media marketing, you've got a relatively open field for your own online success.

FROM FINANCE TO FACEBOOK

My background is a great deal different from most people who work in the social media industry. I graduated from business school and worked for the next ten years at three of the top investment firms in the country. That means, from the beginning, I was trained to focus on the bottom line. Believe me, I wouldn't even be in this field if I didn't already know that social media mastery yields real bottom-line gains.

Ironically, however, my decade in the investment industry actually prepared me for social media. I learned during that time that leveraging my relationships helped me expand my presence, and, by doing so, I was able to achieve really significant results. Fast-forward to today, where I've found a very natural progression to that path to success in social media. It enables you to take extra steps to increase your visibility to people you never would have had a shot at reaching before.

With all that in mind, I founded and became the CEO of Social Media Magic, a social media training provider and done-for-you solutions firm. Our company's success has been incredibly gratifying; we were recently named one of the best social media services by Mashable. com, the top independent online news site, and we're also a finalist for "Forbes" magazine's "Most Promising Companies" list. Our reputation for professionalism and our ability to fully understand business needs has attracted elite clients such as SAP, the largest enterprise software company in the world, who came to us for help in handling their social media marketing.

That reputation comes from insisting on doing things right and that make business sense. I sometimes get frustrated by all the empty propaganda being put out there about social media; most presenters and speakers on the subject are just trying to sell their services without really thinking about how to deliver the kinds of results that are crucial to success.

I understand the importance of these results and we work hard to achieve them for our clients. And it's a complex task, because social media marketing goes far beyond the traditional kind of marketing that was done before the internet; it's one thing to be able to create an effective sales one-sheet, another to master and utilize the multifaceted online interfaces built around social media today.

That's why our Social Media Marketing University only employs individual experts in Facebook, LinkedIn, Twitter and other specific disciplines. This kind of specialization is key to both keeping up with these services and being able to fully leverage them to meet our clients' business goals.

SOCIAL MEDIA BUSINESS STRATEGY

When it comes to an overall social media strategy, there are a few important rules to keep in mind.

First, some basic branding common sense - keep your personality and messaging consistent. You want to build a solid and steady business identity across all services that people can easily identify over time. Whether you're quirky or a straight-ahead professional is up to you and what your brand is all about. Just remember, casual works on Facebook, but not so well on LinkedIn.

Also remember Anthony Weiner and Charlie Sheen - never tempt fate by sending out any questionable content to anyone on your business or personal account. There is no rewind switch - once you click the "Send" button, your message or photo is history - as could you, depending on what that message or photo contains!

Secondly, you shouldn't approach social media with a promoter mentality. You don't have a sale on Tuesday, a two-for-one deal on Wednesday, a special introductory offer on Thursday, and so forth. Constant commercials turn everyone off and that's no way to begin a conversation.

Third, and most importantly, that's just how you need to think about doing social media - as if you're having an ongoing conversation with your potential and current customer base. That conversation must be organic, must be interesting and must be more about your audience's needs than yours.

That conversation, over time, should also establish you as a thought-leader in your particular field or expertise. And it should also be used to help your customers create products they would want to buy from you.

This is where social media can really save you a lot of money. Imagine if you wanted to do a test ad campaign for a product on television or radio - you'd have pay to produce the ads, book the time on the stations, study the results carefully, and do the whole process over again until you felt you were ready to break it nationally.

Or imagine you think you have a killer product that everyone is just dying to buy - so you just roll it out without testing. What happens if it completely bombs? 95% of all experienced entrepreneurs will tell you they've had exactly 'that horror story' happen to them.

Social media helps you prevent either one of those expensive scenarios from happening. Now you can survey thousands of people at one time on a real time basis about a potential product - and get real time feedback. Now, this is different than being a hardcore promoter - in this case, you're engaging an audience and asking their opinion about something they might be interested in. Since there's no sell involved, they're comfortable in answering. And if it's a product worth pursuing, they'll be responsive and let you know what they like about it and don't like about it.

They'll also tell you if they'd buy it. Isn't that a pretty good thing to know?

The truth is that this is all valuable information that's a potential gold-mine to any business - and you can access it at no cost beyond the basic expense of your social media marketing operation.

INVESTING IN SOCIAL MEDIA

By the way, I'm not one of those people that's going to go on and on about how social media is completely free. I don't believe it is free - not if you want to be successful at it. Your company needs to have a sub-stantial social media strategy in place - and that requires a significant investment in that strategy. The Dell computer company is one business that understands that. "We have 10,000 Dell employees trained as social media professionals," says Susan Beebe, Dell's Chief Listener, "but we want a lot more people at Dell trained to be brand ambassadors." In fact, Beebe wants to see *everyone* at Dell trained in social media.

You can't just hand off social media to your current marketing person and expect him or her to take care of it in addition to your overall marketing. You need additional resources, because you probably don't have the necessary skill sets internally - and, even if you do, you and your people probably don't have the time to implement a proper social media campaign.

This is why many companies come to us; because social media training and management solutions is what we do and we're completely focused on achieving success in that arena. We function as a part of our clients' marketing departments to help fulfill their existing brands' power and extend it across the social media services.

Another important thing to remember is that these services are changing all the time. Our Facebook expert wrote a book on the site, and, by the time it was finally published, half of it was already outdated. We have to work hard to keep up with the never-ending changes, and, again, most companies just don't have the resources to keep current on their own. Many come to our Social Media Marketing University just to find out how to make sense of everything and focus on what yields results.

This constant change is why strategies have to be monitored and adjusted as needed. You also have to build to achieve the viral approach that everyone is after. Proper planning, implementation and execution are vital to social media as it is to any other endeavor - but when you see things going sideways, you have to be able (and willing) to change up your strategy so you don't jeopardize the results you're after.

THE 11 KEYS TO SOCIAL MEDIA SUCCESS

At Social Media Marketing University, we provide results-based social media instruction on how to listen, learn and implement successful campaigns. We also provide what we believe to be the 11 Keys to Social Media Success, and I'd like to briefly run down the essentials of those keys right now:

Key #1: Leverage LinkedIn to become a thought leader.
LinkedIn, as I noted, is the number one strictly-business social media online destination - and the way you become a star on the site is to become an active participant in groups. Join relevant groups where you know you'll find your best potential customers. Monitor the discussions,

and then identify areas where you can share your unique perspective in order to distinguish yourself as a subject matter expert. It's a great way to showcase your expertise and attract new business.

Key #2: Use blogs to foster relationships.

Your blog should be a significant part of the social media marketing mix - and that means you should take a social approach to it, by utilizing the commenting feature on other blogs as much as possible. This way you can drive traffic back to your blog site or to your website and also increase exposure to you, your expertise and your brand. It's an excellent method to build relationships and create conversations with you as the leader.

Key #3: Integrate video into your social media marketing mix.

73% of small business owners who are integrating social media into their marketing mix are using YouTube. And they're using it to tell their stories much more effectively and efficiently than they could with written content; keyword title videos also help drive web traffic and improve search engine rankings.

Key #4: Leverage mobile to drive business.

Mobile is now one of the fastest-growing marketing platforms. Not only is it cost-effective, but because of the exponential growth in cell phone usage across the world, mobile has enormous potential to help you reach a larger market, increase visibility and build your business.

Key #5: Use Facebook to find your best customers.

As mentioned, Facebook has hundreds of millions of active users - and these users are interacting with 900 million pages, groups, events and community pages when they log on. Capitalize on this level of activity by creating your own pages, as well as accessing relevant pages to connect with your best customers on Facebook.

Key #6: Integrate Search Engine Optimization (SEO).

SEO raises your website's profile and delivers more traffic, customers and bigger revenues. The keywords you use are the cornerstone to any effective SEO strategy, so you want to make sure you thoroughly research which words and phrases are going to attract your best customers. There are millions of searches performed daily - to get the maximum return, put in place a strong SEO strategy for not only your website, but blog posts and all of your social sites as well.

Key #7: Use high performance Pay-Per-Click campaigns.

Pay-Per-Click campaigns, also known as PPC or Sponsored Search, bring you a lot of benefits. Even though there is a cost involved here, you can tailor your PPC campaign to your budget at the same time you tailor it to your marketing goals, so that it still costs less than traditional advertising. Another benefit of PPC is that you can easily track the performance of your campaign to determine how effective it is, and implement needed changes quickly as needed.

Key #8: Implement powerful email marketing strategies.

Both Living Social and Groupon are huge testaments to the power of email marketing. Even though the latter company hasn't been well run from a business perspective, their popularity has been so huge that Google offered seven billion dollars to buy them out. When doing email marketing, make sure you have a targeted mailing list, make sure that your messaging is consistent and appeals to your target group, and do regular testing to determine the level of frequency that your list will allow. If you do those three things, you'll have great success with email marketing.

Key #9: Use strategic PR that's integrated with your social media presence.

When you integrate social and traditional media, you have the opportunity to spread your message even further than ever before. Before social media, we often relied on the news media to broadcast our messages to mainstream audiences for us. Social media now gives us the opportunity to broadcast our own messages to thousands and, in some cases, millions. Equip and empower your social networks to connect with media contacts that are searching for sources and stories in social media.

Key #10: Leverage Twitter to Cultivate Conversations and Communities

Brands are finding creative ways to drive conversations about their brands on Twitter and increase engagement among their target audiences. Capitalize on this platform by launching Twitter chats to encourage consistent, strategic conversations and reinforce your thought leadership. Also, create hashtags for your brand to help customers follow your conversations and connect with other members of your target audience to create a sense of community.

Key #11: Utilize local marketing for local businesses.

If you're a plastic surgeon or you own a dance studio, you want to be going after customers that are based in your specific geographic region. You can do that easily with local online marketing campaigns, using the previous ten keys, but focusing on area prospective customers who live in your region. Optimize your web pages for a local search and you'll improve your brand reputation and drive more relevant targeted traffic.

Whole books can be written about 'the ins and outs' of each of these keys - there's a great deal that can be done within the confines of each one, and, when you combine the power of them all, you have an unbeatable social media strategy.

Social media marketing, as I've said, is a cultural shift, not a fad. The sooner you learn how to effectively present your brand online, the less likely you'll be left behind as more and more prospective customers go online to find the products and services they're after. The world has changed - and we all have to change with it.

About John

John Paul Souza is the founder and chief strategist of Social Media Magic, the industry's most trusted social media training and management firm. Under his direction, the firm has seen explosive growth marked by a recent Mashable Awards nomination in the Best Social Media Service category, the launch and record expansion of Social Media Marketing University (SMMU), and the exponential increase in the number of clients and students. Since SMMU's launch, thousands of business professionals from across the globe have participated in the program making it one of the largest and most diverse social media training programs in the world.

John is also an author and highly sought-after speaker, and was most recently voted Social Media Marketer of the Year by the Tech Marketing Awards. Over 75,000 rising and established business leaders have registered to participate in his weekly webinars. An innovator and thought leader, he continues to transform the way businesses think about and implement social media, and his efforts have caught the attention of high profile media outlets, including Forbes America's Most Promising Companies campaign and The Michael Gerber Show, hosted by the author of "*The E-Myth Revisited.*"

John is a former finance industry executive who has held key roles at JP Morgan Chase and Bank America Capital Management Group. He is a graduate of New York University Stern School of Business and completed the MIT Entrepreneurship Development Program at MIT Sloan School of Management.

To learn more about John, Social Media Magic or Social Media Marketing University, visit www.socialmediamagic.com and www.smmu.com.

CHAPTER 3

THE "VOLTRON" FORMULA: DYNAMICS OF BUILDING AN OUTSTANDING TEAM

By Mfon Ekpo, Esq.

While I loved "Superman" as a child, I had a special preference for "Voltron." This was because even though Superman was powerful, he was just one man, and my young impressionable heart would threaten to fail every time I watched him being weakened by his nemesis "kryptonite," wondering if this was the day Superman would die – and also wondering why he had no friends to come to his rescue.

This was too much for my little mind to fathom, so I took solace in watching Voltron, where a group of friends transformed into the parts that came together to form an indestructible whole called "Voltron, The Defender of the Universe".

Although, sadly, not as handsome as Superman, I knew that when one member of the Voltron team fell (often because he strayed away from the rest), there was always the certainty that the rest would band together to rescue their troubled team member – until the group was complete enough to cause me to jump up and down excitedly chanting with the television characters:

"Ready to form Voltron! Activate interlocks! Dyna-therms connected. Infra-cells up! Mega-thrusters are go! Let's go, Voltron Force!"

For those too occupied to have watched either Superman or Voltron, I apologize, as all I have written hitherto must sound like a foreign language. However, in my training seminars as in this context, "Superman" represents the lone ranger, the "I can do it all myself," or "if I don't do it no one else will" kind-of-business-person, while "Voltron" represents team, tribe, group, clan or whatever word can be used to describe individuals that come together to achieve specific purposes. Having personally tried both systems in business, I agree with anyone who has taught that teaming up with others is better than doing it alone.

However, what they often happen to leave out is that building a viable team can be hard work. Some business owners in consultation have even suggested to me that it requires some sort of superhuman strength or capacity, and while I would not go that far, I admit that building a working team is definitely not child's play. Notwithstanding, the rewards of having such a team far outweighs the investment made, because having the right team is one of the major factors that determines if a business fails or succeeds.

LETS START FROM THE VERY BEGINNING: LET'S CALL A SPADE A SPADE!

Make no mistake about it, anyone can put together a group they refer to as a team, but not everyone can put together a viable team working at its optimum capacity to deliver outstanding results. This is my concept of the word team, because why on earth would anyone get more people to deliver results that a single person can deliver by sheer hard work and initiative? However, subconsciously and sometimes consciously, this is what most people do.

I had a client who ran his business in this manner. He was always dousing fires created by his "team" members, having to correct the errors of his "team" which most times required his doing their work all over again by himself; he repaired the relationships his "team" had come close to destroying in his absence, and allowed this situation to persist – all the while still clinging forcefully to the idea that he had a "team." This went on until he came close to losing a major business deal that could make or break his company. He finally asked for help, and in consultation was able to admit that the brood he referred to as a "team" was, from an objective point of view, a one-man army with many error-prone foot soldiers. However, until he realized and admitted that, he could not change anything because improvement always starts from admitting the truth about your present circumstance.

So, after embarking upon the imperative task of taking stock of your present circumstance, here is a list of seven keys to put together an exceptional team.

1. ABANDON THE "COUCH POTATO" SYNDROME.

Most behavioral life patterns can be replicated in business. Being a couch potato implies a lazy attitude where one sits and idly watches what goes on. Ironically, even some of the most hardworking business people turn out to be "team-building couch potatoes" in the sense that they can't be bothered to get involved because its just too much trouble.

Building a team requires consistent involvement. It will require the abandonment of the comfort zone of self. It requires you to take the time to place your heart inside theirs or in other words, sell them the vision. It requires you to choose your team carefully, study their differences diligently, encourage them in their strengths consistently, note their weaknesses attentively and put your team first unfailingly, yes, even before any common goal, after all it's the people that come together to achieve this common goal.

However this can be a bit disconcerting because most times, all a business owner wants is 'results.' Team building is like delayed gratification. You wait, you hone, you teach, you train until finally, the type of results you want to see start happening.

2. MATCHING AND MIRRORING

A team produces at the level of their leader. They are like children that mirror what their parents do. Whatever confronts the eyes and ears constantly registers in the mind, and, of all the earth's resources – none is as potent as the human mind. This is one of the main reasons building an effective team appears so tasking. It requires that you be on top of your game constantly, that you operate at a higher frequency, that you are certain in which direction you are headed. You have no time to cut yourself any slack, because where you lead, your team will invariably follow.

3. BE PREPARED TO LET GO

Admit it, it's a bit daunting to watch someone you have invested time and effort in – leave. I have seen this happen time and time again; so that I have come to accept it as part of the team building process.

I recall working in a team with a very naïve lady. She was however, eager to learn, and asked me so many questions on the job. Some times it was flattering, sometimes disturbing and at other times downright annoying. But as time passed by, the barrage of questions reduced, as she learnt to stand on her own feet until one day, I realized she had not asked for my help in a long while and was doing quite well on her own. I felt a sense of pride, but surprisingly I also felt quite sad. Every one wants to feel relevant and sometimes growth of the tutee makes the tutor feel quite irrelevant. Then again, her independence proved I had done my job.

In building a team, most entrepreneurs fail to realize that no one has a monopoly on another person's life's direction. Some stay, others leave, not always out of malice, but because under you, they have developed the confidence required to proceed without you, and stifling the growth of an individual will only cost you eventually. Nevertheless, its critical to endeavor to leave teams, businesses or places of employment on the best of terms. There is always a better way to leave, don't burn your bridges!

On the flip side of things, in getting the best fit for your team, try as you may, you will not always pick the right people, be prepared to protect your investment in the rest of your team and let anyone that does not fit, go…and this is putting it mildly. This is very necessary because one wrong team member, if allowed to remain, can sabotage and cripple all the effort of the rest. People keep wrong people teamed up for numerous reasons and while there are a thousand and one reasons to justify hanging on to someone whose activities threaten to destroy the entire team, none of these excuses hold water. As unpalatable as it may seem, to succeed in business you have to deal with it – and swiftly too.

4. BE GENUINE

Teamwork requires trust. It is critical in team dynamics. Therefore don't be a fake team leader or team player; it destroys the very fabric of the team concept, because being a fake is not as bad as not being a team player, it is worse!

I had to resolve a dispute threatening to destroy the entire structure of a brilliant triangular business team where one member of the team continually sidelined the rest of the team to look good in front of the clients and the chairman of the company. Handling that team made me realize that people who do not allow others to grow or think nothing is worth celebrating if it does not concern them, are generally insecure. They do not deserve good people, neither can they keep them. It may take a while, but team members will eventually detect a fake; its demoralizing and will only send your team running for the exit.

5. STOP PRESS! IT DOES MATTER WHO GETS THE CREDIT.

I know it is said that in teamwork it doesn't matter who gets the credit... but it does...Seriously! Praising intelligent input in a team does not break the team down. On the contrary, if done rightly, it strengthens it. It makes each member strive to perform his or her best. If you are a business owner or leader, allow your team to partake in what you partake of. If you get recognition, allow them to get some. If you sit in high-powered meetings, let them sit in too, the result is worth the inconvenience.

I have been in various musical groups both as a leader and as a member, and there is nothing as gratifying to a band member as when the leader takes out time from being applauded and celebrated to recognize and channel the same applause to their band members, not behind closed doors but right there in front of the audience. Most times it is accomplished by introducing each member of the band to the audience and praising their input. There is nothing as energizing!

The same goes for any kind of team, because what a team member hears at that moment of appreciation, regardless of the words used is "the praise that is mine is yours too, because I couldn't have done this without you, but not only do I know that...I also want the whole world to know that too."

People that make up a team are still very much individuals and human, they are creatures of celebration, tilting towards where they are most celebrated. Team leaders and members should learn to give credit to each other as recognizing and appreciating other people's input has the inherent ability to destroy the kind of egotism and self-centeredness that threatens team unity.

6. PAY, PAY AND PAY YOUR TEAM.

Once you have found your dream team, show that you acknowledge their worth by paying them well. One of the best ways of ensuring that a team stays is by ensuring that their needs are met. Having said that, payment is not just monetary, although that is a major part of it, there are other things just as important. Pay your team by personal recognition, by adding value to them, by showing that you trust their abilities, by respecting them, by appreciating them, by training them, by developing their skills, and by doing whatever you can to make their lives better – to make them thankful that they are associated with you.

It's the things others take for granted, but major success stories have come out of the ability to pay attention to details. A little really does go a long way.

7. THE EMERGENCE OF X-MEN: ALLOW THEM TO GROW.

Going back to my movie analogies, after all is said and done, Team "Voltron," if groomed carefully, will eventually metamorphose to "X-Men." X-Men, as in the movie, represent individuals who have honed their special powers and decided to use it for the greater good. No longer children businesswise, The "X-Men" kind of team is a superior form of teamwork and its what the most successful businesses have been able to achieve.

The difference between the "Voltron team" and "X-MEN team" is that while "Voltron" is made up of dependent parts that need each other to form a whole; X-Men are mature independent individuals who make a choice to come together to synergize their skillfully-honed core competencies. At this time, each member of the team, although able to stand alone, chooses instead (from their independent platforms), to harness the power of synergy and work as a team. At this stage, business takes on an effortless, optimally productive rhythm. It's why a business owner of one company is the company secretary of another company and can still be a director in yet another company. They contribute expertise and create a web of supporting relationships. However, this metamorphosis will not take place if each individual's potential is stifled and not allowed to grow within the team structure.

SUMMARY

There is a distinct advantage in having a team that really works. Having a "Superman" mentality in this fast-evolving business terrain is choosing to ignore that there are better ways of achieving business success. The dynamics of building an outstanding team is not rocket science; it simply requires consistent application fueled by the knowledge that, as Andrew Carnegie put it, "Teamwork … is the fuel that allows common people to attain uncommon results."

About Mfon

Mfon Ekpo is a maritime lawyer and an entrepreneur who juggles multiple roles as a strategy consultant, professional negotiator and mediator, writer, speaker, singer and songwriter. She is the founder of Premier Pioneers Network (http://www.premierpioneers.org), training people in the art of public speaking, writing, negotiation, ideas generation and implementation since 2006.

Mfon is a Best Selling co-author of the book *"Pushing to the Front"* featuring Brian Tracy and other thought leaders. She also serves on the board of several companies and is currently the Director of Strategy at Red Media, a leading Media and Communications Development Company.

A staunch advocate of personal development and a firm believer in the limitless possibilities of the human capacity, she is a founding partner of the John Maxwell Team (http://johnmaxwellgroup.com/mfonekpo/) and a Member of the British Institute of International and Comparative Law. She trains young people on humanitarian issues as a school speaker for the British Red Cross and enjoys expounding life lessons to readers on her blog, *The School Called Life*, see: https://theschoolcalledlife.wordpress.com/

CHAPTER 4

CREATE MORE IMPACT IN YOUR MARKETING BY PROMOTING THE TRUE END BENEFIT OF YOUR PRODUCTS

By William R. Benner, Jr.

In the book *Game Changers*, I taught you how to take an idea, turn it into a product, and then take that product to market by starting your own small business. After that, in the book *Win*, I taught you how to earn more money from the products you already make, by identifying new niche markets, and by modifying your products to meet the needs of the new niche markets.

Indeed, most of my career has been focused on product development, because within my own field of endeavor, I've turned dozens of ideas into products that are the basis of multi-national company operations.

If you've ever seen a professional laser show, then you've probably seen one of my products in action. They are used to create shows at the world's top theme parks and major events like concerts, the Super Bowl and the Olympics. Because of how long we've been in business and our success, I know how to bring brand-new products to market.

However, as discussed in Michael Gerber's book The E-Myth, it's easy for entrepreneurs to get caught up in the myth that by simply creating great products or by simply doing excellent technical work, that these

41

activities are enough to be successful in business. They aren't! Marketing your products and promoting your company will account for at least 50% of your success. To do these things best, you must understand the true end benefit of your product.

What do I mean by "understand the true end benefit"? Well, what I mean is that you must look beyond the immediate benefits that are derived by your direct customers.

I'm sure you've heard that you should ask your customers why they buy from you. Their answers will help you to understand how to improve your products, and how to better market them. Within my company, we've asked this question for years, and we've gotten useful feedback. Our product gives the customer a powerful set of tools that they can use to quickly and easily achieve their goals. Our product quality is very high, so customers rarely have a need for technical support. If the need for technical support does arise, we are available nearly 24 hours a day, from three separate offices in America, Europe and China. Our prices are very affordable, and our products are available from dealers all over the world, so they are easy to obtain.

All of these answers are the obvious kinds of things that you would expect (or at least hope) to hear. This lets you know that you are on the right track. During such a question and answer session, your customer may also give you a different kind of feedback, which you can use as a data-point to help you to understand how to serve the customer better, and how to reach new customers.

However, I've recently learned to look beyond the obvious things mentioned above. Those points exist on a kind of microscopic level, since those answers only account for one link in the chain – the link from you to your customer. But the fact is that your customer also has customers, who must also derive a benefit! Once you understand how THOSE customers benefit – i.e. the TRUE end-benefit of your product, then this can become a very effective part of your marketing campaign.

Let me give you some examples, and then I'll discuss the related concepts that we've applied to our own business and its marketing campaign.

You've probably heard of Intel, the semiconductor company that makes memory chips, microprocessors and interface chips used in computers and other high-tech equipment. Intel sells their chips to companies like Dell, HP, Apple and many others.

If Intel were to ask Dell why they buy Intel microprocessors, Dell would probably say the obvious things that you would expect to hear about pricing, availability and delivery. These answers help Intel understand the implications of their supply chain. Dell might also say some non-obvious things about the packaging of the product – how the connectors are aligned which makes the microprocessor easy to mount within Dell computers, or how they like the fact that Intel has included a cooling fan with the processor, so Dell doesn't have to obtain this from another vendor and figure out how to mount it. These are technical features that help Intel to know that they're on the right track, and helps them to know that they should retain these features in future products.

Unfortunately, these points are on a microscopic level, because they only help Intel to understand how their supply chain or technical details affect one link in the chain – the link between Intel and Dell. These points won't help Intel to understand how their products help the next link in the chain: the true end-users who then purchase Dell computers.

It would be very helpful for Intel to understand how consumers are using Dell's computers – for example, that the use of video is on the rise, so people can watch entire movies on their computer that are streamed over the Internet. Or how consumers are using Skype and other programs for video conferencing and person-to-person video chats. Knowing these things, along with the fact that Intel microprocessors have special instructions that help the computer decode video for faster and smoother display, would help in Intel's marketing efforts. Instead of saying "buy our product because it is affordable and easy to obtain", or "buy our product because it is easy to mount" they could say "buy our product because it makes video look better and thus, your customers will have a more enjoyable experience". Of course this has a much greater impact, because it speaks to the true end-benefit.

Indeed, armed with this information, Intel may decide not only to market their products to their direct customers (companies such as Dell, HP and Apple) but also to their customers' customers – the true end-users of their products. This was the thrust behind the "Intel Inside" campaign that has been running since 1992 and has made Intel one of the top ten brands in the world, alongside Coca Cola, Disney and McDonald's.

Here's another example. Suppose you are in the business of supplying restaurants with tablecloths and napkins. There are the obvious benefits that restaurants need to obtain from these things. They need to be affordable so that the restaurant can buy in bulk. They need to be easy to clean because of all of the messes that customers routinely make at restaurants. It would be easy to get caught up in the microscopic view, that the only customer that matters is the restaurant. But this is not the case! It is the diners who come to restaurants who are the true end-consumers, and oftentimes these diners are not only looking for a meal, but rather an entire dining experience.

Think about a birthday party or even a marriage proposal that takes place in a restaurant. If the table cloths and napkins have special features to them, such as a frilly lace border or a special feel of the linen, then these things become a part of the entire birthday or marriage proposal experience. By understanding that the frilly border and feel of the material make a dining experience and the special occasions more special, these can become a part of the marketing campaign. Instead of "buy our table cloths and napkins because they are affordable and easy to obtain" or "buy our table cloths and napkins because they are easy to clean," it becomes "buy our table cloths and napkins because their look and feel makes the dining experience special." Of course, this has a much greater impact, because it speaks to the true end-benefit of the product.

This concept can be applied to almost any business, because almost everyone has customers who themselves also have other customers. Let me give you one last example that might be completely non-obvious.

In the field of hair styling, you have, of course, the hair stylist and you have customers who come to those stylists. The hair stylists perform services such as cutting, curling, permanent waves, hair straightening and coloring. It would be easy to get caught up on the notion that, within this type of business, there is only one customer – the person who comes to the stylist, but this is not the case! Some of these customers might be well-known personalities such as professional actors or television newscasters, who are of course observed by an audience. And even if the customer doesn't have a well-defined audience, they still have co-workers or family members for whom they would want to look good.

(Indeed, the reason why I kept going back to my last hair stylist was because of the many positive comments made by my co-workers after having my hair cut by her.) With this in mind, the hair stylist's marketing campaign can go from "come to me because I have an open schedule" or "come to me because I have affordable pricing" to "come to me because you'll look better in front of your audience and you'll be complimented by your co-workers." This kind of message has a much greater impact, because it speaks to the true end-benefit of the styling activity.

Let me now turn to how this concept has been applied at my company, Pangolin Laser Systems. We are the world leader in software and control hardware used for creating and displaying professional laser light shows. For years, we concentrated our marketing efforts only on those customers who buy directly from us. Sure, on some level we knew that lasers are used in concerts, clubs, theatrical presentations and special events. But we never fully understood all of the benefits ourselves until we really started asking how it is that THEIR customers (i.e., the people watching the laser shows or sitting in the seats at corporate events) benefit from these activities in the first place. We began looking at the return on investment (ROI) that everybody in the chain derives from using them.

On our journey to discover the true end-user benefit, we heard people say things like putting on an event is like dressing for success. If you want to play in the big leagues, you have to look like the big leagues. And whether you're putting on a corporate event, a concert, a party or a charitable event, you need to connect with attendees on an emotional level, and give them something to get excited about.

For event producers, there are many individual elements that can be added to an event to achieve this emotional connection and create excitement. For example, you could add balloons, printed graphics, plasma and LED video, linens, candles or even things like a three-piece band or a professional speaker. Each of these elements has a WOW factor associated with it, but the WOW factor is relatively low because each of these things has been done over and over at events. However, lasers have a high WOW factor because of the unique qualities of laser light, which makes lasers impactful, motivational and memorable, and thus, the ROI is higher than for any other production element.

With their thin shafts of light and rainbow-pure colors, "Star Wars"-

style laser beams are a dazzling cross between theatrical lighting and fireworks. Lasers can also project animated graphics to communicate in a way that is more eye-catching than conventional video or slides. Indeed, decades later the event attendees can recount exactly how the laser etched out a company logo, or how a beam came down to reveal a product. Essentially, the unique features of lasers help them put the "spectacle" into spectaculars, and the "special" into special events.

(It may be difficult to understand how lasers can accomplish these things easily and inexpensively. In fact, within the last decade there has been somewhat of a revolution. Laser projectors have become portable air-cooled devices that plug directly into normal AC power, and are controlled by a laptop computer running Pangolin software. Very often, the source imagery comes from existing media such as 3D Studio MAX, Adobe Flash, or even normal video.)

After discovering the true end-user benefits for ourselves, we felt compelled to communicate these benefits both to our direct customers – the event planners and producers who decide how to entertain and educate audiences, as well as true end-users – those people who are attending events.

This was accomplished in a variety of ways. Within our brochures, our on-line videos, and our web site, we created a section called "Powered by Pangolin." This showcases the true end-result of our products and helps the true end-users to see how professional companies are using lasers to increase their ROI.

To give you an example of what I mean, the material found in our Powered by Pangolin section highlights large theme park shows at Universal Studios Florida and Disneyland in California. It also showcases the many high profile concerts at which you see lasers being used, including Roger Waters, Trans-Siberian Orchestra, Black Eyed Peas, Shakira, Drake, and Justin Bieber and many others. And it provides new ideas by showcasing the many new settings in which laser are being used, including the nightly shows seen on Carnival Cruise Lines and at the Las Vegas Nightclub Moon. We even showcase the more esoteric end-uses, such as creating true 3D images in mid-air and how laser can be used for industrial applications, such as projecting alpha-numeric characters onto factory floors to communicate production-related information to staff members. Each of these is exciting and speaks directly to the end-user, and each of these also has an ROI, which speaks to our direct customers.

For Pangolin, as a result of this new style of marketing, our sales have increased by 50% and our profits have increased by an even greater margin. Our brand name has also become the best-known brand among our target market of event producers and even among consumers, in the same way that Intel is the best-known brand for computer microprocessors.

This was a very exciting lesson for us to learn. In addition to the marketing changes that have led to clear results, our team members are also more engaged in our business as well as our customers' businesses. As we receive emails and inquiries, we stop and ask more questions of our customers, in an effort to stay 'in tune' and 'up to date' with the true end-benefits.

As I conclude this chapter, I call upon you to apply the lessons that we have learned and presented here. Examine your products and identify the true end-benefit experienced by your customers' customers. After that, identify how it is that your direct customers actually make a profit because of the unique qualities and benefits that your product provides to their end-users. Then craft a marketing campaign that is powerful enough to get the true end-users excited, while also being clear enough to communicate the ROI that your customers derive by using your products. This kind of marketing message will have maximum impact, and can propel your sales and profits to heights never before imagined.

ABOUT WILLIAM

William R. Benner, Jr. is President and CTO of Pangolin Laser Systems – a multi-national organization with offices in the United States, Central Europe and Mainland China. As President, he sets the general strategic direction for the company and oversees all company operations. As CTO, he is in charge of all hardware and software, as well as research and development on new products, which tend to strongly influence the future direction of the laser- and SMS-display industries.

In addition to having received more than 20 international awards for technical achievement, Benner's products are used by some of the best-known companies in the world, including Walt Disney World, Universal Studios, DreamWorks, Boeing, Samsung, and Lawrence Livermore Labs.

Beyond his work at Pangolin, Benner has served as a director on several boards as well as Technical Committee Chairman for the International Laser Display Association. He has also consulted for companies outside of Pangolin including NEOS, Cambridge Technologies, RMB Miniature Bearings and many others.

Benner holds numerous Patents, and has received personal letters of commendation from President Ronald Reagan and Florida Governor Bob Graham. He has also been published in the *SMPTE Journal, The Laserist, LaserFX, US Tech magazine* and Motorola's *Embedded Connection* magazine. He is also co-author of the best-selling books *Game Changers* and *Win!* and was selected as one of America's PremierExperts™ as well as being featured on NBC, ABC, CBS and FOX television affiliates.

He represented the State of Florida in the United States Skill Olympics and represented the U.S. in International Skill Olympics trials, receiving gold medals for each. Benner has also received the International Laser Display Association's highest accolade, the Career Achievement Award.

CHAPTER 5

DARE TO BEGIN

By Chuck Boyce, The Independent Executive

"All Glory Comes From Daring to Begin" ~ Eugene F Ware

At 12:01 am every day, we all get the same 1440 minutes for the next one.

How you choose to use them, and what you choose to start right now, determines whether or not you will find success.

As a serial entrepreneur, I get approached with opportunities and ideas for joint ventures, partnerships and new businesses with some regularity. Many times the person that approaches has a reasonably good idea that they have been kicking around for some time, yet they've done nothing with it. They have made a choice to keep their idea locked up in a notebook or in their head. They have never given it a chance by taking that first step and doing something with it.

This is always so frustrating for me when working with small business owners and new entrepreneurs. I have found that there are generally three reasons that people haven't gotten started working on their ideas.

First is inertia. It takes a huge amount of energy to get out of the day-to-day routine that we find ourselves in. We become so very comfortable. I had a very comfortable lifestyle working in the corporate world. My financial needs were being easily met every month, and it took a great deal of energy and resolve to say, "You know what, there's got to be something better.

The second most common reason for not moving ideas along is failure. It can be a huge obstacle to overcome. No one want to look foolish to their friends, to their families, or to their colleagues – if this thing just doesn't come out perfect the first time out of the gate.

Finally, the third reason I see when working with entrepreneurs is the perception that you need a big bunch of money to be able to start up something new. They are waiting until the bank balance has grown to a certain level. Alternatively they may feel that you need access to a lot of money to get the venture started. In many cases, for the businesses that I work with, that is just not the case.

I find that successful people don't generally sit around waiting to find someone else to help them get a project off the ground. They will start working on something immediately, and look for others that fill in critical gaps along the way. A commitment is made to move forward quickly, and they get started. They dare to begin!

WHEN IS THE RIGHT TIME TO START?

They're not willing to wait for the perfect storm for the perfect set of circumstances to present themselves, to get their next project or the next venture, up off the ground. They're willing to take a little bit of a risk and say you know what - when I'm at that point, the right resources are going to either come to me, or I'm going to go seek them out.

There's never a perfect moment to meet your spouse or partner. There's never a right moment to start a family. There's never a right moment to do certain things and the same is true with a business.

Personally, when I decided to leave my corporate job at Estee Lauder, and start my entrepreneurial journey, it was less than the perfect moment. My soon to be wife was thinking about having me committed.

She asked, "What do you mean you're giving up your nice secure corporate job and you're going to go out and start your own business as we start our life together?"

I've yet to have the perfect moment. There have been times that opportunity has presented itself, and I've been in a position to act quickly, and take advantage of it, but most times it happens when you're not actually looking for it.

A set of circumstances will come up and you've just got to decide, I'm not willing to move in this direction anymore, and I'm going to make a change.

PLANNING VS. EXECUTION

Several years ago, I had the idea to open a computer-based testing center as part of our executive business suite. One of my tenants was a small, regional IT staffing and consulting firm. I thought it would be a great fit in terms of our business needs. I laid a quick plan and wanted to open the doors within 3 weeks. My client agreed it was a good idea, and he could benefit by having a way to schedule his consultants in a priority queue and receive discounts for their certification exams. He indicated he'd get back to me shortly.

While he was performing his analysis, creating forecasts, working the calculations and looking at the project from every conceivable angle, I got to work. About 10 days later, he got back to me and indicated he still wasn't sure if it was a good idea for him, but he was willing to consider moving forward. In that same time he spent analyzing the project, I was done. The center was furnished, the equipment was in place, and we had qualified as an authorized testing center for the big three in Computer-based testing.

I shared with him that the center was done, and unfortunately he had missed out on the project. The testing center continues to generate a nice income stream as an add-on to that existing business. This project was a success, because while he was analyzing, I was doing. I had 'dared to begin.'

The key idea here is that you can always be doing something right now. Stop waiting for the perfect time and get to work.

Now just as this example was a success, there are many occasions where starting something that looks good at the outset turns out to be a mistake.

FAIL FORWARD FAST

"Fail faster. Succeed sooner." ~ Tom Peters

With the steady flow of starting new projects, and constant activity, it is important to know when to let go of a project or an idea. There are times when it is just as important to call it quits. The objective is to Fail Forward FAST.

One of the things that I've always realized is that successful people are impatient. They want results, and they want them quickly. As we move from a very localized, regionalized, nationalized economy to a global economy and in the information age, as information can move so quickly across the globe, it is more important than ever to fail forward fast.

By that, I mean do something, create a set of objectives, analysis tools for metrics that you're going to evaluate it for. See if it passes the test, and if doesn't, call it a failure, and move on as quickly as possible.

When you are starting so many things, it is important to measure progress. If you are moving as quickly as possible, there will be times when a key market, partner or technology is just not ready, stable or receptive to your plans. There has to be a way for you to objectively decide to kill a project.

I think it's important to talk about how failure in this context is taking an action that's doesn't produce the expected results. We'll hear so many times in scientific research when an experiment becomes a failure. And it's a failure because it didn't produce the result that it was expecting.

However there are so many products out on the market that are a result of failures. Take Play-Doh. The brightly colored, non-toxic can of fun was invented in 1955 by Joseph and Noah McVicker while they were trying to make a wallpaper cleaner.

So, you need to embrace those failures, get them out of the way, and keep going forward.

SET YOUR INDICATORS

The indicators you establish are going to vary. I like to have no more than three. Depending on where we're at in the project, we may have one, we may have more.

Generally, when we talk about getting started quickly, and we're looking at that initial launch phase, and we're going to set our initial deadline at two weeks and see how much we can do in two weeks. For this stage, I like to have one key indicator. I want to know there's a willing marketplace for a new information product we're going to roll out. Is there a willing audience for a seminar or event we are planning on hosting?

We may look at that by doing a survey to the marketplace, we may launch a smaller version of the product in those two weeks and put some advertising against it to see what the response is, but we're basically looking to see, hey, do we really have a market here?

Further on in the project, we're generally going to always be looking for, for me, one of my key indictors is a profitably indicator. I don't like to work for free.

I have certain percentages for different types of products and lines of business that we're involved in, where there must be a minimum profitability for a specific task, project, service that we're going to offer. It must meet and hold its own, otherwise I don't want to do it.

Finally, as we get the product ready, we're going to be looking at an indicator that is more technology-based if there's a technology component. If we're trying to do something cool or new, does the technology or the platform exist for us to deliver this product or service the way we want to? Is the automation there, or are we trying to invent something new?

By having a clear set of indicators and a timeline in place, it makes it much easier to decide to end a project, before it becomes a massive drain on your available resources.

NO MORE WAITING!

One of my favorite quotes used by marketing gurus, consultants, coaches and 'arm chair philosophers' is "Insanity is doing the same thing over and over again and expecting different results." Having known my share of certified 'crazy folk', the idea is not really meant to be taken literally. It does point out that most people won't muster the energy required to change their habits and chart a new course. It takes hard work and perseverance to overcome the inertia created by doing the same old thing.

You however, can be different. You can choose right now to make the changes. Here are my recommendations to get you started:-

(…So now it is time to dust off that notebook, go to the whiteboard or jot down that idea you've been carrying around….)

• Write out the list of your three best ideas to bring yourself closer to personal success.

• Take a huge red pen, and cross out numbers two and three. Draw a huge circle, dollar signs, or a heart around number one.

• Put this list up in a prominent place so you see it at least several times per day.

• Take action on your Best Idea for Success right now.

• Make it a giant step and make a public commitment.

• Write down the ONE CRITERIA you will use to determine if this is a success, and the date you will evaluate the project. Chisel this date into a stone tablet, and be brutal when the day of reckoning arrives.

• Ask yourself constantly, "Is what I'm doing at this very moment moving me closer to achieving my goal of success?"

Through this chapter, I have laid out a blueprint and the foundation for you to go from idea to business and become an entrepreneur and small business owner; one that's going to allow you to live out your vision and see your ideal picture of success.

If you do want to take that to the next level, I encourage you to head to http://www.DareToBegin.com, and discover the other resources available to help you along your journey.

Take action to realize your ideas coming to life. I dare you to begin, NOW!

About Chuck

Chuck Boyce is known as "The Independent Executive." After achieving success quickly in the corporate world, he decided to step off of the corporate ladder and make his business work for him instead of the other way around. One of the top alternatives people are using to create wealth in this tough economy is through development of their own small businesses. His DARE TO BEGIN SYSTEM™ and BREAKING FREE SYSTEM™ are helping other entrepreneurs and business owners that have decided to jump off the corporate ladder.

An accomplished speaker and author, Chuck's work has been featured in *USA Today, Newsweek, Inc. Magazine, The Wall Street Journal, FastCompany.com* along with a variety of magazines and blogs.

He has appeared as a guest on ABC, NBC, CBS, and FOX affiliates discussing entrepreneurship, the independent executive lifestyle, and the new American Dream.

Chuck is the co-author of the *Ultimate Success Secret* with Dan Kennedy and Mike Capuzzi; co-author of the best-seller *Power Principles for Success* with Brian Tracy; co-author of the best-seller *GameChangers: The World's Leading Entrepreneurs: How They're Changing the Game & You Can Too!* Upcoming titles include *Building the Ultimate Network* with Dr. Ivan R. Misner, and *You Had Me At Hello!*

Chuck was twice award the Golden Quill from the National Academy of Best Selling Authors.

Chuck resides in Delaware with his wife Angel, and their daughter Ally.

Connect with Chuck!
(800) 495-5267
chuck@breakingfreeblog.com

 http://www.twitter.com/chuckboyce

 http://www.facebook.com/breakingfreeblog

 http://www.linkedin.com/in/cboyce

CHAPTER 6

Managing Your Money - Do It Yourself or Hire a Pro?

By Bryan Sullivan

Why use an advisor to help manage your retirement money when you can do it yourself? Maybe you don't want somebody else to handle your money. Maybe you want to avoid the cost of doing business with an advisor.

I remember when I had just started working and bought my first house. My neighbor came by and said, "I want to buy this new wood burning fireplace insert. They will give me a great deal if I buy two of them. What do you think? Do you want to go in on this?"

Well, I lived up in Oregon at the time. The winters are cold there, my fireplace didn't produce much heat, and an insert really would help. It was a $1000 to buy this thing, and for a couple hundred more bucks they offered to send someone out to install it. So I paid the extra $200 to have it installed by a guy who did it every day. It got done, it looked great, and it worked great.

My next door neighbor was a "do-it-yourself" guy and he decided he was going to tackle the project himself. There was a step in the process when you had to drill through some metal. He didn't wear safety glasses while he was drilling it and a little metal shaving flicked into his eye. He had to go to the hospital and his sight was crippled for about three weeks. He was unable to drive and had to take time off work. Imagine the pain, agony, and expense he went through to save that $200.

Whether you pay someone to help you or you do it yourself there always will be a cost. It is important to weigh the cost of your time and the value of your abilities to manage your money as effectively as a trained professional who does it every day.

Most people don't spend their life managing money. There is more to it than just buying into a process and applying it, and there are many pitfalls that could cost you very dearly. When it's your money you also can't help being emotionally tied to it – which can lead to even more mistakes. A good financial counselor is aware of these pitfalls and has experience providing assistance with almost every type of situation.

You should consider asking yourself, "Am I willing to invest the time and energy to educate myself about money, and do I have the emotional fortitude to make the right decisions at the right times when I'm dealing with my own money?" These are very real and serious questions that a good financial advisor can help you work through.

For some of you the answer still may be, "Yes, I'm going to take the risk and do this myself." Many more of you will find that working with a qualified financial advisor provides more value.

It is unfortunate that so many people are more willing to risk managing their own money than they are willing to risk having somebody cut their lawn or paint their house. When it comes to their money they somehow think they are the expert and are afraid to give up control.

If somebody messes up my lawn it's not going to be the end of the world. It will grow back and I can get someone else to do it or cut it myself next week.

It doesn't work like that with money. If you make a mistake with your retirement money you can't ever get it back, because your earning power is gone.

By hiring a financial advisor you are not giving up control of your money. You still have the final say in how your investments are managed, how much risk you take and how much loss or gain you are willing to accept or try to achieve. These things all remain in your control. Your financial advisor is there to help you protect your standard of living by protecting your money from yourself.

So now you've decided you're ready to find somebody to help you manage your money, how do you decide whom to trust? The most important factor is going to be somebody with whom you have a very fundamental and strong rapport.

Of course you are going to need trust, but trust doesn't come immediately; it happens over time. So to get started with an advisor you first have to start with rapport.

Life is too short to be working with somebody you don't like. A financial advisor may be the smartest person in the world and can help you get excellent returns, but when you call them to talk about how much money you should spend on your daughter's wedding and you get rubbed the wrong way, that's not the person you want to be managing your life savings.

The first thing to put in the back of your mind before you even start your search is that you want to find somebody with whom you can connect, somebody who really understands you, understands your family, takes some interest in your livelihood so that when you do start to make decisions they can help you to make those important decisions. Some type of affinity or strong rapport is the foundation.

There are a couple of ways you can go about it. I love the idea of referrals. Talking with somebody you trust and respect that has a good relationship with somebody they work with is always a good starting point. However, I always recommend talking to many different people. We sometimes have a tendency to say, "Oh, something happened to my car, where do you get your car fixed? ... Okay, I'll take it over there," or, "My cleaning lady just quit, who do you use?"

With a financial advisor you need to take it one step further. I would suggest asking for a referral but also interview several more advisors to get a real sense of how they manage the process – until you find the one with whom you are going to have the best rapport and long term relationship.

Once you get to the point where you are interviewing, also look for things that will matter to you in the long run. What is their availability? What is their policy on returning calls or giving you an appointment? What is their investment discipline? How will they help you make those decisions? Their answers need to not only make sense, but also to reso-nate with you.

If you are an engineer and very structured you may want to know a lot more detail. The advisor should be able to explain the process to you, what technologies they are using to help them manage your money and specifically how they make buying and selling decisions.

I believe that every financial advisor also should bring up the issue of compensation. Are they fee-based advisors, commission-based advisors, flat fee advisors or hybrids?

There also are designations to look at such as education and experience that an advisor brings to the table that help make them valuable to you. You sometimes read in money magazines that you only should hire a CFP. Most people don't even know what a CFP is or what it means or what criteria are required to qualify to get and keep that designation. Designations can be important but having somebody with long term experience is more important than almost any type of designation any-body can have.

You want to work with someone who has experience in the area that you need advice. If my specialty is managing money for retirees, and you come to me about funding a small business and I don't have experience in that area, I am not the right person to help you with that. Similarly, a small business funding expert is not the person you want handling your retirement investments. It is best to have an advisor that has experience with the types of things that will come up in your life. When they do, your advisor will understand and be able to help you better.

Ultimately, it is not so much about the advisor selling you on his or her expertise as it is about you finding the "right fit." The crux of a success-ful relationship with your financial advisor is the relationship. You have the power in the relationship, and the advisor should have to do a really good job of proving to you that they are the right fit. One person may want the type of advisor that is all business, busy managing your money and doing well for you. Another person may want somebody who is more open to meeting in person, answering many questions and giving advice about money. It really is a personal preference.

Some people may think they are more concerned about performance, but in the long term, the relationship is the key. I am not trying to discount performance, but the baseline has to be the relationship and performance is a component of that. Any advisor may have a great track record for five to ten years, but there will always be a hiccup along the way. If the client and advisor don't have a good working relationship that can navigate through that storm, it will be virtually impossible to have a long term relationship.

Here are 7 quick questions you can use to interview any financial advisor to help understand what it is that they bring to the table:

1. How long have you been offering financial planning advice to clients?

2. What are your areas of specialization? What qualifies you in this field?

3. Are you personally licensed or registered as an investment advisor representative with a state(s)/Federal Government?

4. How are you paid for your services?

5. What do you typically charge?
   (Fee: Hourly rate? Flat fee? Percentage of assets under management? Commission?)

6. Is any of your compensation based on selling products?

7. Do you provide a written client engagement agreement?

WHY FEE-ONLY ADVISORS ARE YOUR BEST FRIEND

There are three basic ways an advisor gets paid. There are some hybrid models as well, but the traditional way financial advisors get paid is through a commission process. In my opinion there are some very fundamental flaws in that process. It is still very common today to pay a commission for a stock purchase or sale. So when a broker suggest that you sell stocks to purchase other stocks, you pay a commission to sell those stocks and pay another commission for the stocks you purchase.

Whether those investments are profitable or not, the advisor gets paid. So, in my opinion, there is a fundamental conflict of interest in that activity. The more activity in that account, the more the advisor gets paid. Even if the advisor has done all the right things and gives you the very best advice possible, there is an inherent conflict of interest because the advisor's compensation is tied directly to short term activity and not to the long term performance of your investments.

There has been a movement away from that model and towards a fee-based model over the last ten years or so. This has become more popular because it puts the advisor on the same side of the table as the client.

In the fee-based model, the advisor's fee is calculated as a percentage of the value of the ac-count. The plus side for you as a client is that the advisor's financial incentive is the same as yours. You both want your investments to increase in value. For the advisor to make more money he has to make more money for you.

The fee-based advisor has the least conflict of interest because compensation is tied to performance regardless of the number of trades that are done in an account. It is a win/win situation. Although the advisor still gets paid if your investments decrease in value, the fee paid also decreases. So there is an inherent disincentive for bad performance, and this helps to drive the advisors thinking process in your favor more than getting paid per transaction.

Advisors are required to tell you how they get compensated and fee structures are usually found in the fine print of your contract. A problem with the commission-based model is that many financial products have been created whose commissions are not totally transparent. Often it can be difficult to know for sure how those fees work. Therefore it may not be clear on your statement exactly what fees you paid.

A fee-based advisor clearly defines those fees on your statement. It is very transparent. Your contract with the advisor clearly defines those fees, and that fee arrangement is filed with the SEC.

About Bryan

For more than 20 years, Bryan Sullivan has been a Financial Advisor helping individuals and families achieve their financial planning goals, by providing advice on Investment Planning; Insurance Planning; Tax Planning; Retirement Planning; Estate Planning; Intergenerational Wealth Transfer Planning; and Educational Savings Planning. Working with a network of highly skilled professionals in San Luis Obispo, CA he has dedicated his career to providing high-quality advice and integrated wealth management solutions that simplify and enhance the quality of his clients' lives.

Bryan became a licensed financial advisor in 1992 and worked with several Wall Street firms including Merrill Lynch and UBS until he created an independent, SEC-Registered investment advisory firm in 2009 - Vellum Financial. He is also the author of the book, *"Protecting Your Money From Yourself - A Retiree's Guide to Insuring You Have Enough Money to Enjoy Your Retirement."*

It is his belief that the RIA platform is the final step in the evolutionary process toward providing unbiased investment management to their clients. In creating Vellum Financial, he has created a strictly objective financial advisory firm that incorporates "best practices" of investment management while avoiding the many negatives of the brokerage industry.

Vellum Financial is the embodiment of his uncompromising focus on the client. Bryan aims to provide objective advice, complete transparency and unique access to "best-in-class" subject matter experts.

The firm that he has created gives him the opportunity to shape his own culture and to establish a higher standard of service and performance within his industry. Indeed, Vellum Financial represents an ethical, intellectual and deeply personal opportunity as owner-operator - the opportunity that culminates in allowing them to be a true steward of your assets.

A strong contributor to the community, Bryan has volunteered with the Morro Bay Lions Club and Big Brother Big Sisters organization. Resident in San Luis Obispo since 1994, Bryan and his wife Tricia, and their 4 children share a passion for outdoor activities and spending time with friends and family.

To learn more about Bryan Sullivan and how you can receive a FREE guide called, *"The Critical Questions You Must Ask To Get Your Financial Life In Order"* visit: http://www.VellumFinancial.com/freeguide or by calling Toll-Free: 1-800-546-0123.

CHAPTER 7

When It Comes to Competition You Do Have To Be Different

The Business Elements which Help Differentiate How Buyers Buy: Pricing, Value, Niche and Trends

By Christine Rae

UNDERSTANDING HOW BUYERS BUY

What I have learned during my years in business is that most entrepreneurs are not completely ready to do business when they start out. They think they are – but they are not; it is one of the contributing factors to the statistic - 80% of small businesses fail within the first year. John L Beckley said, "People don't plan to fail, but they fail to plan" and to me, planning involves market research and an understanding that whatever business category you are entering into – essentially you are in sales. Most new business owners tend to assume business will be drawn to them through osmosis – if they advertise, it will magically appear. Most successful business owners learn at some point that it requires a constant nurturing of the sales cycle and client base to maintain business success.

Know, that you cannot sell to people who do not want to be sold to – people hate to be sold to, but love to buy! Your sales closing ratio will improve if you study how buyers buy. Seems like an oxymoron but it is true; people obviously buy for their own reasons, but when you modify your sales approach slightly to reflect their wants, needs and buying style, it reduces the stress for them – making the sale easier to transact.

People buy solutions to problems or to address what is missing in their lives. It was Walt Disney who said "we remember in images," and research supports that we do think in pictures. So by using words and senses to illustrate how it will feel for your client when they make the decision to buy your service/product, is good marketing strategy. The advertising and communication from your company needs to influence the consumers' brain, to focus and support the good feeling they will enjoy when they buy from you.

That means you need to focus your selling efforts on the benefits of your service or product.

Marketing experts agree the reason people generally don't buy is because they are afraid to make a decision – in case it is a mistake or they are just reluctant to change their habits. Helping the client feel better about a change and/or about making the decision, will propel the sales process forward.

Buyers gravitate to success and people want to work with winners and experts. Research shows that 93% of people's perception of success comes from how much they believe you, so showing and telling your targeted market why and how they can trust you is important. Think, what will illustrate your authenticity, honesty, integrity? Skill certification from a credible, recognized source, insurance certificate, code of conduct/ethics, core beliefs/mission statement, testimonials and police clearance certificate are some of the items which come to mind. I have also learned that the best way to overcome objections in a sales process is to raise possible objections before your prospects do, and then provide the answer. Your client may not directly ask to see the proof items; however, by showing them (perhaps online or in a sales portfolio) before being asked, you are subliminally removing barriers to purchase. Let's be honest, today's consumers are frightened; with everything which has happened, they have less and less faith in government and banks, and feel like they have less and less time to manage mounting levels of information, activity and choice.

Note: 75% of all buying decisions are based on unconscious needs and wants, such as prestige, habit or perceived value – so your message should appeal and stimulate at least one of the basic needs.

REMEMBER MASLOW'S HIERARCHY OF NEEDS?

It is usually illustrated as a pyramid. The lower levels comprise of the most basic needs, with more complex needs at the top.

The basic physical requirements including food, water, sleep and warmth form the foundation; once these have been met, people can move on to the next level of needs, which are for safety and security. Moving upwards toward the peak, the needs become increasingly more social and psychological. These needs are for love, friendship and intimacy, as well as the need for personal esteem and feelings of accomplishment.

However, as you process the level your service/product satisfies, remember that no matter how many levels are satisfied, and no matter what the brain says, people will still buy with their hearts – so you really do need to appeal to their emotions, desires and needs. People buy with emotion and support their decision with intellect.

PRICING AND VALUE

Everyone understands the axiom, "you get what you pay for" but who is paying attention? For in the race for market supremacy, a low-price leader mentality has been driven home as the rational purchase determinator. However, if everyone only sells cheap price, quality will disappear forever. Make a decision to stop competing on a lower level and focus on the value you bring to the table.

Example: People recognize the value and know the worth of difference when making a decision to buy a car; all cars have four wheels and get you from point A to point B, so why do some cost many times more than others, and why do people buy them?.... to satisfy a higher level of need. They buy the value and perceived benefits vs. the price. Let's think about a staple in North America like coffee; many of the price leaders are losing marketshare to gourmet coffee houses like Starbucks. Why? ... because a higher value is placed on the experience and taste vs. the price. Consider cleaning and health products, people are not as likely to scrimp when it comes to the health and welfare of their family; the decision to buy is very firmly rooted in emotions.

In the search for securing the best bang for the buck, most everyone will have you believe that today's consumers are looking for the cheapest price. Struggling through a recession, budgets get tightly squeezed, and when 'push comes to shove,' lowering your price may lure you in an effort to secure business and cash flow. When the old mapmakers depicted the world as flat, they wrote along the edges of the uncharted waters – "Beware, beyond here there be dragons".…. That is my advice to you if you ever think about lowering your pricing. Even when variable market conditions exist, low pricing is the bane of business. Low pricing has never topped customer satisfaction surveys and is definitely not a market driver. Lower prices might secure a client, but it is great service which keeps a client. If a client is not 100% satisfied, then low pricing is not a bargain.

Think back, …have you ever ignored your better judgement and bought a cheap priced item only to have it fall apart sooner than you expected? …or you incurred increased maintenance costs on it? A good example is cheap air travel tickets – people wanted lower and lower airfares, so in order to maintain their business, service delivered was reduced. One example is that they started charging premiums for seats, to take your suitcase and you started to expect delays. If these things are important to you and the expectations of service delivery are not met, then price is not an issue. A low-priced bargain option led to disappointment and frustration when we found the parts to sustain it were cost prohibitive or it didn't live up to our expectations. Warren Buffett said, "Price is what you pay; value is what you get." Face it, starting a business in any industry is tough; but starting out with the lowest price puts you in a precarious situation from which many do not recover.

Essentially, people buy solutions to problems; the greater the need the higher the value, so the simplest thing to do is provide the best solution to a problem. Where a market leader exists with little competition, there will always be someone who thinks they can do it for less. Maybe that approach works for a short time, but eventually something has to give; maybe as they become a player in the market the price increases, because they can't sustain the business on low profit margins, maybe their service decreases or maybe they just go out of business. When you are faced with making the decision about whether to lower pricing in order to compete, I urge you to hold fast or even raise pricing then add more value to what you provide. As an alternative, perhaps you provide a menu of services individualized to meet client's needs and budget:

❑ Good   Basic

❑ Better   Enhanced

❑ Best service packages   Premium

Doing this will then make it not a choice of whether to use you; rather it is a case of which service option they will use.

Also, remember people buy their own perception of value – not your perception; your job as a business provider is to uncover that perceived value driver (be it convenience, esteem, wealth, ease of use or peace of mind) and provide the best perceived solution. When you can do that well, you will discover price is not an issue. Consumers never cease the need to consume; they can be encouraged to buy as long as their perception of value is met or exceeded.

NICHE MARKETS:

Michael E. Porter, a professor at the Harvard Business School is considered the leading authority on competitive advantage theory. According to his work, three of the main types of business strategies are: cost leadership, differentiation and focus strategies. Niche marketing is a focus strategy.

What it means to you is that within the industry you plan to work, you pinpoint a segment of the mass market which is not being served or served well, and you provide a solution specific to that need. For example, several years ago someone who was fed up with being sick developed Gluten-free bread. Initially it was a small target market, but definitely an identifiable specialty. That small niche market has now grown exponentially. You can see an instance in almost every industry – real estate is just one. For example, real estate professionals can develop specialized knowledge to work in commercial real estate or certify to work with seniors. By working in a narrower field, there will be less competition and you can concentrate your advertising dollars on the market most likely to hire you.

Niche marketing for any business is the smart business strategy to use; in small and new businesses, it is the best strategy for the most likely sustained success.

No business can be all things to all people, so look for a niche for which your company can provide a solution, but also one in which you can quickly become an expert or specialist. A niche market can be one which serves social or cultural differences. It can be a delivery channel (Nerds on Wheels was a new concept which addressed the need for in-home computer repair and removed a fear from the client), or it could also be exclusive rights to provide a particular program. (CSP International has exclusive rights from the LiveGreen, LiveSmart Institute to present the Certified EcoProfessional program.)

Perception Is Key! It Is What The Client Thinks That Counts

1. By continuing your own education and developing expert status in specialty niche markets, you show commitment to your business and clients.

2. Collaborate with like-minded businesses who need to reach the same target market segment but who do not conflict with your business.

3. Develop specialties to compliment and support the work you want to do and which others in your industry may not have. Doing so:

   ■ Shows commitment to your business and interest in enhancing their business

   ■ Your specialties speak to your expertise

   ■ Your specialties support their expertise

   ■ It shows professionalism

   ■ It adds to their trust in you to help them manage aspects of their business

   ■ It demonstrates collaboration

Once you start positioning yourself as an expert you need to become one. Build your resume and expert status in a variety of ways, because doing so will position you as an expert. Have a great website with testimonials. Using social media, blogging, article writing, pod radio and also speaking engagements within your targeted market will help propel you to the top. Keep in mind, whatever you do – do it well and do it often.

TRENDS:

Trend awareness is used in business planning to help companies understand demand, speed, volume and to develop process to meet those requirements.

Wayne Gretsky said, "A good hockey player skates where the puck is, a great hockey player skates where the puck is GOING." Substitute 'successful business' for 'hockey player' and you have a metaphor for business.

Faith Popcorn is a consumer trend analyst who predicts global market shifts and helps large corporations to develop products to lead the shift. Her book "The Popcorn Report" opened my eyes to the need for me to understand how staying on top of trends would help keep my business from stagnation or disaster. I learned to forecast how global consumer habits and trends would affect the industry I worked in (See book: *TRENDSETTERS*). Keeping your business one-step-ahead-of-the-crowd (or several) requires a study of trends within the economy and society, and not a review of trends in your industry.

Stefan Swanepoel, a trend expert, said: "trends are like ocean currents – you can ride a wave or be sucked down by the undertow." How trends affect business is rather like watching a Tsunami. Someone observes minute shifts in consumer consciousness then predicts how society will respond. Fast-moving companies shift their focus to delivering products/services to feed the trend, thereby providing niche market leadership; consumers develop demand, companies evolve to meet the demand and then a tidal wave of mass-market awareness and acceptance happens, then it tends to subside. Generally, trends last for 10 – 30 years, so missing the mark can severely hurt your market position.

Understanding the economy will help you retool your business, your message and your marketing. Today's consumers are not as gullible as previous decades; they are also more difficult to please. There is too much noise, too much to do, not enough time to do it in and everything is predicated on not having enough money to do it. Consumers are more sceptical; they feel let down and are looking for value. A shift in your business consciousness can help you ride the wave. They are still learning that low price also means lowest value; so you need to create the demand for your services. Work for the results of the future, not the day you are in; where is your business going? …growing?

Look at the results of Soy Milk. In 1992, the industry sold $84million; ten years later the demand created $892million in business.

WOMEN, YOUTH AND MINORITIES FORM FASTEST GROWING SEGMENT OF CONSUMER INFLUENCERS.

Women are the world's largest economy; they make up 52% of the population and buy 85% of everything ….how will that affect your business? What shifts can you make in your business to be ahead in your industry? Don't dismiss the obvious! Christopher Columbus never stopped to ask for direction when he discovered America, however don't forget he was looking for India.

If you think this is all too much work, think of this wonderful story I read in Jeffery Gitomer's book The Little Platinum Book of Cha Ching:

THINK about doing business in 1880

- No computer, fax, TV, no radio, no copiers, no paved roads, cause no cars
- Heat was provided by coal/wood and there was no air conditioning
- If you wanted to go somewhere, you went by train or horse
- To contact someone, you sent a telegram or letter – handwritten – there were no typewriters and the light bulb was one year old
- The telephone was 4 yrs old, but no one had one
- 1880 –there wasn't much of what we have today
- There were no business models, no info gurus and no formulas for success
- Stores kept their money in a drawer and a safe – there were no cash registers, BUT in Dayton, Ohio, John Patterson bought a patent from John Ritty for an invention called a cash register. He formed The National Cash Register Company (NCR) and founded a business and instituted sales processes.

Selling by leveraging emotion and logic, John Patterson didn't sell cash registers, he created the demand for a receipt. **HE CREATED THE DEMAND FOR HIS PRODUCT.** You need to create the demand for yours and remember if you aren't doing any of these things in your business, all you have is a job, and as Michael E Geber says, "and you are working for a lunatic (you)."

Commit to learning how trends affect your business, if you don't. ...

YOUR COMPETITION WILL.

About Christine

Christine Rae is known as the leading expert and trendsetter of the Real Estate Staging Industry. In her role as President and CEO for CSP International, she steered the company to the top of the excellence chart for her industry. The CSP International Academy is known as a successful incubator for 'would be' entrepreneurs with a decorating flair who want control over their own destiny, while building successful, profitable businesses of their own. CSP International provides a safe haven for learning, support, knowledge, best practices and leading market trends. Graduates from the Academy benefit from a reputation of excellence, helping them gain credibility and recognition as they market and develop their own business.

Christine is recognized as the world's leading authority on staging from her global experience as well as through her work in developing standards, examinations, professionalism and trend forecasting. She is the author of *Home Staging for Dummies®* (Wiley press), editor of the world's only Staging Industry Magazine, and is co-authoring two new books in the works for release this fall, *Trendsetters* and *Sold*.

Christine developed and trademarked EcoStaging®. She is an Industry Expert Blogger for REALTOR® magazine, a regular contributor to Real Estate Magazine and is the Green Staging Expert for HomeGain®. She has been a featured speaker and keynote for many industry events including six Stagers Expo's, Real Estate Staging Association, Sydney, Australia Real Estate event, Key Note for a European convention of stagers in the Netherlands and expert speaker at the California Association of Realtors convention. Christine and her unique, signature CSP® Real Estate Staging Business Program has received awards, accolades and recognition – including accreditation by RESA. Currently five US colleges across the country endorse the program. Her book, *Home Staging for Dummies®*, has also been selected as the textbook on staging at several colleges in Canada.

Christine's success stems from her work ethic, desire for excellence, integrity and integral goodness. In a very competitive industry, what sets CSP apart are the differentiators and the driving force to be of service and value to the student. From the outset, CSP International core values, mission, "pay it forward" philosophy and apprenticeship program have been the catalyst to the myriad of differentiators which set CSP apart. Christine has worked with TV House Doctor Ann Maurice. Many of Christine's graduates have appeared on popular HGTV real estate shows, she was recently certified to facilitate Michael E Gerber's *"Dreaming Room"* event, was interviewed by Michael, and had a guest appearance on The Michael E Gerber Show. She also has appeared on ABC, NBC, CBS and FOX television affiliates speaking about staging.

CHAPTER 8

THREE CRITICAL MISTAKES THAT STOP 95% OF REAL ESTATE INVESTORS FROM EVER MAKING THAT ILLUSIVE FIRST MILLION.

By Joe Rickards

Did you know that someone becomes a millionaire every four minutes in North America? Did you know that 93% of millionaires made it in real estate?

You're about to discover my proven roadmap to creating financial freedom buying distressed real estate in Canada and the US, even if you have no money and no credit! I used these closely-guarded strategies to go from flat broke to multi-millionaire; and I'm going to share them with you.

YOUR SHORTCUT TO SUCCESS

The best shortcut to success is by modeling successful people, bar none! Life is simply too short to figure it all out on our own. We want to become great investors, right? Well, let's model the greatest investor that has ever lived - Warren Buffett. In a nutshell, he buys companies, equities and free cash flow at a discount. If at the beginning of Buffett's company, Berkshire Hathaway, you had invested a mere $10,000, you'd be sitting on a cool $50 million today. Can we apply his strategy to real estate investing? Absolutely! I successfully applied the buffettology strategy - Buy, Hold and Prosper - to real estate investing for two decades, so I can tell you it's the safest, most certain path to real estate wealth creation. It's simple. You collect the positive cash flow while your tenants pay down your mortgages – until that glorious day comes when you own your properties outright "free and clear."

WHY REAL ESTATE – WHY NOW?

Why real estate? Leverage! Leverage is by far the biggest reason 93% of all millionaires made it in real estate. The reason being, real estate is one of the only assets that banks will readily allow you to borrow, or leverage, up to 100% of its value (and more if you know how).

Why now? Skeptics have said to me, "But Joe, that was then, this is now. Times have changed." To the contrary, history always repeats itself in predictable cycles, and today's economy presents one of the best real estate investment opportunities in our generation. Why? For one, there are still many distressed sellers out there – in Canada and the US. How do I know? Because I'm finding hot deals virtually every week. Today you're able to buy positive cash flow properties with money you can borrow at all-time historic low interest rates. Whenever you can borrow money at less than the real rate of inflation, like today, the real cost of that money is zero – it's interest-FREE MONEY! So the real question is, how much interest-free money should you borrow to buy positive cash-flowing assets?

READY, FIRE, AIM

It's unfortunate that most real estate investors get caught up in the ready-aim-aim-aim mode… and sadly never pull the trigger on making offers and buying properties… and that is **critical mistake #1**. Years ago during lunch, Canadian self-made billionaire Michael Lee Chin told me something profound that changed my life. He said, "We can only make sound decisions quickly when we have previously developed the framework and experience within which to make such decisions."

Thanks to Michael's wise advice, I went to work on developing my expertise and 'decision-making framework' until eventually I was able to buy great deals sight unseen, and even successfully manage them remotely. To help you develop the framework to make quick decisions consistently, my Power-Team mortgage broker Kyle Green and I teamed up to co-brand our comprehensive Real Deal Analyzer™ tool that allows you to evaluate and make investment decisions in minutes. A free download is available to you at www.JoeRickards.com.

The 'Buy, Hold and Prosper' approach to wealth creation applied to real estate is to control millions in positive cash flow real estate over the long term. The only way you get there is by taking massive action – buying, buying, buying. Some argue timing is everything. It is not. You don't buy the market, you buy the deal. You can find deals in both good and bad markets. Sure it's great to buy at a discount, but not if you're going to get stuck in the ready-aim-aim-aim mode, forever searching for that perfect deal.

To illustrate my point, let's compare 'Joe' who simply buys average deals at 5% below fair market value, which he readily finds because he's not overly picky. He buys on average 4 properties every year. Now let's look at 'Terri,' who only buys deals at least 20% below value. Terri's challenge is that she only finds one of these smoking deals every year. Both Joe and Terri only buy break-even cash flow properties and follow the same investment strategy year-after-year for 15 years. All else being equal, guess who wins? At the end of the day, Joe makes 271% more than Terri.

Successful people make fast decisions. In the long run, the more positive cash flow real estate you own, the more you make, so don't be too picky.

MASTERING OPM

Mastering *'Other People's Money'* techniques is the single most important skill you must master to make it to financial freedom investing in real estate. Failing to do so is **critical mistake #2**. Regardless of whether you're flat broke (like I was when I got started), or you're sitting on hundreds of thousands in cash, you'll soon run out of your own money – then it's game over unless you can tap into OPM! The cheapest capital is bank mortgage financing, so I suggest you master the art of fitting into the banks box first.

PRIVATE MONEY SECRETS

Before you reach the point where banks will no longer give you mortgages to buy more properties, I suggest you work on mastering raising private money. Today there are trillions of dollars in 'scared capital' out there running for cover to 'safe investments' such as Gold, Silver, T-Bill's, GIC's, RRSP's and 401k's. It astounds me that the world is so desperate for 'safety' that investors are buying up 10-year US bonds by the billions at today's meager 1.9% yields. Did you know that over 80% of North Americans are dead or broke by the age of 65, and 63% will depend on welfare or charity for their retirement? I feel bad for retirees on fixed incomes that only invest in these 'safe' investments, because no one has shown them any better alternatives.

Are you asking yourself – how and where do I find these private money lenders? The most powerful way to raise private money is using educational-based marketing. On my website I reveal exactly how easy it is to tap into a never-ending supply of these private Mom 'n Pop private lenders. I walk you through the process so you can go out and tap into more private money than you could ever use. CAUTION – seek the advise of a good securities lawyer, as I've seen investors using this strategy get in trouble with the SEC because they didn't follow the rules.

You can find as many of these private lenders as you need online, right from the comfort of your own home. This is one of the best-kept secrets in the creative real estate investment community.

'CASH BACK' DEALS

'No money down' and 'cash back' deals using 100% mortgage financing are still possible today despite what others tell you to the contrary. How do I know? Because I've been doing it for two decades and I continue to use the exact same techniques successfully today.

Two primary techniques is all you need to do most of these deals. The first technique involves a single contract of purchase and sale, wherein the seller credits the buyer back a sum of cash at closing. The second, commonly called a 'flip' or 'skip transfer' involves two contracts of purchase and sale. In the first contract, the title owner sells YOU the subject property for say $300K. In the second contract, YOU now become the seller and sell the property for say $350K to your end buyer. Both contracts close simultaneously on the same day on what is called a 'flow through,' or 'skip transfer' transaction. You don't need any of your own money to close. Rather, the funds to purchase the property flow through you from your end buyer to the current title owner. In this scenario, your gross flip profit is the $50,000 spread between the two purchase prices.

In a nutshell, that's the 'nothing down' formula and that is all you need to know to go out there and find deals right now.

In order to get cash back on closing, you need to purchase the property at a greater percentage discount than 100% minus your mortgage percentage LTV (loan-to-value). For example, if you're buying a property appraised at $200,000 and you're getting an 80% LTV mortgage ($160K) and you want cash back on closing, you need to negotiate a discount of 20% or more off the appraised value. Say you negotiate a 25% discount ($50K) off the appraised value, then you can get $10K cash back on closing ($160K mortgage - $150K price). The bigger the spread between appraised value and your purchase price, the more of the bank's cash you can put in your jeans at closing.

Over my two-decade creative real estate investing career, I've maintained a 100% success track record on countless 'no money down' and 'cash back' deals. I disclose everything to the bank and they lend based on value. At the same time, I don't want to mislead you into thinking that this is 'a walk in the park.' It's simple, but not easy. If you don't know exactly what you're doing, precisely how to write up the contract, or you don't have your Power-Team of lawyers, appraisers, and mortgage brokers in place – attempting this simply will not work. During my years in the trenches doing deals, I've perfected a system that allows these 'cash back' deals to go through smoothly every single time. Feel free to reach out to me. I'll gladly joint-venture with you to show you exactly how I do it, and we'll make money together. I only make money when you do.

GO TO JAIL, DO NOT COLLECT $200

Bank fraud is one of the most taboo topics in the whole creative real estate investment niche. The bottom line is this. As long as you fully disclose the buyers 'credit back' to the bank underwriting your deal, you're fine. Unfortunately many investors do it the wrong way. They write up a buyer credit back at closing clause on a separate addendum and then they don't send that addendum to the bank or their mortgage broker. That's duping the bank and it's mortgage fraud, plain and simple. My Power-Team lawyer, Rick Ledding, is a highly respected real estate lawyer that has done countless creative deals. At www.JoeRickards.com, you can watch Rick's video special report revealing – "*3 Massive Mistakes Real Estate Investors Make That Kill Their Deals.*"

THE HIDDEN TRUTH ABOUT APPRECIATION

I'm going to bust a very old myth wide open. Using the most accurate sources of historical national US data – US Census, NAR and Case-Schiller, I found the historical real estate value appreciation data contains such an invisible wild card that analysts can swing real estate price data either way. From 1950 – 2004, average new home sizes exploded from 983 to 2,349 sq. ft. That means that a big chunk of house price increases wasn't appreciation at all. Larger homes obviously sell for higher prices, which has positively skewed the price data, making it appear house prices were appreciating, when in fact they really weren't.

US house prices have historically appreciated at an average annual rate of 3.8% versus a 3.9% average core rate of inflation, which means *the "real rate" of real estate appreciation has historically been essentially nil.*

THE POWER OF LEVERAGE

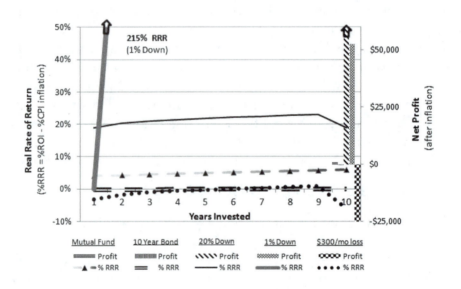

SECRETS GRAPH REVEALS –

1. Even assuming a 0% rate of appreciation, positive cash flow real estate still outperforms all other investments in its low risk class!

2. Positive cash flow real estate strategies are safe, secure and powerful wealth builders, while negative cash flow can send you to the poor house.

3. The power of leverage; 20% DOWN returns 1.9% RRR/yr VS. 1% DOWN returns 21.5%/yr.

4. Conventional 'safe' investments are robbing you blind.

For you 'left brain' data lovers, here's the 'nitty gritty' details of my above analysis.

The graph above represents my comparison of the "real rate of return" (RRR), or ROI less core inflation, for the following low risk class investment vehicles over a 10-year period:

1. Bonds (1.9% current 10 year US bond yield).

2. Stocks or Mutual Funds (assume 7% average).

3. $200/mo positive cash flow real estate with 20% down (at today's 10 yr fixed mortgage of 5%).

4. $200/mo positive cash flow real estate with 1% down (at today's 10 yr fixed mortgage of 5%).

5. $300/mo negative cash flow real estate (at today's 10 yr fixed mortgage of 5%).

The two real estate investment scenarios above – #3 and #4 – use the purchase of one $200,000 investment property at market value (no discount) and a $200/month positive cash flow after all expenses. I applied the 0% historical average appreciation and factored in all costs – closing costs, carrying costs, insurance premiums, taxes and selling commissions.

Our typical investor who puts 20% down, yields a $89,524 profit, or 1.9% RRR per year (%RRR = %ROI - %CPI inflation) from a cash investment of $40,000. Now let's compare your creative purchase with only 1% down ($2,000). You get a whopping $64,573 profit, or 21.5% RRR per year while only putting $2,000 of your own money into the deal. Now that's what I call having a money tree!

Lastly, let's compare the $300/mo negative cash flow investment at 20% or $40,000 down. It actually loses $25,074 over a 10-year hold.

TENANTS, TERMITES & TRASH

Real estate values are predictably cyclical, and you're sure to encounter mountains and valleys along your road to financial freedom. Canadian billionaire Michael Lee Chin said to me, "What I do is simple, but not easy. It's not easy to be successful because it's not easy to be committed, focused and persevere over the long run. But those are all essential ingredients to be successful in business and life."

One of the fundamental secrets to success through real estate is having positive cash flow properties to ensure you can weather the real estate market storms when they inevitably hit. Not having a sound, long-term positive cash flow strategy to make sure you can hold on for the long-term is **critical mistake #3.**

For most real estate investors, "tenants, termites and trash" poses the greatest risk to breaking the hanging in for the long haul rule and throwing in the towel before 'reaching the end zone and scoring the touchdown.' Ask me how I know that.

After having hundreds of tenants, my day-to-day property management hassles became unbearable. I felt that my tenants were robbing me of my passion for real estate. I am excited to reveal that recently I discovered an amazing strategy that allows you to build your portfolio to hundreds of doors, virtually hassle-free. You literally have no tenants and no headaches at all, and I am not talking about rent-to-own strategy here. Sounds too good to be true? At my website you'll find my video revealing this well-guarded secret strategy.

I'd like to gift you more content and empower you to go out there and make deals happen. Go to: www.JoeRickards.com and you'll get FREE access to my content-packed 3-part video series that REVEALS:

1. How to tap into millions in private money to do your deals.

2. How you can pocket thousands of dollars cash back on closing.

3. How you can borrow over $500,000 unsecured at 4% or less.

4. How to turn your properties into 'cash cows' and sell them for profit, even before you buy.

5. How you can buy and own distressed properties completely hassle-free. No tenants and no responsibilities whatsoever.

6. How you can get your deals funded, up to $600,000 per deal. I refer you to my personal private money lender.

7. How you can easily find more smoking hot deals than you can handle.

IF you are an action taker and need help solving a deal challenge, or making it happen, reach out to me for help at www.JoeRickards.com.

I'd like to leave you with a few words of wisdom from Tony Robbins. "If you do what you've always done, you'll get what you've always gotten."

You are your success,
Joe Rickards

About Joe

Joe Rickards has been featured as America's Premier Real Estate Expert on FOX, NBC, CBS, ABC, CBS News, Forbes.com and has been inducted into *The National Academy of Best-Selling Authors™*. World-renowned business expert and bestselling author Brian Tracy has referred to Joe Rickards as "one of the foremost leading authorities in real estate and finance today."

Flat broke and straight out of university, Joe caught 'the real estate bug' and bought his first investment property with no money down. He went on to become a self-made millionaire in his late twenties while also climbing the corporate ladder at leading Fortune 500 companies. After making more in one creative real estate deal than his annual job income, Joe quit his successful engineering career and has been happily 'unemployable' for almost a decade.

Joe's unique business model focuses on mentorship, action and deals as the foundation to creating profitable win-win joint ventures. Joe's proprietary marketing machine – *The Real Deal Finder™*, is helping his JV partners find hot real estate deals across Canada and the US.

"Joe's JV mentorship program changed my life forever. In 2010 I was able to quit my executive job with the positive cash flow income from my multi-million dollar real estate portfolio and now I'm living the dream", says Darryl Torhjelm, one of Joe's apprentices.

Visit www.JoeRickards.com to receive your content rich FREE 3-part video series revealing Joe's closely-guarded secrets and proven strategies he used for two decades making millions using little to none of his own money.

CHAPTER 9

Creating Multiple Streams Of Income

By Nick Berry & Pat Rigsby

As an entrepreneur, you essentially accept the fact that you're trading the security that comes with a steady job for the opportunity that comes with owning your own business. But what if we told you that security and opportunity don't have to be mutually exclusive? Our experience is that not only can you have the best of both worlds, but you can do it more quickly and easily than you probably imagine by creating multiple streams of income.

About the time we launched our first business together, our *"The Only Business Book You'll Ever Need"* co-author, the legendary Robert Allen, released his best selling book: *Multiple Streams of Income,* which served as inspiration for us as we embarked on building our new personal training business. We were opening this business in a town of just 23,000 people in Central Kentucky, not exactly a perceived hotbed for personal training, so we knew from the beginning that we needed to have multiple ways of generating revenue if we wanted this venture to be a success. So instead of simply relying on selling one-on-one personal training services like most people who owned similar types of businesses, we created a number of different revenue streams, including:

- One-on-One Personal Training
- Group Personal Training
- Weight Management Programs

- Sports Performance Programs
- Dietary Supplement Sales
- Smoothie Bar
- Workshops
- Corporate Fitness Programs

This approach quickly propelled us to a point where we had over 400 clients in a town where utilizing the typical approach to this type of business might have yielded 1/10 that amount.

And that's where things really started to take off. Soon, health clubs and personal trainers were seeking us out to consult and share some of the strategies that we'd successfully utilized so they could employ them in their own businesses. These consulting opportunities opened our eyes to the vast opportunities that were available sharing our systems and strategies through information marketing and business coaching.

Over the next few years we developed a variety of coaching programs, information products and seminars helping personal trainers grow their businesses. Most recently we launched two separate personal training-based franchises, one targeting the youth fitness & sports performance market and the other targeting the adult fitness market. As of the time that we're publishing this book, both are among the fastest growing fitness franchises in the world.

Once we'd positioned ourselves as industry leading providers of business coaching and resources for fitness professionals, we would be presented with opportunities to obtain ownership in other business in the industry where our expertise would be of value. Now, along with our business coaching and franchises, we also have ownership in a leading fitness certification organization, an equipment company, several niche fitness information-marketing businesses and a handful of other businesses, collectively providing us well over 100 different income streams.

Now we teach thousands of fitness professionals around the world to employ the 'multiple streams of income' approach and how simple it is to integrate into a business. While you're probably not in the fitness industry, the 'multiple streams of income' approach will work in your business too, perhaps even better than it's worked in ours. Really it simply starts by answering these two questions:

1. What 'problems' do your current offering(s) create?
2. What opportunities do your current customers / clients / patients present?

By answering those two questions you'll easily be able to identify potential income streams for your business. Let us give you examples of how we might have answered those questions in our personal training business.

What 'problems' do your current offering(s) create?

One-on-one personal training is potentially too expensive for many consumers so offering small and large group personal training allows those than can't afford one-on-one personal training similar benefits while being available at a much lower price point. Also, personal training focuses on the exercise component of physical improvement, but there are other factors than can impact someone's success while trying to achieve fitness goals like nutrition, supplementation and recovery. By offering weight management programs, supportive nutrition solutions though our 'smoothie' bar, dietary supplements and workshops, we can address the other factors that will help our clients achieve their fitness goals more quickly and easily.

What opportunities do your current customers / clients / patients present?

Many personal training clients are either business owners or business decision makers, so they can open doors to opportunities to provide corporate fitness programs or off-site weight management programs at their companies. Additionally, many clients have children and / or are in positions of influence (teachers, school administrators, coaches, etc.) for the youth population and would see the benefit in, and help promote, youth fitness and sports performance offerings.

Hopefully you're already getting some ideas for income streams you can develop based on those two questions. Another great way to get ideas for potential income streams is to simply look at other businesses and see what they do.

Here are a couple examples:

Automotive dealerships don't just sell cars. They do repairs. They do preventative maintenance. They offer financing. Some dealerships even provide things like detailing or car rental programs.

Amusement parks don't just offer rides and attractions. They sell food and refreshments. They sell a variety of retail products from theme-related attire and toys to sun block and sunglasses that visitors might have forgotten to bring. They also offer paid parking, photographs taken during guest stays, and many have their own hotels that guests can utilize during their visit.

There are thousands of businesses employing the 'multiple streams of income' approach, so learn from the successes they're having so you can create your own.

Once you've determined some general ideas of what other problems you could solve for your customers / clients / patients or the opportunities that they could create for you and your business, then you need to decide on the models for your income streams.

Basically there are five types of Income Models you can implement:
- Service Based
- Product Based
- Coaching / Consulting Based
- Information / Knowledge Based
- Affiliate / Referral Based

Each of these Income Models has it's own set of benefits and drawbacks and some may be more appropriate than others for your business, but you should have no problem choosing a couple that you can integrate into your business and add additional revenue – in some cases almost immediately.

So let's take a look at each of these Income Models in greater detail. We'll share an overview of the model and an example of how we've integrated it into our own businesses.

Service Based – This is typically the easiest to add to a business, as it often requires little set up and relies primarily on you or a staff member utilizing skills that you (or someone on your team) possess and will be of benefit to your customers / clients / patients and typically compliments your primary offerings. The upside to this type of Income Model is the ease of start up and integration into your business. The downside is that it's time and skill intensive.

When we had our first personal training business, the easiest and most obvious Income Model for us to integrate was a Weight Management Program. This program was basically a nutritional education program delivered by our staff members that helped our clients reach their goals faster and was the perfect compliment to the exercise based coaching that was our primary offering.

Product Based – Product based models are potentially very simple to integrate into your business as well. The upside to the product based Income Model is that it usually doesn't require any special skill to offer products beyond some basic product knowledge and this model isn't as time intensive as the others.

The first potential drawback to the product model is the fact that most products or similar competitors will be offered in other retail outlets so there isn't as much price elasticity as with the other models. The other drawback to the product model is that it usually requires an upfront investment for inventory.

Our initial use of the Product Based Income Model was through selling dietary supplements to our personal training clients. Our clients were regularly investing in supplements to help them reach their fitness goals and often consulted with our staff when choosing what supplements to purchase, so it became obvious very quickly that we should carry our own line of quality supplements and direct our clients to purchase from us. Not only were there financial benefits to this, but we also now could direct our clients to products that we knew and trusted. A great win/win.

Coaching / Consulting Based – Coaching / Consulting Based Income Models are great if you've established a successful business and are willing to share your business systems and knowledge with other entrepreneurs. The primary benefit to this Income Model is that the potential financial upside of business-to-business coaching /consulting is typically much greater than providing services to consumers. The other real upside is that it allows you to leverage what you already know and do in your own business by sharing it with others.

The potential drawback to the Coaching / Consulting Based Income Model isn't really a drawback at all. It's more of a pre-requisite. To ethically coach or consult you should have experienced some success running your own business. If you've successful owned your own business and have a systematic approach that others can model, then this approach is very powerful.

We first employed the Coaching / Consulting Based Income Model by teaching other personal trainers and health club owners how we'd successfully built our personal training business. This Income Model eventually merged together with the Information / Knowledge Based Income Model and evolved into our two franchises: Athletic Revolution International and Fitness Revolution International.

Information / Knowledge Based – In the Information / Knowledge Based Income Model you simply document what you know and do successfully and package it to be shared with others. There are many advantages to this model. Some of the biggest are the fact that you can develop information products to offer to people that normally couldn't be your customers / clients / patients due to geographic constraints, so essentially the whole world is potentially your market. There is great leverage with this type of Model too. You can create a product once and sell it over and over again. Typically the margins on offerings in this Model are very high too.

If there is any downside to this Income Model, it is that while your market is no longer limited by geography, the same goes for your competition. When offering an information product or program you will be competing for your prospect's attention with many more marketers than you would typically face when just selling products or services locally.

We began with the Information / Knowledge Based Income Model with two different offerings at about the same time. One of our offerings was directed to other business owners sharing our systems, strategies and tactics for building a successful personal training business. The other offering featured Pat's wife, Holly, and was a consumer product called Fit Yummy Mummy, which was a fitness program specifically designed for moms. In both cases, we simply packaged the things that we'd done successfully in our own businesses and shared them with people who could benefit from the knowledge, but couldn't work with us face-to-face.

Ultimately both of these initial products laid the foundation for new businesses that have each become category leaders in their respective markets.

Affiliate / Referral Based – This Income Model is very simple to integrate into your business as it basically just requires you to find a product or service that you can refer your customers / clients / patients to, which is complimentary to your offerings. The upside to the Affiliate / Referral Based Income Model is the fact that it requires very little work on your part to generate additional revenue. The 'partner' that you are referring business to will provide the service or product while paying you a referral fee. The downside to this Model is that you are putting your relationship with your customer in the hands of someone else. If they provide an inferior product or service, then you will suffer the ill effects of that. Therefore, if you employ this Income Model, be certain to only refer only businesses of the highest quality.

We initially utilized this Income Model by referring our personal training clients to a massage therapist. The massage therapist provided a quality service to our clients that we did not offer and paid us a referral fee for every client we sent. In addition to those benefits, the massage therapist also referred their clients to us for our services to make this a great reciprocal relationship.

By determining what problems you could solve for your customers / clients / patients or the opportunities that they could create for you and your business and the income models you can employ to address them, you can not only add tens of thousands of dollars to your bottom line and better serve the people you work with, but you may also lay the foundation for businesses that enjoy even greater successes and profits than the one you have now. We certainly have.

About Nick

Nick Berry has spent his entire career as an Entrepreneur in the fitness industry. His experience has given him the opportunity to become a Business Coach and Consultant, and co-owner of dozens of other businesses, which have allowed him to help thousands of other small business owners, both in and out of the fitness industry.

Nick co-founded, co-owns, and continues to build the Athletic Revolution™ and Fitness Revolution™ franchise systems. Athletic Revolution™ (www.myathleticrevolution.com) is a youth-based sports performance franchise which began in 2009 and currently has over 40 franchise units. Fitness Revolution™ (www.fitnessrevolution-franchise.com) is an adult fitness franchise, which began in January 2011, and currently has over 75 franchise units.

Nick partnered with Pat Rigsby in 2005 and they continue to operate Fitness Consulting Group, (www.fitbusinessinsider.com) from which they offer their fitness business consulting programs. He has helped build and co-owns the International Youth Conditioning Association, which is considered the premier international authority on youth conditioning and athletic development (www.iyca.org). He also was a co-author of the International Best Selling *Total Body Breakthroughs* book in the spring of 2011.

He and Pat Rigsby currently partner in a dozen other businesses, primarily in the fitness industry. They continue to focus on surrounding their primary companies with valuable services and products from reputable and dependable vendors, and to create relationships that are valuable and beneficial for all parties involved – the customers, the vendors, and the primary companies themselves. This philosophy has been built around the concept of "A rising tide lifts all boats," and has lead to many of their current interests in these additional businesses.

About Pat

Pat Rigsby is an author, consultant and fitness entrepreneur as well as the Co-Owner of a variety of businesses within the fitness industry

Pat co-founded, co-owns, and continues to build the Athletic Revolution™ and Fitness Revolution™ franchise systems. Athletic Revolution™ (www.myathleticrevolution.com) is a youth-based sports performance franchise which began in 2009 and currently has over 40 franchise units. Fitness Revolution™ (www.fitnessrevolutionfranchise.com) is an adult fitness franchise, which began in January 2011, and currently has over 75 franchise units.

Pat also Co-Owns the Fitness Consulting Group, (www.fitbusinessinsider.com) which provides coaching, products and programs for entrepreneurial fitness professionals. He has helped build and co-owns the International Youth Conditioning Association, which is considered the premier international authority on youth conditioning and athletic development (www.iyca.org). Pat is also author of the International Best Selling *Little Black Book of Fitness Business Success.*

Pat and Nick also host a number of conferences, webinars and write a blog and newsletter that reach over 65,000 fitness professionals on the topics of fitness business development and fitness marketing, and other business topics. He has been seen on NBC, ABC, CBS and in the pages of industry publications like Personal Fitness Professional, Club Industry and Club Business International. You can learn more about Pat & Nick's coaching programs and products or to download their collection of free business-building gifts by going to: www.FitBusinessInsider.com.

CHAPTER 10

Three Keys to Unlocking *Your* Total Business Mastery

By Forest Hamilton

"It is a terrible thing to see and have no vision."
~ Helen Keller

I think we can all agree, high school is one of the most influential periods of your entire life. During this intense four-year span you make many of your lifelong friends, career choices, and largely determine how you will view yourself for the rest of your life. As a senior in high school, I was more focused on the Friday night lights of the Homecoming football game than I was on schoolwork. Scoring a touchdown was much more gratifying than any boring class could ever be. However, our school district found a way to swing the balance back in schoolwork's favor when they implemented the Senior Project. Even with passing grades all year long, if we received a failing grade on our Senior Project, we would not graduate. If I did not graduate, I could not pursue my athletic career. Suddenly, school became important. My motivation to pursue my dream of collegiate and professional athletics forced me to focus on school.

BREAKING IT DOWN

My search for the perfect Senior Project took me on a journey from Skydiving to Quantum Physics. Then I met Lucy. Lucy was in the third grade at Stillwater Elementary. In the year that I spent with her she never said a single word. Lucy was autistic. I was fascinated, intrigued, and intimidated. Autism is a pervasive developmental disorder that is characterized by impaired social interaction or communication. I spent two hours a day with Lucy for my entire senior year studying her and learning about Autism. But she means much more to me than the tearful standing ovation I received from the School Board while giving my successful Senior Project Speech. You see, Lucy taught me one of the most valuable lessons of my life. She taught me that in order to understand something fully, we must break it down into small parts and then rebuild it. She was 9 years old and couldn't speak, but she could take a working rotary phone apart until it was in 100 small pieces and then put it back together again in a matter of minutes in perfect working order. I have spent the last 18 years of my life following Lucy's lead. Anytime I encounter something I don't understand, I break it down into small pieces, examine them, learn to understand them, and then put them back together. What I have found is that when I put the parts back together as a whole, there is always an extra piece. That extra piece is me. I become a part of whatever I am studying, and in turn, *it* becomes a part of me.

I recently attended Brian Tracy's Total Business Mastery Seminar in San Diego. Brian invited me to speak on stage with him after I graduated from his Speaking Academy. It was quite an honor and I spent over 50 hours preparing for my speech to the hundreds of business owners and entrepreneurs in attendance. Much of my effort and research never made it to the stage. But it didn't go to waste. I have published almost every word of it in books, blogs, seminars, and newsletters. By totally engaging in the monumental task of speaking at my mentor's seminar, I was able to break down multiple subjects and when I put them back together again, they became a part of me. Many times, by breaking things down, you are able to gather the insight necessary to take your next step towards success. Part of the research and preparation process that I went through was to break down each word in the name *Total Business Mastery*. What I found was truly amazing. The following pages detail my findings that will help you apply The Three Keys to Unlocking *Your* Total Business Mastery.

1. RESPONSIBILITY - YOU ARE THE SUM TOTAL OF YOUR ACTIONS

"Our lives are a sum total of the choices we have made."
~ Wayne Dyer

The first key is to take total responsibility for your entire life. You are exactly where you are in life because of your actions, reactions, and inactions. This is a tough one to swallow at first. We are trained by society, television, and many of our peers to blame others for our failures. I mentor and coach a diverse group of men and women ranging in age from 15-80. Without fail, when I ask them why they have not achieved their goals or dreams, the culprit is always outside of themselves. The younger generation tends to blame their parents, while the older generation blames their children. The middle-aged group blames the government, the economy, their bosses, or their employees. As long as you give circumstances and other people power over your future, you will have no control of your own destiny. The moment that you wrestle control back from the outside world is one of the most exhilarating and terrifying moments of your life. No longer can you blame your clients or your boss or the economy for your lack of success. It is your fault you aren't succeeding.

The beautiful thing is, if it's your fault, you can fix it. If it's not your fault and you have no control, you will take no action. What would be the point? As hard as you might work, and as right as you might be, if you believe someone else controls your success then you will eventually give up. Only when you choose to believe that you and your actions are responsible for everything in your life can you work through the obstacles fully. Ok, so now you recognize that your current life is the exact sum total of your actions up until now. But what does *total* mean and where did it originate?

There are multiple ways to define total. All of them contain a life lesson within their meaning. Here are a few of the definitions:

to-tal /ˈtotl/
    Complete, entire, absolute.
    Comprising or constituting a whole.
    Sum. An amount obtained by addition.

The origin of total is from the Medieval Latin word *totalis*, meaning "entire." *Summa totalis* is 'the sum total'.

If we are all the sum total or *summa totalis* of what we put into our minds and bodies, then whether the input is good or bad, it becomes a part of us. If you are conscious of the thoughts, feelings, and foods that you allow into your sum total, you can have absolute control of your life. If you do not like your weight, you must simply evaluate your current caloric intake and quality of food and choose to change your diet. By being disciplined and consistent, you guarantee a change in your total weight. You can also accelerate this change by adding or subtracting exercise from your daily routine. There are thousands of diet plans available, but with a small amount of research, you can find the one that best fits your specific desires.

This same concept applies to your business. Picture your business like a mound of clay that you are shaping into a beautiful bowl set in your mind's eye. If the bowl is too thick or too thin, or starts to lose its desired shape, you don't just accept it as permanently flawed and walk away. You simply apply pressure, time, and energy to it until you have literally created the bowl of your dreams. *Choose* to not give up control to the circumstances of your market, clients, employers or employees. Stay focused on what you want to accomplish. *Constantly* evaluate yourself and your business. Make the necessary adjustments to your daily thoughts, feelings, and actions. Only then will the sum of the parts multiply in your favor, adding up to *your* total success.

2. CLARITY - CLEARLY DEFINE YOUR BUSINESS

"Your mind, while blessed with permanent memory, is cursed with lousy recall. Written goals provide clarity. By documenting your dreams, you must think about the process of achieving them." ~ Gary Ryan Blair

The second key is clarity. Clarity is the single most important asset you can possess in your business. The level to which you are absolutely clear about who you are and exactly what you want to accomplish will be consistent with your level of success in business and in life. In order to achieve the highest level of clarity for your business, you must break down what "business" means to you and why you are in it to begin with. Let's start by defining it and learning its origin:

Busi-ness /'biznis/
    Purposeful activity: busyness.
    A person's regular occupation, profession, or trade.
    An immediate task or objective.

The origin of the word business is derived from the Old English word, bisignes, meaning, "careful, anxious, busy, occupied, and diligent."

Using a combination of the definition and origin of business, imagine your day at work like this: You wake up early after "carefully" preparing a list of "purposeful activities" the night before. You are "anxious" to get to the office to get "busy" with your plan. You walk in with your head up and shoulders back, a smile on your face and 'pep in your step.' As you pass people in the foyer, they can see by the intent look in your eye that you are proud of your "profession," and are passionately pursuing a worthy "objective." Throughout your day you stay engaged and "occupied" with completing your most "immediate tasks". By the end of your day your "diligent" pursuit of success has netted you confidence, respect, and results. This is a description of a day in the life of almost every consistently successful businessman and businesswoman in the world. It doesn't matter what field you are in or what level you are at in that field. People that fill their days with the definition and origin of business have business success. People that fill their days with the opposite actions receive the opposite results.

Become absolutely clear about who you are and what you want to accomplish in your business. The reason most people don't have clarity is because they never actually sit down and made a decision to acquire it. Something magical happens when you grab a pen and a pad and begin to write with intent about who you are and what you truly want. Writing them down forces you to think about the process necessary to achieve them. Once you have that specificity of purpose you are able to make specific, purposeful, decisions that will make your days look happily similar to the one described above. Commit and choose to live the definition of business in your daily life and watch your productivity increase exponentially.

3. COMMITMENT -THE ROAD TO MASTERY

"Only one who devotes himself to a cause with his whole strength and soul can be a true master. For this reason mastery demands all of a person."
~Albert Einstein

The third and final key is to learn how to achieve *mastery* in any given subject or field. Notice that I did not say the key is to achieve mastery, rather it is to learn how to achieve it. Mastering a subject is wonderful and gratifying, but the real treasure is not in mastering a specific subject, it is the knowledge that you can master any subject through a specific process. There has never been a human that was born a great doctor, teacher, inventor, or salesman. Two of my favorite Brian Tracy quotes are, "Every master was once a disaster," and "Everyone at the front of the line started out at the back of the line." Which brings me to some of the most insightful definitions that I have ever encountered.

mas·ter·y /ˈmast(ə)rē/
    Possession of consummate skill.
    Comprehensive knowledge or skill in a subject.
    Full command of a subject.
    The upper hand in a contest or competition

So what *is* mastery? The possession of consummate skill? I love that definition. It does not say, the possession of consummate God-given ability, talent, or giftedness. It clearly states the word *skill*. Which means you *only* achieve the ownership of mastery through action, not birthright. So what actions must you take to gain the full command of, and comprehensive knowledge in, a given subject? First you must decide if you want to just become good at something, or if you truly want to master it. There is a monumental difference in the two. I've heard it said that 80% of the world becomes just good enough at their trade to not get fired, and then they never get any better. Around 19% continue learning and become some of the highest paid and sought after experts in their field. Only around 1% become the masters in their fields of choice. I say "fields of choice" because once you are a master of one field, you have learned the secrets to accomplishing the feat and can many times repeat it in multiple fields. You become a "serial entrepreneur." Unfortunately, society looks at the masters as special and immediately finds all the reasons why their success is not repeatable. It is easier to find an excuse why you *cannot* do something than it is to overcome the fear of failure and then do the hard work necessary to accomplish it.

THE THREE ROADS TO TOTAL MASTERY

The first road is a slippery, foggy, frustrating road that many times dead ends in a career change. It is the unfocused, unclear, uncommitted road that most people take when they decide to *try* and master something. Obstacles and outside influences quickly stop this wanna-be-master soon after departure.

The second road is a long, winding, methodical road with many rest stops along the way. This committed, diligent, plodding, turtle of a master eventually arrives at the desired destination. Generally, this type of master has accepted that it will take him or her their entire life to finally reach master status and their thoughts become their reality. He or she slowly studies the entirety of the field, but often spends days, weeks, or even years on unnecessary tangents.

The final road is reserved for a very special type of master. One who is open to alternative methods of learning, thinking, and acting. This master achieves master status by applying the Three Keys to Total Business Mastery on a consistent basis. There is a repeatable path that you can follow this master down to achieve the same level of enlightened success, happiness, and fulfillment.

Take total responsibility, *achieve* absolute clarity, and *consciously* commit to Total Business Mastery even in the face of massive adversity and it will be yours.

"You cannot control what happens to you, but you can control your attitude toward what happens to you, and in that, you will be mastering change rather than allowing it to master you."
~ Brian Tracy

About Forest

Forest Hamilton was literally delivered into his father's hands. When the midwife was late in arriving, David Hamilton had to find a way to bring his boy into this world. Through fear, uncertainty, and an umbilical cord wrapped around his son's neck, he found a way. Raised without running water or electricity into his teens, Forest followed his father's example and continued to persevere. His father taught him to be the hardest worker on the farm, the most competitive athlete on the field, and the most dedicated student in the classroom. This work ethic, coupled with his mother's consistently encouraging ways, helped him find his way to Texas to pursue his dreams at an early age.

Forest Hamilton is now an Assistant Director of Universal Coin and Bullion, Ltd. in Beaumont,Texas. He has held many positions in his nearly 15-year career with UCB, one of the world's largest gold, silver, and rare coin investment firms. Beginning his career at UCB as a teenager, Forest has been awarded numerous honors for sales, teamwork, and customer service on his way to becoming an invaluable resource in every department. He has helped propel his company from a five million dollar a year business into a multi-national, award winning, sixty million dollar a year industry leader.

Forest is also a partner and co-founder of David Hamilton Winery, LLP in Mt.Vernon, Oregon. This family-run winery specializes in organic fruit wines of the Northwest. He truly enjoys working with his family in the acquisition, production, distribution, marketing and drinking of their unique wines.

Forest and the love of his life, Stormy, have two beautiful daughters, Taylin and Tinsley, and are expecting their third child in March of 2012. Forest is a dedicated husband and father and applies the same passion to his personal life that he does in his business life.

Forest, co-author of the best-selling book, *PUSHING TO THE FRONT,* was recently awarded the 2011 Thought Leader Of The Year Award from the National Academy Of Best-Selling Authors. He is one of America's Premier Experts and has been featured in *USA Today.* He is known to many as a "Perpetual Positive Emotion Machine." His goal is to help others realize that happiness and success are direct results of choices, not chances. He considers sales, communication, and coaching to be art forms and is constantly striving to master each of them in an effort to better himself, his family, his businesses, and those that come to him to be mentored.

If you are interested in having Forest Hamilton help YOU find a better way in life, business, or wealth preservation and diversification in Gold and Silver, please visit foresthamilton.com or universalcoin.com. You can also call 800-248-2223 or email Forest directly at foresthamilton@universalcoin.com

If you are interested in learning more about organically grown fruit wines with no added sulfites, visit davidhamiltonwinery.com or call 541-932-4567.

CHAPTER 11

Business Success Maxims

By Mark Cole

Having a lot of money equates to success! At least that is what I thought when I started my first job many years ago.

When I was 12 years old, I started my first business: cutting grass in my neighborhood. Even though I was very young, I had no problem knocking on doors to get new customers. Soon, my business expanded and I started shoveling driveways to keep up with customer demand throughout the year. The income was steady and I was a hard-working, disciplined kid who loved having some extra money.

Now 30 years into my professional career, I remain very committed to running a successful business, but my focus has changed. I have realized that true business success comes not from promoting myself, but rather from promoting others. I have discovered that my real purpose and mission is to help other business owners and members of my community reach their goals.

FINDING THE OPPORTUNITY...AND THEN THE LESSON

Back in 2005, I had put in 19 years at a local manufacturing company; a leading global supplier for the automotive industry. Though the pay and benefits at this company were very good, I saw the writing on the wall with the auto industry's eventual collapse in 2008. I quickly realized that looking ahead, there were practically no career opportunities if I stayed with this company. For someone like me – a person that was always looking for the next opportunity professionally as well as financially –

I knew I had to do something. But unlike many other auto-industry workers who later found themselves in a career transition not by their choosing, I embraced the opportunity to try something new. I decided that I would be the one to make the first move, instead of hoping for the best and later being out of a job without a plan B.

I approached my insurance agent at the time about selling insurance and opening up my own agency. Even though I had no background in insurance or financial services, I decided to leave the "stability" of my company job. So I put in my notice, studied for my insurance exams and became a multiple line insurance agent and registered representative.

The excitement of this new chapter in my career faded pretty fast...soon I found myself in my new office with nothing but empty filing cabinets, few clients and a lot of free time. It didn't help that our country was facing really tough times. To make matters worse, I was starting my agency in Youngstown, Ohio – the #1 economically depressed city in the country at the time I chose to start my business.

It became pretty obvious to me why 85% of those who start out selling insurance do NOT make it past the two-year mark. It's highly competitive and it is a very slow process of building a successful agency, even in the best of economic times. You have to invest a lot of time and energy upfront before ever seeing any results or much income. And the truth is that most new agents get frustrated when they don't see the immediate benefits.

I decided early on that I was going to commit to the process of building my agency the right way. I knew that I was going to have to pay my dues for a few years and really work hard. But I thought back to all the different business ventures I had been involved in...the grass cutting, owning and operating a roofing and seal-coating company, buying and selling rental properties...every business experience I had up to that point had become successful in large part due to my ability to network...being really good at getting the word out and meeting a lot of new people. I figured that with insurance, networking would be just as critical to my success.

So I started my own local networking chapter of Business Network International – the largest networking organization in the world, and tried to meet as many new people as I could. This decision turned out to be a major turning point in my career as well as in developing my professional brand. What started out as a goal to find new clients quickly became something much greater – the opportunity to truly partner with other small business owners in my local community. I was a natural at not only building relationships with other people, but also at connecting people together to help them benefit from each other. In fact, I did such a good job in my networking chapter that I was given the opportunity to take on a regional leadership role within BNI.

My networking activity quickly attracted the attention of other local service organizations. I became an active member in these other groups as well, and the more that I contributed my service and my knowledge to the other members, the more I saw my circle of influence grow. And as my business expanded, so did my ability to teach people my key drivers of success.

I made it a point to set up as many individual, face-to-face meetings with my new contacts as I could on a weekly basis. And during every one of these meetings, I would learn what other people in my community and other local business owners were trying to accomplish – what their challenges were and different ways that I could help them. I would often get asked, "Mark, how do you do it? How do you get all of your work done and still have time to volunteer and make a difference?" I found myself advising and really becoming a resource for people. Every time I had a meeting or even a passing conversation with a client, business partner, friend or prospective customer I would take the extra time to listen, offer my words of wisdom, and share my knowledge to help them in any way that I could.

KEY DRIVERS OF SUCCESS

Through my 30 years of professional experience and countless conversations and interactions, I have discovered that there are three key drivers that are critical to business success:

— The Ability To Network.

— Community Service And Involvement.

— Consistent Business Building Activities.

1. NETWORK, NETWORK, NETWORK.

The concept of networking has been around for many years, yet too many business professionals and even business owners don't make networking a priority. For many, networking is a nice to have instead of a must have. There are tremendous benefits to be gained from networking activities, but many people don't "get anything out of it" simply because they don't put much into it.

Networking helped me launch my start-up insurance agency much faster, and helped me expedite my production results above my competition. I can honestly say that much of my business success is the direct result of my commitment to networking, and I've seen it help many of my friends and business partners similarly.

Here are some reasons why you need to be networking to build your business:

Relationships Still Rule
Social media can only do so much. Posting status updates and composing tweets may help you reach more people, but truly building a relationship with potential customers can only happen in a face-to-face context. With an increasingly competitive marketplace, customers need to have a certain level of trust before they make even minor purchases today. Meeting with someone in person is the fastest and most effective way of establishing that trust and rapport that is so critical in business relationships.

Build your personal selling team
Networking multiplies your selling efforts by at least 10. The more people you meet and make an effort to build a relationship with, the more you are expanding your sphere of marketing influence. The real secret about networking that many people don't understand is that networking should be part of a long-term business development strategy, instead of something that you do when you are trying to land a big sale.

Think Long term
Many people join a networking organization or participate in networking activities/events with the expectation that their business will reach some major milestone – either through increased clients or from a significant increase in revenue – within too short of a timeline of the net-

working activity. When this anticipated business 'boost' doesn't happen, many become disappointed and frustrated, and either discontinue future activities or drop out of networking groups altogether.

However, networking should be thought of as an ongoing strategy to build contacts and brand your business. You won't see the benefits overnight, but you will see the many advantages over time, such as more referrals and a stronger business brand and reputation.

Surely there are networking groups and organizations in your local business community. Talk to your friends, family and business partners; even your clients. Find out which ones they think are worthwhile and make a commitment to do some type of networking activity at least once a month.

2. SERVE YOUR COMMUNITY.

Communities across our country rely on competent business professionals like you to give back. What's great about community service though, is that it can have many benefits for you too.

I joined my local Rotary club a few years ago because I wanted to get involved and give back to my community. Since then I have traveled on a mission trip and taken on leadership roles where I've gained invaluable experience. I knew that it would enhance my life personally, but what I didn't realize was how much it would benefit my business and brand my name in the community.

Most business owners who are strapped for time and cash may think that their time could be better spent on other priorities. But, there are several reasons why you should be making community involvement one of your top priorities.

Community service helps strengthen your business reputation
A company's business reputation is very important, especially in this tough economy. Customers tend to reward businesses that have good reputations by purchasing products and services at their businesses. One way to increase your company's visibility and exposure is to get involved and volunteer at community events and local charities. The experience is not only personally fulfilling but also helpful in getting your business name out there.

Community service helps customers to recognize your business

Prospective customers will buy products from a company that they know, especially a company that cares about their community. Being affiliated with a well-known service organization can really expedite your efforts when it comes to name recognition and building your brand.

As an insurance agent in my community, standing out among thousands of other agents was and still is very important to me. My community involvement has really helped me differentiate myself amongst my competition and build my brand.

Community service offers an opportunity to improve your community

Everyone benefits when people in a community come together to make it better. By volunteering your time and effort, you will reap many rewards in terms of better relations with the community and a stronger business reputation.

There are so many great service groups out there who need your help. Invest some time in reviewing what your local community offers to figure out where you would like to make a difference. In the meantime, donate money to the community scholarship fund in the name of your business or help the local soccer team buy their uniforms. Both you and your community will be better off for it.

3. REVISE YOUR BUSINESS-BUILDING ACTIVITIES.

My motto has always been "activity drives success." Setting and visualizing your long-term goals is the key component of consistent activity. Knowing what you are working towards by doing the daily "grunt" work will give you the motivation to keep striving toward your goals. It helps you justify doing whatever it takes on a daily basis by reminding you that you are getting closer and closer to the end result.

Your goals don't need to be long. They don't need to be fancy. They just need to be relevant to you, to keep you going today, tomorrow, and on into the future.

Take time now to write down 5 goals you MUST accomplish with your business this year. Next, think about what activities are required to get you there and create an activity plan. Here's a sample template that you can follow:

Average Amount of Commission or Salary Needed per Month:

Commission Earned on an Average Sale:

Number of Sales I Need Each Month:

Then...

How many appointments must be scheduled to complete one sale?

How many conversations does it take to schedule one appointment?

How many prospecting calls does it take to schedule one in-depth conversation?

HOW MANY PROSPECTING CALLS MUST YOU MAKE EACH MONTH?

Using these questions is a great way to create a practical plan for your business behavior. The trick is to focus on your activity, not on your challenges. Someone in business once told me that in sales, there are things that you can't control, but also things you can control. You can't control the economy, you can't control company or personal budgets, and you can't control what your competition does. What can you control then? Your activity. If you remember this simple yet powerful fact, you will be persistent with your activities and you WILL achieve your desired outcomes with your business.

About Mark

Mark Cole is a Financial Services Specialist and Multiple Line Agent with the Mark Cole Agency representing American National Insurance Company. He has over 30 years of professional experience creating and managing several of his own profitable companies and is currently the co-owner of Next Level Unique Marketing, LLC.

Mark is very active in his local community and has a tremendous passion for helping others. He holds several leadership positions including Area Director with Business Network International and incoming 2013 President of Rotary Club of Austintown, Ohio and many other local business organizations. Mark also chairs several 501(c)(3) organizations. For more information, please visit: www.markcoleconsulting.com.

CHAPTER 12

Leaving Complacency... Forever

By Grace Daly

One of the biggest factors that I see holding many people back, aside from the notorious and familiar Fear, is its villain partner: Complacency. Fear feeds on the unknown, the possibility of unfavorable results; paralyzing people to attempt any action for an unfound and at times illogical assumption of failure. Complacency is an acceptance, a satisfaction for the way things are. Complacency advocates that everything is acceptable and fine, just the way it is and there is no reason for change. The old "Why fix it if it's not broken?" is the motto for complacency. Complacency affects all aspects of our lives: relationships with families and friends, health and overall well-being, financial success, career growth or business expansion. In this chapter, I'm going to share with you ways to move away from this silent, invisible 'dream killer': Complacency.

There are two approaches to leaving complacency:

1. The first approach that many people take is to avoid pain in their current situation. They will move out of their comfort zone only for pain avoidance. Sometimes because they may have been living in complacency for a lengthened period of time – their threshold for pain or discomfort can actually raise higher, meaning that they may have lowered their standards of what is acceptable in their specific situation. Some may wait until their situation becomes absolutely dire before taking action for change.

2. The second approach operates from a completely different driver. These people seek to implement change for a greater desire or goal, to achieve more than where they're at now. Instead of operating from a drive of pain avoidance – they operate from a positive drive of achievement and victory. They focus on and work towards bigger dreams.

Ideally, one can argue that either approach: pain avoidance or greater desire - both can lead you to step out of complacency. Now, having coached hundreds of people, as well as experienced both approaches, I highly recommend the greater desire approach. The holistic difference is in the perspective; which affects the overall process in itself. When you're focusing on pain avoidance - you're problem solving; however, operating from a positive stance for a greater desire – you are empowered, your possibilities become infinite because you're creating.

As a native New Yorker, born and raised in Chinatown, one of my favorite childhood foods has always been the sweet buns that are traditionally sold in the neighborhood's local bakeries. These sweet buns are also referred to as sticky buns because their light sweet glaze left your fingers sticky - especially when you ate one warm and fresh out of the oven. Baked to a golden perfection, there's a large variety of fillings; some of the more popular fillings are red bean, egg custard or roast pork. Other Chinese bakery delights include: delectable almond cookies, vanilla cream sponge cake wheels and the celebration cakes that were flawlessly frosted with the lightest freshly whipped cream, intricately adorned with fresh fruit and accents of drizzled chocolate.

Now with my career background in the retail design, construction and facilities industry, I've directed the build-outs of hundreds of new stores and managed facilities for multiple retail brands across the country. So of course, it made sense to combine my innate skill for aggressive store development with my passion for these buns. I started to wonder – why aren't these bakeries available outside the Chinatowns across the country? What if we took these buns, branded it with an incredible store design to open multiple bakeries throughout the country? Hmmm, how would that work? Right there an idea was born: a desire to learn this bakery trade with the intention of future store expansion. I wrestled to postpone this: I'll do this in a few years; I'll do this later when I find a partner; I'll do this when I have more time; I'll do this when I have more capital, etc. However, no matter how much I tried to postpone this idea, I could not stop this inner voice that just softly whispered two words that posed all possibilities: "What if?" This idea of the bakery took root in my mind, and started to take a life of its own. I couldn't stop thinking of it; the idea just kept growing. I found myself dreaming up names, doodling logos, sketching out floor plans. Then my fantasizing took deeper root and I started calculating the minimum required square footage for the kitchen and the sales floor, what permits would be needed if the bakery had a few tables for service? I found myself researching the cost of bakery equipment, refrigerated bakery showcases and raw supplies that came in 100-pound sacks. I found myself working up budgets as if I were really opening a bakery. At that time my current job directing design and construction for new store openings across the country became monotonous after I opened the 550th store in my 7 years with the same retailer. This was a fresh fun project; this was my project and pure creation at its best. Armed with a healthy blend of curiosity, courage and adventure, I came to the only sensible conclusion to satisfy this inner voice. I had to learn more about this, I had to try. I know me and this would haunt me for the rest of my life if I did not do it. I discussed this with my family, who has always been supportive, and for the next 8 months I planned my transition out of my fulltime job in corporate America. When the day came and I announced I was leaving, many colleagues in my retail development industry were shocked – "Are you sure you want to do this?" "Are you serious?" "How long have you been planning this?" "Why are you leaving a Director's salary and bonus to go chase a dream?" "If you're bored, just stay there until you find another job to build with another retailer." Just as they could not talk me out of it with their opinions that mostly feed on fear or ego, I could not explain this pure inspiration to them. I had to work this through. I was confident in my skills and the fact that corporate America will always be there for me should I decide to return.

I asked my mother if she had the recipes for these sweet buns or knew of anyone who did. She replied in her typical animated Cantonese "No, your daddy and I know people in the restaurant business – which is entirely different than the bakery business. You need to find a Bun Si-fu." Si-fu? What's a Bun Si-fu I asked her? "A Bun Master, these are trade secrets passed on from many generations of bakers!" I went back to my old stomping grounds in Chinatown with 100 freshly printed business cards. I went up and down the main drag of Mott and Canal Streets; then I hit every little street, nook and cranny in between. I went into these bakeries, introducing myself as best I could in the "Americanized" Cantonese I spoke. "Hi, I'm Grace. I would like to intern at your bakery to learn the trade. In return I will work hard and also share with you marketing strategies for your business." Many folks were surprised and puzzled; some of them were skeptical and quickly shooed me away thinking I was attempting to solicit products to them. A few of them spoke the Mandarin dialect of which I politely reiterated, as best I could, that I only spoke Cantonese. Six days later, I received a call from a baker who spoke some broken English mixed with Cantonese. Somehow one of my business cards ended up with a small family run bakery on Clinton Street, close to a mile away. Two days later I met with the bakers, who were also the owners, one early evening before the bakery closed. I introduced myself, and gave them background information on who I am and what I did. They were impressed by the major national chains I built for and how eager I was to share marketing strategies with them. The Bun Master, in his early fifties with more than 30 years experience in his trade, had opened many locations in Hong Kong for a large bakery chain. In the process, he taught and launched the careers of many other bakers. We decided that we would start this internship / partnership the following week.

I got up at 4 am every morning and drove 1-1/2 hours into the city to start the ovens at the crack of dawn with the other bakers. I learned and did everything I could - no job was above me, no job was beneath me. I swept the floors, wiped down the café tables, mixed large vats of dough, and actually made the various buns. Now each of these delectable sweet buns is actually hand formed. It was amazing to watch the bun master work; he was swift, agile and filled pan after pan of buns lined up neatly to go into the proofer before going into the hot ovens. The Bun Master would start with a piece of precut dough, knead it and work it into a ball. In one swift motion he would slam it down onto the long stainless steel table and there would be a perfectly flattened, leveled round piece of dough. From a large aluminum tray, he scooped the prepared filling, placing it in the middle of the dough and ever so gently but quickly - with the tips of his fingers he would fold up the edges of the dough, perfectly pinching it closed and binding the bun together. He'd place it upside down on a large baker's tray and the perfect ball shaped bun would be waiting to be proofed, then baked.

It took a while for me to get this right. The first few times I did it - I had to change out the piece of dough because I over worked it and it became too warm and soft in my hands. When I tried to slam it onto the table to fill it – it was an odd square shape or I slammed it too hard and the dough broke through with a hole that obviously could not hold the filling. I'd scrap it back off the table and try again. There was a constant stream of laughter amongst us and soon I came to my own conclusion that they appreciated my entertainment more than anything else! When a freshly baked tray of buns came out – they'd call out to me in Cantonese "Fresh out of the oven, Gracie! Eat, eat one while it's hot." and so I ate… and ate. I mean – how could I refuse? This was comfort food to me! Usually by the time 10 am rolled around I had already eaten 3 or 4 varieties of buns. For lunch the bakers would take turns cooking traditional Chinese foods. We'd take off our aprons and sit around the long stainless steel table and eat family style with rice bowls and chopsticks. Because I was limited in what Chinese foods I cooked – I would always volunteer to do the dishes afterwards. One time I made oven fried chicken for lunch. That was the first time they had fried chicken without going to a fast food chain to buy it. They'd watch me place the pieces of raw chicken in a plastic bag of seasoned flour and thoroughly shake. When the chicken came out of the oven, hot and crunchy – I encouraged them to eat, and eat it while it was hot.

So at the end of this internship, 4 months later and 10 lbs heavier, I discovered I really did not want to open a bakery and sell these sweet buns. The truth was I just enjoyed eating them! But you see – I would have never reached that conclusion unless I worked this through. I would never have worked this through unless I stepped out of my comfort zone to try something new. This story has been shared in most of my keynotes because it's the epitome of my curiosity, creativity and leaving complacency.

This one ability to recognize and leave complacency is a propelling force to massive accomplishment. People who leave complacency are playful folks, there is no traditional sense of "failure" to them – as they have an insatiable appetite to learn and experience. They benchmark that they feel is a limit, and they work at pushing beyond it. They recognize this race they are running is only one of their own. They are engaged in experiencing life – all of it: the good, the bad and the ugly. And because they are extreme optimists – they find beauty and learning in every aspect of life.

Here are the seven keys to keep you stepping out of your comfort zone and leaving complacency…forever:

1. Create an incredible drive to positively affect your life. Don't wait for pain avoidance; operate from a source of creating which opens to all possibilities.

2. Recognize and focus on the desired outcome that far outweighs any risks.

3. Seek that gift within yourself that brings you fulfillment. This is your life's purpose that you were put on this earth to share with others.

4. Crave to understand yourself – seek inward. Find what you feel are your strengths and then stretch those capabilities just a little bit more each day to constantly challenge yourself.

5. Maintain a certain level of entitlement for answers. Simply ask yourself the question that poses all possibilities: What if?

6. Recognize monetary gains are not always the greatest rewards or even the most sought after. Learning and understanding a new skill, pursuing and developing your passions and trying something new for pure enjoyment in itself is a reason to step out of your comfort zone.

7. Embrace wonderment. We're all here to learn, so possess a playful, curious energy that cannot be alleviated until you give something new a try. There is no such thing as a failure or waste of time; everything is a good time, a good story or a good learning experience. Live to build up these incredible experiences in your life's portfolio.

About Grace

With more than 25 years in the retail industry, Grace Daly, also known as America's Retail Facility Coach™, is an inspirational speaker, coach and best-selling author who helps individuals maximize their full potential by harnessing the power of their innate strengths. Her latest coaching program, *Actualizing Your Full Potential*, designs a blueprint to success and fulfillment for the client.

Grace Daly International, Inc. was founded in 2008. In addition to her acclaimed inspirational writing in her published books: *The Seven Success Keys for the Retail Facilities Professional* and *Everyday Inspiration*, her signature keynote: *Rediscover and Share Your Gift Within™* encourages her audiences to seek within for the empowerment and creativity to boldly pursue the life of their dreams. By sharing her life experiences, Grace shows her clients how to work through the challenging times in their lives and utilize that same energy to propel themselves to spiritual and career growth. Grace also teaches a writing class, and partners with diverse organizations to coach individuals and groups seeking her advice on business, life balance, and at times, just the necessary "shot of inspiration" when faced with difficulty in various stages of their careers. Grace holds a degree in Advertising & Media Communications from F.I.T. and is a Dale Carnegie HIP & GA certified graduate. She received her coaching certification from Certified Coaches Federation. Grace is the recipient of various awards for her written work and has been inducted into the National Academy of Best-Selling Authors™.

Grace's coaching expertise is regularly sought by business colleagues through her writing published in leading industry trade magazines. Her heart-rending keynote speeches of leadership, service and inspiration are sought out by business leaders who want to impact their teams to take positive action. A passionate coach, inspirational speaker, award-winning writer and best-selling author, Grace is dedicated to 'paying it forward' to her community and working with those who courageously pursue the life of their dreams. *Get Ready, Get Inspired!™*

To learn more about one of the country's leading authorities in inspiration and fulfillment, Grace Daly, please visit: www.gracedaly.com or email: grace@gracedaly.com

CHAPTER 13

In the Referral Marketing / Networking Lab

By Bertrand McHenry

Somewhere around the fifth person I asked, "So what is your target market and who do you need to meet?" I realized I had reached my quota of being answered with blank stares, and I decided to go into recon mode. I was at an after-hours mixer of one of the local chambers, and it's not like I hadn't come across this before, it's just that tonight I decided I had had enough and decided to do what I rarely endorse engaging in at a mixer…people watch. It's mostly ineffective however. I identified a handful of "networker species" that evening and proceeded to test my theories in the wild, oh all right…subsequent networking mixers. After carefully considering my control groups and setting up my labs, living in the jungles of the Mixer, I came to the conclusion that there are 5 distinct species of networkers. Let me share them with you and you decide if you recognize anyone you know. No, don't raise your hand if you spot yourself…sheesh!

Ready? Here we go:

1) *Homo buymystufficus:* This species is characterized by an overly aggressive nature, a predator's gaze always looking for a weakness in his/her prey. He leads his introductions with his business card and brochures, cramming them in your personal space until you are forced to reach for them and then…BAMM! The close, I mean you must be interested right? This one is difficult to evade once engaged, but I have become quite adept at distracting him with fresh prey.

2) *Homo noeyecontacticus:* You'll never forget this fella once you come across him. Formerly known as *Homo noliferus,* this harmless looking guy is anything but! Try having a productive conversation with him...go ahead, try. You'll get zero information from this one. You'll have to fight the urge to wonder aloud... "WHY?" as you walk away shaking your head. Unlike *buymystufficus* this one is easier to slip away from, but you'll find your energies have been depleted...must...get...rest.

3) *Homo collectawadicus:* This one is just plain and simply deluded. She believes that "She who leaves with the most business cards...WINS!" I'll say this, she clearly has a goal and mission...to collect everyone's business card, and I mean EVERYONE! I mean how could she possibly consider the mixer a success if she did not have a trophy to haul into the office tomorrow? Sales Manager: "Susan, may I see your forecast for this month please?" Susan: "Oh yeah!"(Turning her purse upside down and dumps 1100 business cards on the desk) "BAMM! What? Oh yeah baby!" Sales Manager: "Uh what's that...exactly?" Susan: "That? That is all the prospects I developed last week!" (Skip to next week) Sales Manager: "Susan where are all of those prospects you had last week?" Susan: "Oh I dumped them in the trash...you didn't expect me to haul them around the rest of the month did you? Don't worry there's another mixer tomorrow and I'll get more...lots more!" Let's lower the curtain on this one...too painful.

4) *Perennial scaredtodeatherus:* Yep, I went plant on you and the name says it all. This one is totally uncomfortable in crowds, yet believes somehow that just going to the mixer is productive. You can spot them when they enter. They usually come in meekly, and bee line for the food table, fill their plate, back up to the wall and proceed to go on a comfort binge. Watch your fingers!

5) *Homo Flappergumaximus:* Do I really need to explain? You will not get a word in edge-wise! There are more, but I only have so much space and I've made my point. Let's set this example on the lab table for a moment and make sure we are speaking the same language before we go any further.

Networking is a word which has been tossed around pretty loosely for the last 15 – 20 years. Most of us use the term and there are as many definitions of the word as there are people using it. Mostly though, people equate the word networking with the activity of "professionally mingling."

Almost all business people I meet are very well intentioned and want to be productive, yet there is this one area where we've muddied the waters. Many times we think "gift of the gab" is a skill set of networking. By the way, what is gab? The dictionary defines it as – to talk idly or incessantly as about trivial matters, idle talk, or chatter. Not exactly words I want associated with my business activities. People collect names, numbers, and business cards as if that attainment is an actual measurable unit of work.

Referral Marketing is a newer term, related to networking but an entirely different species (pun intended)! Before we go any further, I want to make sure we are speaking the same language so allow me to define these two terms. According to bestselling author and international speaker Dr. Ivan Misner in his book, World's Best Known Marketing Secret *"Networking is the process of developing and using contacts to increase your business, enhance your knowledge, expand your sphere of influence, or serve the community. Networking in this context is a vital business activity to help generate referrals, but let's be clear it does not mean direct prospecting!"* New York Times bestselling author Mike Macedonio in the same book says that *"Referral Marketing is a business strategy to attract new customers through a process of building relationships which result in a flow of personally recommended business."* So, where do these activities / strategies fit into your business? Finally, what exactly is a Referral? I'll be brutally honest with you here…most of what business people pass off as a referrals are really just leads. I can get leads myself, it's easy! I did it myself for years, and it only takes money and or work. What none of us are able to do is get introduced to referral partners and future clients whom we do not know at this point, and we need motivated referral partners who want to, have the time to, and have a data base to make introductions on our behalf! Again, according to Dr. Ivan Misner, a "Referral is the opportunity to do business with someone in the market to buy your products or services: it's not a guaranteed sale, but a chance to discuss your product or service with someone." How do we take these terms and make sense of them for our purposes? I mean I've been told early on that it's not how much you know but who you know, or something like that, so networking, aka schmoozing, must be important to building my business right? Wrong! Great questions though, and I'm about to make sense of them, give you some clarity, a framework, and a couple of tools that, if used, will make a difference in your business production and networking experience this week!

Dr. Misner notes that *"A referral is the opportunity to do business with someone in the market to buy your product or service: it is not a guaranteed sale, but a chance to discuss your product with someone."* If Referral Marketing is your strategy, then Networking is a slice of that strategy. At the Referral Institute of Houston, I teach a relationship business model called V.C.P. and it stands for Visibility + Credibility + Profitability. It is important to note that V.C.P. is a sequential process. That is to say, when forming business relationships we are either looking for clients or referral partners and either way we must move the relationship through the model beginning with Visibility to Credibility and only after we have fully arrived at the first two can we then move to Profitability.

I will tell you this, I have yet to meet anyone who has attended a networking function and moved through the V.C.P. model in any stage while at the function. Let me define these terms. Visibility: If I meet you today and we have a brief conversation, and tomorrow I can recall your first and last name, your company name, and what you do for a living, we are only at Visibility. Ok great, we now know one another's names, places of work, what we do...can I sell now? Let me ask you, have you determined if this person is a suspect, prospect or a referral partner? A referral partner is someone who, if properly motivated can and will bring you many referrals! Once you know what category they are in you will still have to move the relationship to Credibility. How, you ask? How about asking yourself or them, how you can add value to their experience? What can you bring to the table? This should be the first question you seek to answer before you attempt to sell anything! This model of doing business has a philosophy driving it. The philosophy is simply "Givers Gain." Simply put, I give to you and eventually you will reciprocate and give to me. Remember, *Referral Marketing is a business strategy to attract new customers through a process of building relationships..."* Aha! You are getting the picture!

So how do we move the relationship from Visibility to Credibility? Moving to Credibility involves activities which initially exclude you helping yourself to their wallet! Ask yourself these questions: Have you supported them in their efforts to build their business? Have you used their service (where appropriate) as a gesture of support and so that you can refer them intelligently? Finally have you referred them business? I mean real introductions to at least one person you have a real relationship with and who has a real opportunity to purchase their product or service. Once you have met these criteria and they are tracking with you in this activity, you are at least close to Credibility. Stay in this stage for a while, continue to add value, develop the relationship and the Profitability will come.

You may even have a conversation with this person at some point about systematizing this "Referral Relationship" so that the activity and results are more predictable. Most business people I meet at mixers are there to do one thing and that is to sell! However when you start the sales process before moving through the V.C.P. model, you actually move backwards from Visibility! You move into a stage we at the Referral Institute call I. or *Irritability Marketing.* It's a very ineffective way of building business or securing sales. Then why do so many engage in it? I believe it's always been done that way, and in this hyper-competitive market place we feel we must "pull the trigger" as often as we see a prospect. Remember the ABCs of sales? Always Be Closing. Referral partners can assess needs for you, tell stories about you, edify you, roll out the red carpet for you, and shorten the sales cycle and the time you spend developing a "suspect into a prospect into a client." I'm going to go out on a limb here and say that you might consider going to a mixer or event like it, in order to stay at Visibility with larger groups of people and begin to select a few people (future referral partners?) to begin to systematically move through the V.C.P. model. Hopefully this relieves the pressure of needing to close a sale at a mixer or from a mixer. We can even use the V.C.P. model to drive a client relationship. Now that we have a new paradigm or framework, let's take it and revisit the mixer.

1) You first decide on a goal for a mixer. Decide how many people you need to meet. Be specific here, you may want to meet two C.P.A.s or even specific professionals by name. Do a bit of research and find out if these people belong to the group hosting the event or are planning to be there. In any case, setting this goal gives you intentionality. You are on a mission and once accomplished, you can leave.

2) Try as much as possible to get "referred" to the people you'd like to meet. Go with a buddy and ask her who she'd like to meet at the mixer. Then share with her who you'd like to meet and how you'd like to be introduced and ask them to make those introductions on your behalf when possible. It is important that you

actively seek introductions on your partners behalf...it's called moving to Credibility remember?

3) Once introductions have been made, try these questions on for size: "Tell me about your business." "How did you get into this line of work?" "What do you like best about what you do?" "Who is your target market?" ...and once you get enough information, how about: "How can I help you?" or "If your target market is _____, would an introduction to _____ be helpful to you?"

Congratulations! You are at the beginning of the V.C.P. process and you are set to make your sales, revenue, earnings and income very, very predictable and maybe even more importantly, you are one more researcher on my team ready to help me make extinct the ancient species I categorized earlier and actually create two new species...How about *"Giver Deluxicus"* and *"Earnaloticus"*? Sounds good to me...see you in the lab!

About Bertrand

Bertrand McHenry is known as the Referral Marketing Strategy Ninja. He is a published author, hosts a weekly CNN radio show called *"Business Builders Radio,"* and is the President/Owner of the Referral Institute of Houston - a referral marketing training company. He takes entrepreneurs and business owners and applies his three core competencies to their goals: 1) Making sure they get the right Referral Marketing Education. 2) Accountability and Immersion in the information and actions, and 3) Getting their networks trained. Pairing Referral Institute information and curriculum with these three core competencies is a combination that is transforming revenue, earnings, income and lives!

To learn more about Bertrand, his company and how he can transform your business visit him at: www.referralinstitutehouston.com , follow him on Twitter at @bertrandmchenry , email him at: bertrand@referralinstitutehouston.com , or call him at 281-401-9852

CHAPTER 14

BUILDING YOUR MARKETING MACHINE

By Abdoul Diallo

No one had ever been given anything better than Patience/Endurance.
~ Prophet Muhammad (SAW)

Many entrepreneurs will start and stop businesses almost as often as they change clothes. They look for whatever the next big trend might be – and lose perspective on what they've already begun to accomplish.

My experience has proven to me that focusing, concentrating and following through on an enterprise that has the seeds of success pays off in ongoing rewards. Each day you work hard at your company becomes water for those seeds – which will eventually grow not only a very profitable company, but also a strong and vibrant business network that can aid you in whatever you choose to undertake as the years go on.

It is this network that is the power behind the perfect "marketing machine" – it provides the contacts and reputable image that allows you to do more business more easily. You can create your own marketing machine if you are willing to "go the distance" and not give up on a good thing.

BUILDING MY COMPANY

Five years ago, I began my company, FMI TRADING, in New York City – a company that sells sugar, iron ore, gold, cement, rice and so forth. Many people back in my home country of Guinea in Africa wanted to buy many of these commodities from the U.S., so I could see the business potential of being the middleman in these transactions. That was really the motivating factor behind starting my own company.

Even though the demand for these commodities was strong, my business itself was relatively unknown when I began it. And even though I had been in America since 2000, it was still a hard operation to get off the ground. For the first year of FMI's existence, I worked very, very hard to the point of exhaustion. I was dealing with people located in different time zones around the world that I had be in touch with constantly – which meant I could never get a good night's sleep. Instead, I relied mostly on short naps to keep as rested as possible.

Today, it's a different story. I have ten people working for me, as well as agents around the globe to help represent my company - but, back in those days, I was the only one I could really depend on. There was a huge upside to this constant labor, however – and it was that, the more I worked, the more I stayed "in the zone." I would constantly think through the next steps I needed to take and how to take those steps to continue to build my operation.

More importantly, without even realizing it, I started to automatically build a network of people who wanted to work with me. This is incredibly important for any business. When people work with you and learn that they can trust you and also become confident that you are good at what you do, they come back to you. Not only that, they will refer you to other potential customers, who, in turn, will bring you more people who want to work with you.

I attribute a great deal of my ability to attract the right kind of people to my work ethic. Suppliers and investors alike saw how much of myself I put into growing my company and they respected that. They knew I wasn't going anywhere – that I was totally invested in my business and was willing to do what was necessary to make sure they were taken care of. Eventually, there were more than enough people who wanted to deal with my company.

Internally, as I went through the process of building my company, I also learned the business basics of how to appear as trustworthy as possible. I didn't start out at a large American investing company so I could see how they made themselves look good to prospects. I had to learn for myself. For example, when I was finally able to go live with a high quality website containing all of our correct, up-to-date information, it made a huge difference.

Taking the time to create a professional appearance really helped me connect with more well-established clients. And again, as I said earlier, the longer I was in business, the more those well-established clients were willing to deal with me, as well as give me valuable referrals to their associates. Of course, I had to deliver to really gain their trust – and I worked hard to make sure I always did.

But it was a process – a combination of being persistent and getting the opportunity to work with the right people. When you're just starting out, you're not entirely sure who those right people are or how to get to them. That was one of the reasons I had to work so hard in the beginning; I didn't have a plan to reach those desirable clients, so I responded to everyone as if I were a machine. I didn't yet have my own "marketing machine" completed!

LESSONS LEARNED

If I had it to do all over again, I would have thought more strategically and concentrated more on the clients I eventually wanted to work with, rather than put so much energy into deals that were either just the one-time-only kind, or were, more likely than not, to fall apart. Of course, the flip side of that coin is that, if I hadn't worked so hard, I might not have been as successful. I know I would not have learned as much as I did.

For example, just as I had to be in my business for a certain amount of time to gain certain clients' full trust, I had to make sure the people I worked with had been in their businesses for a certain amount of time. So I began qualifying people for my network – they had to have been in the business for at least three years and had already closed transactions for me to take them seriously.

Also, I had to make sure the people I used as part of my team understood my business and my particular procedures. It was important to spend quality time with my representatives to teach them how things work. That way, they could easily explain the process to my current and potential clients; that would give those clients the all-important confidence that my people knew what they were doing.

Finally, I learned that your business relationships should be about more than business. You have to work towards great friendships as well. Yes, business is very much about dollars and cents – but, as they say, "people buy people." For the beginning years, I was the main representative of my own business. Brokers, clients and suppliers had to believe in who I was and what I was doing – they also had to like me and trust me. That required making a genuine effort to connect with them.

YOUR NETWORKING IS YOUR MARKETING

This brings me to my initial point and the reason I wanted to write this chapter. Building these strong contacts and creating your own network that feeds business back to you is really the strongest way to market your company. The ultimate marketing machine is one in which you create a fan base that goes out and "sells" you without your doing a thing.

They readily recommend you and your company not just because they like you, trust you and think you are good at your job. There is also an element of self-interest here; it's good for them to be able to have a name at hand when a friend asks if they know someone who provides a particular product or service. When they have a referral to share, it makes them look connected – and, if they really believe that you're good at what you do, they know it will ultimately make them look better if their friend enjoys working with the referral.

But, again, it takes time for all those relationships to form into a network with lasting power. Think about the closest business contacts you have – and how long it took for them to become as strong as they currently are. Now think about the ones you trust the most when it comes to actual business transactions – and how that trust is a result of their longevity and consistency when it comes to their own individual companies and endeavors.

BUILDING YOUR MARKETING MACHINE

Here are a few tips I've learned along the way on how to network the most effectively and create the strongest possible relationships – relationships that will, in turn, provide the power for your marketing machine.

- **Use open-ended questions when networking.**

Go beyond "yes" and "no" questions, or questions that can be answered with a simple fact, when meeting or talking with a new business contact. Asking them the "why" and "how" of something causes them to open up more and reveal more about themselves, rather than soliciting simple information that you might just be able to get from their website. It also sparks a deeper conversation as you exchange thoughts.

- **Represent yourself professionally.**

As I noted earlier, just the simple act of creating a quality website helped my company's image tremendously when it came to new clients wanting to check us out. First impressions are important, so you always want to look like a responsible, professional business person. It opens the door for networking potential.

- **Provide useful advice and resources**

Some businesspeople are very guarded about what information they will share and what they will do, unless they are first paid to do it. I think this can be a mistake. I have gained a great deal of experience and know-how when it comes to the commodities business – by sharing information and ideas with others, I have become known as a reliable source and have also increased my visibility in my field.

- **Be clear in what you are looking for and what help you would like**

Everyone networks, so everyone is after certain kinds of contacts that can help them expand their business. There is nothing wrong with that, or in putting the word out that you are looking for a certain kind of individual or company to work with. Just make sure you are asking for that help from the right level of people. You do not want your time wasted with those who aren't connected in the right way, but pretend they are.

- **Follow up efficiently on referrals and contacts that are provided**

When someone you trust and like does give you either referrals or important contacts, you should follow up on those leads as soon as possible. And you should also let the person who gave you the names know that you did connect with them. It's a matter of simple respect and politeness - and it will encourage that person to continue providing you with valuable resources that will help your business grow.

- **Do not misrepresent yourself when networking**

It can be tempting to oversell yourself and your business when meeting new and important people. After all, you want to impress them as much as possible. However, that usually catches up to you and puts you in a less-than-trustworthy light in these high-level circles. There are always ways to promote yourself effectively without harmful exaggeration, so there's no need to engage in it.

- **Set overall networking goals**
Think through the kinds of people you want to meet and what avenues might bring you in contact with them. Setting down networking goals and detailing the ways you might be able to achieve those goals will help you focus and achieve your objectives.

- **Create a loyal "core group"**
There are three people I trust above all others that I work with. I rely on those three people to provide me with the truth as well as to deliver on what they promise. Every businessperson can benefit from having this kind of core group in their network as the "heart" of their marketing machines.

When you take the time and put in the work to build the right kind of network, you've build the ultimate marketing machine that will improve your profits and grow your business. Once it is in place, you only have to maintain it and add to it when desirable – in the meantime, every day, it will be out there putting your name and your business in front of new clients without you having to do a thing.

The longer you stay with your business, the longer you stay focused on your objectives and working as hard as you can towards those objectives, the larger and stronger your network will grow. The more you deliver for that network, the more it will invest in you and the more it will recommend and refer you. That's a marketing machine that will never break down – and will continue to create rewards for you for years to come.

About Abdoul

Abdoul Diallo is also known as a "cash flow master," bestselling author and Business marketing and consulting expert that is regularly sought after for his opinion on: how to start and create a profitable business, and also how to expand a company.

In 2007, He founded a commodity trading company well known around the globe called www.fmitrading.com. His company is known for offering great services and products to his customers. He also acts as a consultant to many different companies around the globe and teaches them how they can improve their cash flow and avoid losses.

To learn more about Abdoul Diallo "the cash flow master" and on how he can assist you in your business, please email: adiallo@fmitrading.com
or call +1-347-853-0390.
www.fmitrading.com

CHAPTER 15

Key Lessons For Building Your Dream Business

By Ed Alfke

When I first realized I was an "entrepreneur," I was in the process of building my third business, Rent-A-Wreck. I am now a "serial entrepreneur" (someone who builds a series of companies), a mentor, and one of the leaders in the Angel Investment movement. Over the years I have raised tens of millions of dollars of Angel Investment, invested millions of my own and had a series of successful companies and a couple of failures. I have created 3000 jobs, and hope to help you create some of your own! By contributing to our environment and other business owners building our communities and the economy, I feel a kind of self-fulfillment and success that I hope you will experience as well.

Those of us who have become successful entrepreneurs (small business owners), didn't know everything and did not become successful without making many mistakes, as you will too. What we did do however, is start! It all starts with the decision to begin. We began with the best knowledge we had, could not foresee all the challenges we faced and, most of all, did not know for sure if it would work. This chapter is not about me, it is about you and the tools and inner characteristics you have within you to build your future. You will learn the key things you need to do simply, quickly and consistently, so that you can build your business. Success supported by using 'smart' tools will take your dreams where you want them to go. Dream your dream and begin!

I would like to share with you some pivotal lessons I learned through my business experiences. Many lessons were learned via mistakes I made, however I also made many of the right decisions. The true lesson is to do it the "smart way." I built many companies and experienced the highs and lows, all the while learning from the "hands on" experience of "doing." What I know now is that if I had the knowledge and a template to success, I would have saved myself time, money and a whole lot of frustration as I built my businesses. Success is dependent on a combination of things all going on at the same time and working in unison, or not. This is true if you are in business at present or creating a new business.

Most importantly, keep it simple and make a commitment to get started now! It doesn't need to be the perfect plan, just good enough to take action. Good enough is good enough, a decision is better than indecision. Allowing fear of over-analysis can paralyze your dream from the onset.

When I was 19 years old, I began my first partnership with my brother in the restaurant business. I had no clue about the food and beverage industry. In my 20's, I opened a clothing store chain with no retail experience, but had partners who did. This was followed with the creation of Rent-A-Wreck despite having never worked with cars in my life. As my experience grew, my knowledge grew. How did I create all this opportunity? What carried me through on those days when I was challenged and feeling lost? I learned I had a powerful internal force driving me to success. I want to share with you the tools you need to succeed in your own business.

Entrepreneurial Need-To-Knows:

1. The four internal characteristics you must possess.

2. The two key rules that you will encounter.

3. The "how-to's" to get you there.

4. Financing: Angel Investors

The necessary internal characteristics critical to my success and yours are:

1. PASSION

2. COMMITMENT

3. PERSERVERANCE

4. POSITIVITY

Passion: the energy that comes from bringing more of YOU into what you do. Find something that you love and care about and follow THAT dream. Success is more enjoyable if you are passionate and enjoy what you are doing!

Commitment: your promise to yourself and your future to do what you have chosen to do and stay the course. There are going to be many days you call on your own commitment for strength and guidance.

Perseverance: what keeps you going day after day, year after year? "Never Give Up" is the common mantra all successful people have in common.

Positive Outlook: stay positive and surround yourself with positive people who are succeeding in life. Do whatever it takes to keep you in a positive space...whether it be enjoying family time, sports, travel, friends, hobbies...whatever gives you a positive and happy space.

Looking back over the years, these elements were common to every business venture I was involved in. Take these intrinsic ideas and make them your own. You will have days that will be hindered by dark clouds, however as you build your tool box, you will have insight to help you with the next two key rules!

Every enterprise encounters these two key rules. Accept and embrace them:

1. Murphy's Law: "That which can go wrong, will"

2. Ed's Law: "Shit happens"

You need to learn how to handle these inevitable challenges. There were many times that I asked myself, "Why am I doing this? It's hard, no fun, how am I going to deal with this problem?" At the time, I didn't realize what was pulling me to the other side of these challenges were the four internal forces: the keys to success. Believe in yourself! Trust you will find a way to deal with issues that come your way.

First, it is valuable to detail the experiences that you want to have in your daily life:

I personally want _____.

I am motivated by _____.

Draw a three to five-year life plan, including elements that are important to you such as your business, financial, health, family, community, spiritual, etc. Commit to this exercise. Re-read what you have written, amending it twice a year. Having a clear understanding of your true purpose will help you arrive at your dream life. This exercise is as much about values as it is your goals, regardless of whether you are in a pre-start up phase or a business veteran. Set your sights on objectives that are truly important to you; it is not about the money! REMEMBER: Money comes AFTER you do what you do well. Money is a result of your efforts and part of the overall picture, but it is not the only reason why you have chosen the life of an entrepreneur.

Be honest and get to really know yourself. Understand your strengths and weaknesses and write them down. Build your business on your strengths and get the rest done - by someone else!

MARKET RESEARCH: STARTING A NEW BUSINESS OR IMPROVING YOUR CURRENT BUSINESS

Regardless of what stage you are in your business, there is a simple key to success regarding market research.

Clearly define your product or service. Identify the specifics. Even well-established businesses may need to re-visit this concept.

Define or redefine your ideal customer:
- Why are they your ideal customer?
- What is YOUR value to YOUR ideal customer?
- Are they having any difficulties with "X" and, how do you solve this issue for them?
- How do you show them an ROI (return on investment) from you?
- Why would they buy or how can you get them to buy more?
- Find out who your competitors are, what they do, how they do it, and what they charge.

What is the productive way to execute 'market research'? Talk to twenty of your customers or potential customers!

Ask objective questions:

- Concerning your product/service/pricing: Listen to what your customers say without trying to 'sell' them on the product or idea.
- Regarding your competitors: what they like about them and what issues they might be having.
- Ask permission to contact them once you have had time to reflect on the input that you receive from your customers.

This is valuable information that will re-define your ideal customer's wants and needs. Once you figure out how to provide these specifics, you will gain that customer and many new customers to follow.

Chart the Information

YOUR COMPANY	THE COMPETITION
Benefits/Strengths, Advantages	Benefits/Strengths/Advantages
Costs and weaknesses	Costs and weaknesses
= your value	= their value

LESSONS FROM A SEASONED ENTREPRENEUR

Recently I worked with a well-respected owner of a software company. He has been in the business for several years. We re-evaluated his business using current market research and it became clear he needed to change his business model. He has spent millions of dollars developing a sophisticated software and has a great customer base, however, he realized he could grow faster if he found a new way to deliver his products to present and future customers. The obvious question here is where he would be today had he re-evaluated his market three years ago? Kudos to him for exercising the courage along with the passion and commitment to his customers to change his way of doing business. He will now become a leader in his field for being at the forefront of what needs to be done in his industry. He is persevering!

Many companies I have mentored simply need to go back-to-basics and do some market research. If you are in a start-up position, I would recommend you spend significant time doing research and evaluating your market research. You need to determine if there is a customer base and demand for your product or service before making a final commitment. If the customer demand is not significant, it would be prudent not to begin, so re-invent your idea. Unfortunately, there are times that it is in your best interests to simply shut down your idea sooner rather than later. For those of you currently in business and not seeing the success that you had hoped for, then evaluate your product and customer base again. Make it right, so you can experience more growth and success moving forward.

Planning and Goals:

Project your business plan out to include the next three years. Be very tangible and concise as this tool is a reference guide to your dream – allowing you the life and freedom of a true entrepreneur. Planning is paramount, as Murphy will show up somewhere in your deal. You can handle whatever comes up! Your business plan ties into your life plan, so ensure that your desired goals 'fit' and complement each other. Your life plan deals with family, money, health, community and things that are personally important to you. Both your business and life plan need to work together for a successful life. Read over your business and life plan twice a year and assess where you are. You may need to make changes as you may not be on course, or you may be ahead of course due to your great planning!

Goals:

Spend time evaluating your goals and write them down. What are your goals for this year, this month, this week, today? Do they intertwine with your plan? It is critical to have them written down and refer to them often. Focus! Say "No" to everything that is not directly related to your goals!

Sales and Marketing:

No Sales equals No Business - it's that simple. As a business owner you will need to sell every day. Even if sales are not your best strength, no one will sell like you can when you are passionate about your product and business. The rest of the sales skills can be learned along the way. Ask yourself the question - exactly how will I market myself to my customers? How many different ways can I come up with to be effective? Become an expert at this! By researching my competitors, I learned that 2% close the deal on the first call, 81% close after the 5th "touch or call." This tells you that being tenacious and reaching back to potential customers pays off. I also discovered that 90% of my competitors gave up after the 4th call! Use this to your advantage! Don't be easily discouraged, keep in touch or call potential clients.

Cash Flow Projections:
It is critical to understand the cost of creating a business as well as how cash flow coming in and out will affect your business. It will take twice as long and cost about double what you think...yes, really. So be prepared for this and keep track of your cash flow and profit/loss every month.

FINANCING YOUR BUSINESS: ANGEL CAPITAL

Angel Investors
Start your business with your own money first before seeking a bank loan or for family and friends to invest with you. If you still need funding to reach your goal, then 'pitch' your dream to Angel Investors.

Angel Investors are often successful entrepreneurs and others who invest in high-risk early stage companies. It is patient, friendly capital and complimented with exceptional assistance and resources. I have been an Angel investor for many years as well as a CEO, and a mentor to CEO's whom I help to become successful. I am one of the leaders in this space of thousands, who want to help and invest in new companies. Angel Capital Association in the USA, National Angel Capital Organization in Canada and European Business Angels Network in Europe are some of the excellent resources available.

Most cities have a local Angel group as there are approximately 250 groups in North America. Angel Investors are the largest source of early stage capital and are an amazing network of wealth and knowledge of early stage business.

Personally, I have been both an investor and funded by investors. I have received an abundance of support from Angels with contacts, doors opened, and advice from those who have "been there - done that." My website: www.mentorinc.ca offers you free resources on how you can benefit from this information.

In summary, start with the basics and surround yourself with reliable people. Find mentors, advisors, and coaches. Seek out advice from those who have built a company, preferably in your business segment. When you choose experienced guidance, your success will come sooner with less costly mistakes. It is that simple! I continue to have personal coaches and mentors who advise me to this day. The learning never ends, every day is a new and exciting beginning.

"Today is the oldest you have ever been. Today is the youngest you will ever be." Do it now! Good luck with building your Dream Life!

About Ed

Ed Alfke, serial entrepreneur and CEO, is an early stage company growth expert, business turnaround expert, leader in the angel investment space and sought-after international business speaker. Ed has been featured in over one thousand media reports on NBC, CBC, *The National, Entrepreneur Magazine, Canadian Business Magazine,* the *Financial Post* and *The Times of London*, to name a few. He has successfully raised over $50 million in investment capital, founded 21 companies, including Rent-A-Wreck, and is the winner of multiple prestigious awards, such as BC Businessman of the Year Award and the Crescordia Environmental Award. Ed is a guest speaker at numerous Universities, and his business achievements, which include doubling corporate growth for ten consecutive years, were the subject of case studies in many University MBA and Commerce programs across the country.

Although Ed became a self-made millionaire in his early twenties, he admits he did it the hard way, on his own without the guidance of mentors. After more than 35 years of building companies, Ed acknowledges he has learned more from his business failures than he has from his successes. Today he is passionate about helping his CEO Mentees learn from their costly mistakes, turning their challenges into victories and fast tracking their success. Ed's most recent project was recognized as one of the 'Top 10 Early Stage Companies in Canada and has won multiple awards for technological innovations.

Ed lives in wine and lake country and enjoys time with family and close friends. He enjoys heli-skiing and windsurfing and is learning to kite board.

In his FREE special report – *"5 Critical Factors That Make or Break Your Company in Today's Economy,"* Ed reveals his best golden secrets, strategies and tactics in this proven, step-by-step roadmap to fast-track early start up company growth.

To receive your FREE copy, visit: www.edalfke.com

CHAPTER 16

Connecting Your Way to Success

By Larry Benet, "The Connector"

Not many people get fired for what they do best. But that's just what happened to me in 2006.

I was "selectively outsourced" for doing too much networking.

Yes, today I'm known as "The Connector to Billionaires and Millionaires" – but back then, my primary skill only connected me to the unemployment line!

To be fair, my job back then wasn't supposed to be about networking – it's just my natural instinct to do it. And it was a vivid example of the axiom that you should always pursue whatever your passion is. That job had nothing to do with my passion. My current work, however, is all about what I love to do best.

Connections. How would any one of us have advanced in life if we didn't connect with certain key people that believed in us, inspired us, taught us and helped us move forward?

Successful people are successful for a reason. I make connections to the kinds of phenomenal personalities that make things happen – I learn from them – and I share their wisdom and techniques with those who connect with me. And I also put in a lot of hours using those connections to help raise money for important international charities that save lives.

Connections are about helping yourself and helping others – and this chapter is about helping you make those connections. I'll be sharing with you some of the secrets that have enabled me to build relationships with some of the best and brightest people in their fields.

CONNECTING TO MY PASSION

I want to return to that time in my life after I lost my job. I was in a very negative frame–of–mind and not sure what I was going to do with my life. I began to learn from people like motivational guru Mark Victor Hansen in an attempt to find my way.

But it wasn't until I watched "The Secret" movie – from the bestseller of the same name – that I really made the turn in my own head. As all of you probably already know, "The Secret" is all about deciding what you want and applying a positive focus to that goal. It inspired me to finally drop the negativity, apply that positive focus and be open to the possibilities in front of me.

A few days later, businesswoman and TV host Merry Miller conducted a seminar with Donald Trump at the Learning Annex, an event that I decided to attend. I had the opportunity to put a question to Mr. Trump, so I asked his advice on how to handle the kind of adversity I had been experiencing. He gave me a very good, thoughtful answer.

But *my* Q & A with the business mogul wasn't the one that stuck with me. It was the exchange he had with the guy behind me. He asked Trump what he would do if he lost all his money?

Trump's answer was delivered without hesitation – "I would be rich. That's all there is to it. Next question."

That was a light bulb moment for me. I realized Trump's belief system in his being wealthy was so strong, nothing could crack it. And I knew I needed that kind of unshakable belief in myself and my ability. I decided that I would focus on building relationships and make that work for me.

I had my first opportunity to put my new plan into action shortly after that. I heard that Virgin CEO, Sir Richard Branson, would be at a charity event and I made it a point to attend.

I quickly saw that it was going to be incredibly difficult to make the connection I was after. Branson was in the middle of a dance floor, surrounded by security guards, with music blaring so loudly it would be difficult to talk to him. But I managed to get through his entourage and speak to the man himself. I only managed to get 30 seconds to speak to him directly. But by the end of those 30 seconds, I had Sir Richard's email address. And later, to my shock, I realized it was his *private* email address.

What was important about those 30 seconds wasn't the 30 seconds themselves – but *what I had done prior to the event to prepare for them.* I had researched Branson extensively online to see what would be of value to him – and, when I talked to him, I offered a way to help him raise money for his Virgin Homeless fund. In other words, I was giving him something – not asking for something for myself – and it was the beginning of building an important relationship for me.

Some time later, I met Larry King at another charity function. Again, I had done my research on what charity was important to him and spoke to him about helping out. A few days later, I found myself having breakfast with the TV legend in Beverly Hills.

And finally, since good things come in threes, I met the world's 23rd wealthiest man, Bill Bartmann, at another event. I asked him two questions – what was most important to him and what was he the most passionate about? From the discussion that happened as a result of those two questions, I ended up helping him launch his speaking and authoring career, which he's been incredibly successful at.

This was the big turning point for my career – and, in just a little over two years, I've created important connections with such major personalities as Tony Robbins, Jack Canfield, Warren Buffet and many, many more.

HOW DO *YOU* CONNECT?

As I've said, my success began when I developed an unshakable belief system that I could make important connections with powerful people. That gave me the confidence to approach people like Larry King and Sir Richard Branson.

That confidence is important to have. It enables you to have the courage to approach a powerful person – but it's not enough to make the connection you're after. A lot of people approach the rich and famous, but the first reaction of these superstars is usually to be polite but distant. They simply can't handle the overwhelming number of people who want to be close to them.

That's why confidence is only the first step to truly connecting with them. Believing is important – but finding a practical way to build that connection bridge is essential. This is how I make it happen:

• Find a Way to Make a Personal Connection

You'll notice I met many of these powerful people at charity events. The trick is to find a venue where you can actually have some "face time" with them – and a fundraiser is an excellent place to do that. Emailing and cold calling these people is a futile endeavor – again, the demands on them are endless. You need to find the opportunity where you can just walk right up to them and have a conversation.

• Find Out What's Important to Them

As I did with Sir Richard Branson, you should research the personality you have an opportunity to meet – before that opportunity occurs. Find out what engages them on a personal level – do they have a cause they're passionate about? Chances are they will be attending a charity event precisely because it is a cause that they have a large personal interest in.

• See How You Can Help Them

Most people approach celebrities because they want something from them. That gets very old very fast for them (or anyone else, for that matter – it's why parents get tired!). If, instead, there's some effort or project they're spearheading with which they would welcome some help, that's what you need to focus on.

• Determine How You Can Add Value

It's not enough to offer help – you need to determine exactly what you can do to help before you encounter the person. What do you have access to that might help them reach a goal? What talents or contacts can you add to the effort? Have specific answers ready.

• Practice "The Art of the Follow-Up"

Your objective, when you encounter the person you want to make the connection with, is to leave with a viable way to contact them, as I did with Sir Richard. From there, you have to follow up with the person. They're very busy people, obviously, so you usually have to be persistent – leaving just one message doesn't work.

Leaving a memorable message helps – one I left for a busy executive I know quite well was, "I spoke with God today – how come I can't speak with you???" Of course, a message like that only works if you already have a familiar relationship with the person.

DON'T STOP BELIEVING

By understanding who the people of influence were and how I could add value to them, I've been able to power myself to the top of an industry I just started in a little over two years ago. I also make sure not to ask for something for myself from these important people until long after I've added that value to them.

And again, I will credit my strong belief system. Whether I'm talking to a rich and powerful business CEO or someone just off the street, I always believe I can add value in some shape or form to that person. It may not happen immediately, but I try to make it happen as quickly as possible to cement the bond.

I'd like to give some final advice to every businessperson and entrepreneur out there - to help them keep their belief system strong and keep the kind of the positive focus in place; that's what has helped me achieve so much in so little time.

• Play to Your Strengths and Focus on Your Passion

My turning point was deciding to do what I did best – build relationships. You should also work with whatever gifts you have, don't try to force yourself to do something you don't like to do or aren't very good at. Delegate to other people the stuff you don't want to do or can't do very well.

• Get an Advisory Board of People That Can Help You

I have a number of coaches I work with to help me be better at what I do. The more associations you build with successful mentors who can help you to the next level, the better off you'll be. You can either try to do it yourself – and waste time and money on the mistakes you'll invariably make – or you can learn smart, effective short-cuts to achieve what you want from people who have already been through it all. Mentors tell you the quickest way to get where you want to go.

• Watch Your Words – Watch Your Environment

Never say you don't have enough money. Never say you can't get what you want. If you're in a negative environment, surrounded by negative people who constantly tell you how you're not going to make it, change it up and find a more positive group to associate with.

• Don't Watch TV News!

At least, don't watch too much of it. Yes, I'm serious. Years ago, Ted Turner was so frustrated by the relentless stream of negative stories on the news, he began a weekly show on TBS called "Good News" that ran for many years. If the man who founded CNN thinks TV news is too depressing and downbeat, we should all listen. In general, I firmly believe that the less TV you watch, the more money you'll make.

• Have Good Systems

Most entrepreneurs became entrepreneurs because they didn't want to work the 9 to 5 grind. Unfortunately, because they don't implement good systems into their business, they end up working non-stop – and often for less than they'd make in the corporate world. Good systems will help you work less and achieve more.

Connections have blessed me a thousand times over in the past two years – and I hope you have learned something from my successful journey. Connect with your passion, connect with your dreams, and connect with the people who help you channel that passion and bring your dreams to life.

Believe you can do it – and you will!

About Larry

Larry Benet is known as the Connector.

He is CEO of the Speakers Author Networking Group, a group of some of the most successful speakers and authors in the world. Tony Robbins, Les Brown, Peter Guber, Jack Canfield, Mark Victor Hansen, Harvey Mackay, Tony Hsieh of Zappos and Paula Abdul have all participated at SANG.

Larry is a great connector of people, and has been referred to as America's Connection Expert.

His goal is to raise a billion dollars over his lifetime for worthy charities and causes thru his connections, ideas and money. One of his goals is to eradicate homelessness in this country. He is the past Chairman of the Tsunami Disaster Relief Project where he brought top business leaders together to raise money for the victims of the Tsunami.

He has also supported the Larry King Cardiac Foundation, served on the advisory board of the Wyland Foundation and the Soul of Africa, and has helped raise money for the Richard Branson charity, Virgin Unite.

website: www.larrybenet.com and www.sangevents.com

CHAPTER 17

WHICH TAX CODE DO YOU WANT TO USE?

By William Kustka, CPA, CCPS, MBA

Disclaimer: *The following information refers to the line numbers on 2010 IRS forms, and the current Internal Revenue Code (IRC) as of the date of this writing. You should check with a qualified tax expert before implementing any of these strategies.*

It has been said there are two distinct tax codes: one for the informed, and one for the uninformed! It's your choice whether to learn and understand these differences, or to be a victim of them. Don't expect anyone to care more about reducing your income taxes than you!

The tax code is heavily stacked against wage earners and favors business owners. Take a look at your most recent Form 1040. (Google: IRS Form 1040 for the latest version.)

If you are a wage earner, the IRS takes withholding on the gross amount earned each payday. Your gross earnings are taxed as earned, and included in your Adjusted Gross Income (AGI). Your itemized deductions come on page 2 of Form 1040 (Line 40).

Your AGI determines your eligibility for various credits, serves as part of the calculation for whether your Social Security benefits are taxable, and is a key determinant in whether you are subject to Alternative Minimum Tax (AMT).

If you own a business, your taxable income is the **NET** after you have taken your business deductions (Line 12 for a sole proprietor, Line 17 for rental real estate, royalty property, a partnership, or S-Corporation, or Line 18 for a farmer). Business deductions are much more valuable than itemized deductions!

The business owner gets their deductions on page 1 of Form 1040; the wage earner gets their deductions on page 2. If you don't have a business, you should start one. Owning a business is one of the best tax shelters available from the IRS. A home-based business is easy to establish and will provide an escape hatch if you lose your job. It will allow you to spend more time with your family. Perhaps most importantly, it will save you taxes.

The tax strategies we will discuss revolve around shifting income to lower tax bracket taxpayers or changing itemized deductions that are taken on page 2 of Form 1040, to business expenses that are taken on page 1 of Form 1040. Our objective is to reduce your AGI; this will reduce your income tax liability, improve your eligibility for income tax benefits that are phased out at higher AGI, and reduce or eliminate your exposure to the dreaded AMT.

TAX REDUCTION STRATEGIES:

Some of these strategies are employee benefit programs that require you to offer the plan to all employees. Some can be discriminatory and cover only selected employees. Remember this is a team effort; don't try to implement these strategies without competent professional guidance. The IRS will disallow tax benefits if you don't follow and document the requirements.

For 2011, you "graduate" to the marginal 25% tax bracket at taxable income above $69,000 ($34,500 if filing single). You are in the 28% tax bracket at taxable income above $139,350 ($83,600 if single). Our strategies are saving you taxes at your marginal tax rate plus self-employment tax rate. For simplicity sake, let's assume you have not maxed out on Medicare withholding (2011 wages not above $106,800 per spouse). Your savings with these strategies will save you approximately 40% (combined income tax bracket 25% - 28%, plus Self-Employed Tax bracket - 13.3% in 2011, back to 15.3% after 2011). For the rest of our illustrations, we will use a flat 40% tax savings. Since you will probably have state tax savings as well, the 40% for our illustrations is reasonable, and will save space explaining each calculation. We expect the tax code to change at least annually, and the tax rates to change, so the 40% tax savings may be higher in future years.

Optimizing Your Interest Deduction: The mortgage interest deduction has been part of U.S. tax policy for decades. In general, the IRS limits the interest deduction to the interest on $1 million for home acquisition, and $100,000 for home equity loans. The IRS has additional stricter limits that are determined by the fair market value of the residence. The recent decline in fair market value of real estate may trigger these stricter limits. (Google: IRS Pub 936).

Because of the phase out of itemized deductions at higher incomes (reinstated in 2013), the AMT and/or the IRS limits on deductible mortgage interest, many taxpayers cannot deduct all of their mortgage interest.

Most taxpayers deduct their mortgage interest as an itemized deduction. With proper planning you can categorize this interest as business expense.

There are several different categories of interest:

- Interest on your principal residence or second home is deductible on your Schedule A as "qualified residence interest". This is commonly known as mortgage interest.
- Interest incurred in your business is deducted on your business tax return.
- Interest on rental property is deductible on Schedule E subject to passive loss limits.
- Investment interest is deductible (limited to investment income with a carryover available) on your Schedule A.
- Student loan interest is taken as an adjustment before AGI with a phase out at higher incomes.

In general, the IRS has rules that allow interest deductions depending on how the loan proceeds are used; these are known as "tracing rules".

Mortgage interest is the exception to the general rule. Unless you tell the IRS otherwise, your mortgage interest will not be subject to the "tracing rules" and will be considered "qualified residence interest" regardless of what you use the proceeds for (other than buying tax-free investments).

The IRS allows you to opt out of this exception, and opt into the general rule, so you can elect to treat your home equity loan interest as one of the other categories of interest if you can "trace" the proceeds to a specific category.

A home equity loan is probably easier to get, and has a lower interest rate than a business loan. A taxpayer can elect not to treat interest on their home equity loan as "qualified-residence interest", and subject the loan proceeds to the "tracing rules."

If you can trace the proceeds of a home equity loan to your business, it becomes deductible business interest.

Proceeds of the loan should be placed in a separate account. Do not mix loan proceeds with other funds. Do not use the loan proceeds for personal expenditures. In order to substantiate the use of the loan proceeds, you should have separate accounts for your business, your rental properties, your investments, and your personal items.

Let's say you get a home equity loan of $100,000, and you pay $7,000 interest on that loan. You decide to treat this as business interest by electing not to treat the loan as "secured by a qualified residence." You use the loan proceeds to purchase furniture and equipment for your business allowing you to trace the entire loan proceeds to your business, making it business interest. The results: minimum $1,050 in tax savings (No self-employment taxes), up to $2,800 ($7,000 x 40%), if you cannot take the full mortgage deduction.

Not a bad result for adding one more page to your tax return!

Health Reimbursement Arrangement (HRA) under IRC Section 105: This strategy allows a business to deduct 100% of family medical expenses as a business expense. It includes your medical insurance deductibles and co-pays, all dental and vision costs, prescription costs, and non-covered services (lasik surgery).

To qualify for an HRA, a business owner must legitimately employ their spouse in the business. Qualifying business types include sole proprietors, partnerships, LLCs, and corporations. The plan cannot reimburse for medical expenses incurred before the employee enrolls in the plan. This strategy pays your spouse to be involved in your business, and gives them credits toward their ultimate collection of Social Security, increasing the amount they would otherwise receive.

A partnership between a husband and wife will not qualify for the plan. The benefits of hiring your spouse in an S-Corporation are limited.

The HRA is a written plan that includes the following:

1. Description of the benefits.
2. Description of eligibility
3. Description of the claims procedures.

Remember your itemized deduction for medical expenses is reduced by 7½% of your AGI. If your AGI is $70,000, and your medical expenses are $5,250, you are allowed zero medical expense deduction. (The first 7½% of your AGI does not count – 7½% of $70,000 = $5,250.)

By implementing an HRA, you have successfully moved the $5,250 to page 1 of your 1040, and reduced your tax by $2,100.

As your medical expenses increase, the tax savings increase. As you move into higher tax brackets, the tax savings will increase. There may also be the benefit of reducing state income tax.

Hire Your Child: This is a wonderful way to teach your child about your business, about budgeting, and about how the economy works. It teaches them responsibility and job skills. It will also give the child experience they could never be taught in school.

This strategy uses income shifting to move income from the parents' higher tax bracket to the child's lower tax bracket. It is a powerful tax planning strategy. There are some IRS guidelines you will need to follow to qualify.

The child has to perform a legitimate function or service for your unincorporated business; you cannot deduct payments for chores done around the house. You can hire them to clean your home office, maintain your files, or do computer work for the business.

You have to maintain the payroll forms and procedures you have for any other non-family employee. If you already have employees, you are just adding another one. If you have never had employees, Google: IRS Publication 15.

You should have a formal employment agreement detailing the duties the child will perform, and outlining the compensation for those duties. You should maintain a time card or other record of time devoted to these duties the same as you would for any other non-family employee.

You can pay them a reasonable wage for performance of these duties but never more than you would pay a non-family employee. So you can't pay your 8-year old $5,000 a year to clean your office, but you could justify that amount for using their likeness in your business advertising. If you pay a reasonable compensation for the services rendered, the IRS will have no problem.

You should pay the child from your business checking account. The income belongs to the child, so you should set up a separate account for the child. They can start or add to their savings account or start a college savings fund. Since your child now has earned income, they can even start an IRA or Roth IRA.

Besides income shifting, this strategy also allows you to avoid Self-Employment Tax on compensation to your children under age 18. According to the IRS, payments for the services of a child under 18 who works for his or her parent in a trade or business are not subject to Social Security and Medicare taxes if the trade or business is a sole proprietorship or a partnership in which each partner is a parent of the child. (Google: IRS hire child).

If your business is neither a sole proprietorship nor a partnership of the parents, then the compensation will be subject to Social Security and Medicare taxes, but you would still receive the benefit of shifting to the child's lower tax bracket. So your family benefit is the difference between your tax bracket and your child's tax bracket.

By implementing this strategy, you can hire a child for up to $5,700 and the child's tax will be zero. You have reduced your AGI by $5,700, lowering your tax by $2,280 ($5,700 x 40%).

If the child contributes to an IRA, they can be paid $10,700 and still have zero tax, since they are eligible for a $5,000 IRA adjustment. Your family has effectively saved $4280 in taxes. These are your savings per child, per year! In addition to these savings there will be savings on your state income tax return if applicable.

Deduct Child's Car As A Business Expense:

If you are providing a car for your child's use, why not get a deduction for it? With this strategy your business can buy a car or use one of your existing vehicles.

You have hired your child, and some of their tasks include delivering to customers, picking up supplies, going to the bank or post office. The employee can use an employer's vehicle for business purposes and it will be considered to be non-taxable (Google: working condition fringe benefit).

The value of the company car is a deductible business expense to the business owner, and is not considered taxable to the employee. If the employee uses the company car for both business purposes and personal use, the employer still gets the full deduction, but the personal use portion will be a taxable fringe benefit to the employee.

The value comes from the IRS Annual Lease Value Table. If you provide the vehicle for less than a full year, you would prorate the value for the number of days the vehicle was made available to the employee (Google: IRS annual lease value table).

The key to this allocation is the substantiation of business use. The employee should maintain a vehicle usage log of mileage driven that includes specific information (Google: IRS mileage log).

The more information the employee provides on the form, the more likely you will satisfy the IRS requirements. Entries for business use of the vehicle should be made to the form as the mileage is driven, not at the end of the month. If you get an oil change or other maintenance performed at close to the yearend, you will have a document that corroborates the odometer reading, and will enable you to justify total mileage during the year.

Let's use a vehicle valued at $14,900. The value from the Annual Lease Value Table is $4,100. During the year, the employee-child drove a total of 12,000 miles of which 9,000 were personal miles. Your business will deduct the full $4,100. Since 75% of the total mileage was personal use, the employee-child will have $3,075 included in their W-2; the remaining $1,025 was received tax-free as a working condition fringe benefit. The child-employee could receive an additional $2,625 in wages and would have zero federal tax liability! If the child had wages of $7,625 and contributed to an IRA, the child would still have zero federal tax. The $4,100 auto deduction saves you $1,640 in taxes.

There are many other strategies available, but in this limited space, with four strategies, this business owner saved between $7,070 and $8,820 in federal taxes (more if the child opened an IRA). Is that a good return for the cost of this book? Please contact me for additional strategies?

About William

William Kustka, CPA, CCPS, MBA often starts a meeting with a prospective new business client with a brief outline of his background as a problem solver and asks, "When was the last time your previous tax advisor gave you an idea that saved you money?" This is usually followed by the client explaining their business issues and what they are hoping to achieve. Bill's goal is to show clients strategies that legally save taxes based on IRS rules, something most business owners have never been shown.

He is the founder of Bill Busters LLC, a firm devoted to showing business owners how to increase their revenue and reduce expenses, including the cost of their payroll, bookkeeping, and credit card processing.

Bill is a licensed Certified Public Accountant (CPA) in NY and NJ and has owned and managed an independent CPA and tax planning office for over 20 years. He has an MBA in Advanced Accounting. Bill has completed the rigorous certification process of the National Institute of Certified College Planners, and has achieved both the coveted CCPS (Certified College Planning Specialist) designation, and the prestigious "College Doctor" title. This training aids him in showing parents how they can qualify for more college financial aid.

He was the founding President of Le Tip of Middlesex County (a business owners networking group), He is also the former President of the Monmouth-Ocean County Chapter of the Institute of Management Accountants.

Prior to being a self-employed CPA, Bill performed financial audits with Coopers & Lybrand (now Price Waterhouse Coopers).

After a brief stint with the Treasury Department, Bill joined the US Navy. He served as Supply Department Head aboard ship, Bill was responsible for the procurement of everything from toilet paper to ice cream to electronic repair parts that had to be aboard before leaving homeport.

Bill served as an auditor with the Naval Audit Service where he performed operational audits on military bases. These audits consisted of verifying compliance with existing regulations, and making recommendations to improve results with limited resources.

These experiences served as the basis of his developing strategies to solve business owners' problems, reduce expenses and improve their bottom line results.

He is the author of the forthcoming book: *"Winning The College Game: Discover The Secret Guide To Having The IRS Pay For Most of Your Kid's Tuition."*

You can contact William Kustka, CPA at: BILLBUSTERSLLC.COM

CHAPTER 18

THE FOUR POWER POINTS FOR GROWTH

By John Ledford, CFP

I began my career in the investment business 17 years ago. In that time span, we've entered a new century, even a new millennium and, quite frankly, it feels like it. How business was done is no longer good enough—not when the competition is stronger, money is tighter and so many of the rules have changed.

At my firm, Ledford Financial, we've managed to not just survive turbulent times, but to also thrive. I began this company in 2002 overseeing $9 million in assets. Now, we are one of the "Top Financial Planning Firms" in Central Florida, according to Orlando Magazine[3], with more than $125 million in client assets and growing. And I believe we've accomplished all that by embracing the new, certainly not by getting mired in the old.

Frankly, the old ways of running this kind of business haven't led to significant long-run growth for most companies. For the majority of financial planning firms, initial growth generally dead-ends in a plateau—which then leads to a dramatic stagnation. It's very challenging to break the back of that paradigm. There aren't a lot of coaches or experts to help you do it. We've had to carve out our own path and, luckily, we've made the right choices.

I'm going to share those choices in this chapter, breaking them down into four "Power Points for Growth" that apply not only to my business, but to many others as well. These are four action items that I focus on in my day-to-day leadership and that have paid off in tremendous growth for our hard-working staff and myself.

GROWTH POINT #1: DEVELOP RESIDUAL REVENUE

Imagine a baseball player, someone who's a great hitter, who has a primary goal to finish the season batting .350 – a great average for any everyday player. Now imagine all he has to do is bat well in the very first game of the season and he'll have locked down 80% of that season-long average in those initial 9 innings.

Let's say he does hit over .300 in that one game. He'd be pretty happy and confident the rest of the season. Having that kind of stress off his back would allow him to be comfortable and relaxed at the plate and maybe cause him to get more hits than he normally would. He'd be willing to take more chances and wouldn't get overly-concerned about any short-term slumps along the way.

Creating residual revenue as the focal point of your income is your opportunity to feel like that batter. When you lock in a large percentage of your annual income right away, you manage your business much more effectively. It's easier to realistically analyze the people, the process and the business itself if you have that comfort level already in place.

Not only that, but just like that hitter, you have a tremendous amount of confidence about what you're going to do moving forward. You're more energized about acquiring new business, because of the business you already have.

As I said earlier, ours is one of the "Top Financial Planning Firms" in Central Florida, and our business is typically 75 to 80 percent recurring revenue through monthly or quarterly fees that our clients agree to pay. It's a business model I've purposely pursued.

Residual revenue is a relatively new concept to most businesses. In the old days, insurance was one of the few businesses that employed it—obviously people had to keep paying for their policies on a regular basis. It is, however, a concept that is now suddenly gaining widespread acceptance in some surprising sectors. For example, my barber no longer charges me per cut, but instead, charges me a monthly fee for his services. Even the person who recently painted my house suggested a monthly payment plan that would include touch-up or other necessary work down the line.

Leveraging your current customer base into providing a steady cash stream is always easier than trying to constantly find new customers, which is where businesses traditionally concentrate their efforts. Even the investment business, at least when I got into it, was virtually all transaction-based. An advisor would sell something one day and then the next, start all over again at ground zero to try and sell something else.

My partner in the late 90's and I changed that up, and created a residual income-based fee structure, both in the way that we managed assets and how we did financial planning. By doing things predominantly for an ongoing fee and predominately for recurring revenue, there was no sense of having to re-invent the wheel on a daily basis, instead, we had a continuous built-in cash flow that allowed us to do our jobs at a higher level of achievement.

Think about it; if you have a million dollar business and you already have around $800,000 committed to you as of January 1st, you'll enter that New Year with a pretty bright outlook. You also lose a lot of the stress that your competition is plagued with and you end up having a lot more freedom and flexibility in running your business.

As well as a lot more fun.

GROWTH POINT #2: DEVELOP RESIDUAL REFERRAL SOURCES

Referrals are the most powerful way of developing new business and finding new clients. However, for most companies, it results in something of a dead-end.

That's because most of your clients that will actively refer you, only have a limited number of contacts to refer you to. Once those wells dry up, you're out of referral sources. This is a significant reason why businesses such as ours are so vulnerable to a growth slowdown. Not only that, but trying to drive referrals from your clients can be difficult—and those clients can also perceive it as not necessarily being in their best interests. They don't want a whole lot of new clients taking your attention away from their money.

That's why it's much better to create and cultivate a group of business owners as your referral source. Other business owners are like-minded professionals who understand the need for referrals, both within their businesses as well as others. They prefer to work collaboratively toward that end if it benefits everyone involved. And if they continue to grow their businesses, they have a theoretically endless supply of new referrals to send your way. One more key advantage; business owners tend to refer up (higher-income people), whereas clients tend to refer down (lower-income people).

The average financial advisory firm grows at a rate of 9 to 12% per year, typically by organic client referrals. However, a "super-growth" company will usually grow in excess of 25% per year, with the vast majority of that growth coming from professional referral sources, rather than client referrals.

Here's how we created our own successful professional referral group. Several years ago, we formed an organization called, "The 11 to 1 Club," basically a lunch club that would meet once a month (I realize there are already organizations that do this kind of thing, but I believe it's better to create your own rather than join something that's already there—it's good for your visibility in the business community).

I invited CPAs, attorneys, CFOs, and high-level insurance, real estate, banking and venture capital people—the kind of professionals who are out there in the marketplace and already dealing with the type of person who could easily become one of our clients. At first, I only asked 12 people by special invitation and, fortunately, all were excited to be a part of this new group.

Well, we experienced explosive growth in our business as a result. Our revenue more than doubled in the first 3 years of its existence. More specifically, we gained 7 million dollars from the group in the first year and over 30 million dollars in the second. And, because I began to build strong relationships with these kinds of business people, I ultimately forged a partnership with one of the members that continues to fuel our success today.

GROWTH POINT #3: EMBRACE NEW TECHNOLOGY

The financial industry was a bit of a late adopter when it came to computer and internet-based technology. There were a lot of reasons behind that, some of which were related to mandates from regulatory agencies, in addition to there wasn't a lot of great software out there in the beginning that would significantly help us do what we do.

Today, it's a completely different story, at least at our offices. Everyone has at minimum two flat screen monitors on their desk, while the administrative staff has at least three. We all use Smartphones that are integrated with our company's databases. Now, rather than waiting for the technology to find us, we go out and find it—like attending iPad seminars in which we learn how to use that device in the most effective and efficient way possible.

Our internal communication is also second to none and our research capacity is constantly being elevated and leveraged through technology. A significant part of our infrastructure budget is allocated towards adopting new technology and testing new software, instead of waiting until it's out to the general market.

The result has been that our access to information is amazingly quick and every level of our organization has been positively transformed. Our internal systems and processes are cleaner and quicker than in the past and, overall, we're a lot more efficient than ever before. Best of all, we can identify potential clients and find out all about them on the internet before they ever come through our doors. And, of course, they can do the same with us.

The new technology has enabled us to do what we do a whole lot faster and better. By having access to more information more quickly, we can serve our clients better and meet their needs at a higher level.

GROWTH POINT #4: SOCIAL NETWORKING IS THE FUTURE – AND THE FUTURE IS NOW

As a result of the technology boom, social networking is the new norm. Last year, I attended a Facebook seminar where I learned that this premier online community was made up of 500 million members. Now, it's over 750 million today and on track to become the largest organization of people on the planet, exceeding the population of China.

Our company is very much aware of the social networking phenomenon and how powerful—and necessary—it is for a business. If we're going to intersect with our current clients, if we're going to find new clients, if we're going to allow people to find us and learn about us in a non-invasive way, then we have to get on board with social networking way beyond what we're doing today…even though we're doing way beyond what we were doing just a few short months ago.

To that end, we're active on Facebook and LinkedIn, and we've just started a Twitter account. We have Facebook and LinkedIn integrated with our website and every email or newsletter that goes out has featured links to our pages on both services. We also download databases and crosscheck them against both sites and we also use them to find out more about people who come in to see us for the first time. We're also pushing information through those sources and using educational elements to help our clients understand more about the world of finance, as well as extend our media reach.

Beyond Facebook and LinkedIn, the opportunity to trumpet our "brand" through such online media as YouTube videos and internet radio is limitless and helps us distinguish ourselves from our competitors.

The truth is, however, this is a fast-moving world that you need to keep on top of or you end up waking up one morning to find that the world has passed you by. That's why it's important to figure out what social media works best for which marketing objective—whether it's education, community service, attracting new clients, etc.—and also to determine what resonates the most for your client base. Staying ahead of the curve as far as you can, helps you be the most effective when it comes to social media.

And there are significant side benefits to it as well. Whether you realize it or not, "old media" news outlets often use social media to help beef up the content of their stories. Recently, the stock market had a particularly volatile day and one of our social media campaigns was noticed by the news staff of a local TV station. The result was, an hour or two later, I was on the news being interviewed as a financial expert and ideally positioned for the benefit of both my current clients as well as some potential ones who may have been just getting their first exposure to me.

Yes, that exposure was on the good old-fashioned television set—but it turns out there are still plenty of people watching it.

When correctly put into action, these four "power points" work together to build and grow a healthy business. Developing residual income gives you security as well as a tremendous amount of breathing room, allowing you to be a better business person and build a better company. To continue that growth, creating professional residual referrals enables you to add clients and revenues at an optimal rate.

When you've used those two power points to build a stable cash-rich company with incredible growth prospects, you now have to have great technology and systems in place to serve your clients at a high level, making sure nothing falls through the cracks and allowing you, as a business owner, to take full advantage of the opportunities in front of you.

Finally, social networking is the future of how we're going to do business, whether we want it to be or not. If you ignore it, you ignore it at your own peril. Understanding how to leverage Facebook and the like is critical to your ongoing marketing efforts.

Of course, this chapter can't begin to address all the ins and outs of running and growing a successful financial firm. If you run a financial planning company and would like some more insights into how to achieve a new level of success, I encourage you to contact me directly at john@ ledfordfinancial.com.

Times may have changed. But success is always obtainable.

Ledford Financial is located at 605 East Robinson Street, Suite 640, Orlando, FL 32801 and can be reached at (407) 999-8998. Securities and advisory services offered through Commonwealth Financial Network, member FINRA/SIPC, a registered investment adviser.

About John

JOHN E. LEDFORD, CFP® is President of LEDFORD FINANCIAL. John's career in finance began at the age of 19 with a major Wall Street brokerage firm. From there, he quickly advanced to a trust officer with one of the nation's largest trust and investment banks. In 1996, John joined Financial Advisory Service based in Winter Park, Florida. In 1998, he became president and co-principal of Conte-Ledford Financial Group (formally known as Financial Advisory Service). He held this position until July 2002, when he formed Ledford Financial.

In 2011, *Orlando Style*[1] magazine selected John as one of Orlando's "Featured Wealth Managers." In 2009, John was a top 10 finalist for *Registered Rep's*[2] "Outstanding Advisor of the Year" for which he was recognized for his work providing funds to micro banks throughout Latin American and the Caribbean, which spurred the creation of Change MicroFund, a nonprofit micro financing entity of which he is a founder. In 2008, Ledford Financial was honored by *Orlando Magazine*[3] as one of the "Top Financial Planning Firms" in Central Florida. Also in 2008, *Boomer Market Advisor*[4] named John "Socially Responsible Advisor of the Year" again for his work in micro-lending in emerging-market countries.

In addition, John is a frequent contributor to both national and local news outlets—including regular appearances on Central Florida's 24 hour news station, CFNews 13. He is a member of the Financial Planning Association (FPA), on the executive board of the Center for Memory Disorders and a former member of the Gulf Coast and Space Coast Estate Planning Councils.

John attended North Texas State University and is also a graduate of the University of Central Florida and the College for Financial Planning.

John currently lives in Winter Springs with his wife, Valerie, and four children. Away from the office, he enjoys diving, music, coaching, flying, and just about every sport.

[1]*Top 5 Advisors as chosen by Orlando Style magazine's editors.* [2]*John's broker/dealer, Commonwealth, submitted him for nomination. Nominees had to complete a form that included questions about how they have been of service to their community. Winners were selected by the magazine's editorial staff.* [3]*Orlando Magazine chose the top 20 firms based on its own internal criteria that included assets under management, length of time in business, and reputation in the community.* [4]*John's broker/dealer, Commonwealth, submitted him for nomination. Nominees had to complete a form that included questions about how they have been of service to their community. Winners were selected by the magazine's editorial staff. John's registrations include FINRA Series 6, 7, 24, 63, and 65. He is a Registered Securities Principal and Investment Adviser Representative with Commonwealth Financial Network®, and a CERTIFIED FINANCIAL PLANNER™ practitioner. The financial professionals of Ledford Financial are registered representatives and investment adviser representatives with/and offer securities and advisory services through Commonwealth Financial Network, member FINRA/SIPC, a registered investment adviser. Fixed Insurance products and services offered by Ledford Financial are separate and unrelated to Commonwealth.*

CHAPTER 19

Perseverance + Action = A SUCCESSFUL ENTREPRENEUR

By Nicholas Rodriguez

PERSEVERANCE: The steady persistence in a course of action, a purpose, a state, etc., especially in spite of difficulties, obstacles, or discouragement.

ACTION: an act that one consciously wills and that may be characterized by physical or mental activity.

When tackling the business world there are certain activities, actions and commitments that put every single entrepreneur (both aspiring and seasoned) on the same playing field. Often times aspiring entrepreneurs encounter difficulties in getting their businesses off the ground, having people not believe in their goals and dreams, and/or just not having people even know that their businesses even exist! What's the good news in respect to these difficulties? Almost every successful entrepreneur in our world has been through the trials and tribulations that come with building a successful business along with the activities, actions and commitments that are absolutely needed to be successful in the business world. From my experience in the business world, the *two most critical commitments that an entrepreneur must commit to is the act of Perseverance and the commitment to Action.*

I, for sure, am no exception to these trials and tribulations. As the President and CEO of YoungBiz, I routinely tackle circumstances that test my perseverance and my commitment to action. We at YoungBiz provide financial literacy and entrepreneurship curriculums to public, private and charter schools across the USA. We also provide year-round programs, camps and workshops in the areas of youth money and business education, as well as professional development training to teachers and training professionals. In our business space, rejection is higher than the norm. Why? Because our country does not value the importance of preparing our youths for the real world financially. This goes for our politicians, education administrators and parents. I applaud the very small percentage of politicians, education administrators and parents who do take financial education seriously, but because of this lack of attention to prepare our young ones financially, we at YoungBiz have to not only deal with the trials and tribulations that entrepreneurs deal with, but also the task of bucking the status quo of accepting the industrial way of thinking, and not allowing the rejections to kill our company's mantra of changing the way the USA views money and business education for youths.

When I am hit with rejection (and trust me I am rejected more than the average entrepreneur because of my high activity level), I usually ascertain what caused the rejection, what could I have done differently or better, and if we really had a chance to have our services accepted in the first place. Once I run my brain through that gambit, the only thing that makes me feel better is to meet that rejection with a severe arsenal of action! By that I mean I either disengage, modify or go after that rejection again with a new game plan or I refocus my actions in another manner that helps my company achieve the same goal but in a different way. Notice that there is never any thought of quitting or giving up! Never! We as a company view rejection as a challenge, or a way to test our resolve and commitment to serving our market. There is no doubt our company would not be the young and emerging brand it is today if it weren't for our perseverance.

When I acquired the rights to the YoungBiz brand in the United States, the company was in disarray with no steady stream of sales, poor morale and internal disputes that were destructive and demoralizing… a true test for myself as a business person. Close friends and mentors advised me that I was crazy and that I shouldn't deal with or get involved with such a mess that would take endless time and energy to turn around. But I saw something different. I saw a brand that needed a new voice, a new hand and a new lease on life. A brand that could change the lives of youths and how America perceived youth financial education. The one plus I had in YoungBiz was its established curriculum. So I at least had something to work with. To sum it up, I saw in YoungBiz what a real estate investor sees in a beat-up run-down property. Potential and future value. I knew the task at hand would be tough, but I knew I had the perseverance and commitment to action to take on the challenge. The turn around of YoungBiz is such a large topic that it deserves to be discussed in its own published book at a future date, but it serves as a great example of what perseverance and a commitment to action can provide you.

It's ironic how in today's world all you usually hear are the success stories and the end results of how a person is reveling in the new wealthy lifestyle they have as a result of their successful business, but all too often, little is said of the journey that person may have gone through to achieve such success. Like most, I like to read about success stories and the good things that are happening for successful entrepreneurs, but I do love to read about the journeys these people have gone through – their challenges, obstacles and how they had to persevere to reach the pinnacle of their success. Learning about these journeys not only have inspired and motivated me, but they also have taught me. It has taught me that what I have experienced as an entrepreneur is normal, and more of a test as to how badly I want it.

To further emphasize the high levels of perseverance displayed by great entrepreneurs, I want to share with you two well-known pioneering entrepreneurs whose perseverance played a crucial role in their success: Ray Kroc (Architect and visionary of the McDonald's empire) and Shawn Carter – better known as Jay-Z.

• In 1955, Ray Kroc opened his first McDonald's in Des Plaines, Illinois. From that year, Ray Kroc went nearly 5 years without making a profit at the outset of his McDonald's venture. He had constant internal turmoil with the McDonald's brothers (the original founders of the McDonald's restaurants) that led to constant disagreements and animosity between the parties – not to mention Ray Kroc was in his 50's while undertaking such a venture! Now take a second to thoroughly consider this. In today's day and age of instant gratification, Ray Kroc persevered with almost no cash flow, internal conflicts and 60-hour plus workweeks in his mid 50's! Why? Because his vision was so strong and absolute that his perseverance and commitment to action was second to none. Just note this great quote from Ray Kroc himself: "I was an overnight success all right, but 30 years is a long, long night." Ray Kroc's life work had an effect on American Culture. This effect would not be with us today if it weren't for his tenacious perseverance that is exemplified in the McDonald's corporate culture some 50 years later.

• Today, we all know Jay-Z as the most acclaimed and accomplished 'hip hop' star of all time to include his vast business ventures that prove his business acumen. But like Ray Kroc, success didn't happen overnight. Jay-Z personally persevered through his teenage years growing up in the Marcy Houses of the Bedford Stuyvesant section of Brooklyn NY. Drugs, violence and crime were the environment that surrounded the future music mogul. But Jay-Z didn't succumb to his environment as a long term solution. He knew life offered more. Though it wasn't easy, Jay Z made a decision to go after it. Truly a decision that proved to be a great one! At the outset of Jay-Z's career, no record labels were interested in signing him. He received his share of "No's" just like any aspiring businessperson. Rejection after rejection led Jay-Z not to quit or abandon his aspirations to be a successful hip hop star, but instead, he planned, persevered and eventually banded together with two other partners to form their own independent record label known as Rock-A-Fella Records in 1996. And the rest is history! Today Jay-Z is considered one of the most influential individuals in the music industry with a net worth upwards of $400 million. Not so bad for an inner city youth hailing from Brooklyn NY.

I encourage you to research more successful entrepreneurs and study their journeys. Our society loves to publicize the present, but you can learn so much by just understanding how these pioneers did it, what they went through and most importantly, how they persevered.

To ensure you give yourself every chance to succeed as an entrepreneur, here are the six most critical actions I have learned and want to share with you, so you can refer to them when your perseverance is tested:

1. Take rejection as a lesson. When you receive a "NO" in regards to

your business endeavors, view it as a lesson to do it better on the next go-around. And remember, the more "No's" you receive shows your activity level is up, and you are putting in the work so as long as you are learning from each and every rejection. It doesn't matter if you get 100 "No's," it's that one "YES" that can help you have an effect on the world.

2. Do not let negativity or worrying affect you. Part of persevering is keeping the negativity away and controlling the amount of worrying that will seep into your thoughts. You're human so it will happen. Control negativity by controlling your thoughts, with whom you hang around with, and keeping your mind on the big picture. If you are 100% focused on the big picture, you won't have the time to deal with negativity or the late night 'worry' sessions. Your activity and persistence toward your goals will keep you afloat during the rough times.

3. Quitting is not an option. Just like we all will do anything for our families, you must categorize your business as part of the family and just like you wouldn't abandon and quit on a family member, you must never quit on yourself and your business. What can quitting solve other than creating regrets? Re-analyze, adjust your plan, raise your activity level but under no circumstance is quitting an option, especially if you serve as an example for family and friends. In that circumstance, you must buck the system and prove you can achieve your goals not matter how lofty they are. It's your responsibility to your family to create and leave a legacy behind and quitting will never give you the opportunity to do that.

4. Engage your network and mentor(s). While striving to achieve business success, always stay engaged with your network and mentors. Your network can help to open doors for you, create opportunities for your business and share their trials and tribulations with you. Engaging your mentor(s) can help you to see first hand that you can succeed at what you're doing (since your mentor should be someone who has been there and succeeded). Ask your mentor questions, bounce ideas off them, and try to duplicate the strategies they implemented when things got tough or complicated with their respective businesses. This will help your perseverance grow stronger and remain consistent since you're getting tried-and-true advice.

5. In order to consistently persevere and succeed, you and your team must all be uniformly committed. Persevering can only be a massive force if you and your team are unified as one. This is where each person commits to not letting the team down, picking each other up, and everyone handling their responsibility toward the common goal reinforces your will to survive the hardships of entrepreneurship – thus persevering as a company.

6. Get to Work! There's nothing better than setting out and reinforcing your perseverance with action, action, action! Make that tough phone call or knock on that door that you've been intimidated to knock on all these weeks! What's the worst thing that can happen, someone else says no? Get to work so that you can put your head down to rest at night knowing the world got your best effort today and that tomorrow they'll be getting even more of you.

Perseverance and committing to persistent action are qualities all entrepreneurs must have. My perseverance has been strengthened by the countless roadblocks and rejections I've received in the business world. Fortunately for me and my company, rejection only spurs me into persistent action that can only create future success. Failing, mistakes, and rejections don't scare me because I am constantly learning and committing to action – which doesn't allow me to be affected by temporary setbacks. I also refer to my six critical actions when the going gets really tough and I always seem to get through those days that test my perseverance. Always remember, your perseverance and actions should always be a at a high level, but when your perseverance is tested with failure or rejection, kick it into a new gear and use persistent action to persevere – thus keeping your business goals on track for eventual success.

About Nicholas

Nicholas Rodriguez currently serves as the President and CEO of YoungBiz USA. YoungBiz is known as a world leader in business, entrepreneurship, and financial literacy education for children, teenagers, young adults and adults. YoungBiz publishes and provides youth financial literacy and entrepreneurship curriculums to public, private and charter schools across the United States. YoungBiz also provides year-round programs, camps, workshops and professional development training. Nicholas is also the Founder of BusinessMind Creations, the managing company for BusinessMind Greetings and Baby Biz Wear.

Prior to YoungBiz, Nicholas served as the Co-Founder and President of Commercial Lending Group, a Full Service Financing Company specializing in the financing of business acquisitions and start-up business loans.

Nicholas serves on numerous boards for youth-oriented organizations and is a high demand consultant to organizations in regards to developing and implementing financial literacy and entrepreneurship programs for youth and young adults.

Nicholas is a graduate of St. Francis College in Brooklyn NY. He resides with his wife Jacqueline and their family in Staten Island, New York. Nicholas and YoungBiz can be contacted at: www.youngbiz.com and/or at 1-800-878-4982.

CHAPTER 20

SWITCHING CHANNELS: CHANGE UP YOUR MEDIA AND CHANGE UP YOUR BUSINESS

By J.W. Dicks, Esq., Nick Nanton, Esq.
and Lindsay Dicks

"Every company is its own TV show, magazine and newspaper."
~ Jay Baer

How do you sell who you are and what your business is all about?

If you're like most entrepreneurs or professionals, you hit on a few marketing approaches that work, like Yellow Pages ads, email campaigns or networking meetings – and you stick with them. If they're making you some money, what possible reason is there to change it up?

Well, there's one really big reason – to make *more* money.

For example, the three of us had been primarily marketing our Celebrity Branding services through live seminars, webinars and teleseminars. These marketing channels (distribution methods), had worked very successfully for us in the past so it was natural to start a new project with what we were comfortable worked and test our promotions there first.

The type of services we offer are fairly unique and wide-ranging, so we felt seminars were a great platform to explain it all. Once you develop a consistent process using a specific marketing channel, it is wise to begin testing another channel against it. You don't stop what you are doing, but you test the metrics of one against the other to see which one produces the highest return for the dollars spent.

This process of testing is both an art and a science. The science potion is in gathering the data on your marketing campaign, and the art is making a decision based on that data – which marketing channel you go with. Logic first tells you that you go with the one that produces the highest return. If you have limited resources, that may be true. However, it is also very important to have diversity in your marketing because invariably marketing stops producing for one reason or another, and if you only have one channel that you are using, your business will suffer before you can crank up another media channel. An example of this is television. You can be doing great one month and then the Presidential elections come along and the price of television sectors goes up so high your ROI calculations don't work anymore. This is a dangerous place to find yourself. What you discover is that diversification in media buying is as important in marketing as it is investing.

With the diversification rule in mind, we made a decision to begin testing Social media as a specific marketing channel, and in particular, Facebook ads. We had just added a new partner, Greg Rollett, to our Agency team and he had very good success with Facebook ads promoting other products. Since it was clear to us all that Social media is growing into a strong marketing force, it was an easier decision than it might have been. Facebook was also the easiest choice among the alternatives within the social media category, because of its size and ability to target market specific demographics. With over 800 million users, Facebook has a population that's bigger than all the countries in the world, except for India and China.

The final factor that tipped the scale for us selecting Facebook was the cost of testing. For as little as $25 to $50 a day in advertising expense, we knew we could begin to develop specific metrics to compare to our seminar marketing numbers.

For our first program, we selected financial planners as a niche we felt would be responsive to our ads, because they responded well to the tele-seminars program we run, and we had many successful clients from that field. Knowing you target client is very important to help you craft your message, and if you do know your market, Facebook will put you directly in front of their Facebook page for you to offer your product/service.

To help you understand the process of creating a Facebook campaign, we have reproduced parts of it for you to see. You'll probably recognize the format of the original ads we created – you see ones just like it on Facebook all the time. This is a good way to enter any new marketing Channel. Study the successful ads that are running and design your similar to those that run a lot. If the ads weren't pulling, people wouldn't keep running them.

Here are the three we ran, designed to appear on a financial advisor's page when he or she logged onto the social media site:

You'll notice, in all three, we focus on a primary offer of a free download of our best-selling "Celebrity Branding You" – and we tailored the offer to financial advisors. There's no real mention of us wanting to sell anything. This approach inspired a lot of click-throughs, which took our target audience to this page:

You have to figure that if financial advisors were motivated enough to click-through for the free download, they would go ahead and give us their names and email addresses in order to get that download. After they entered that info, they were taken to the actual business offer, shown here:

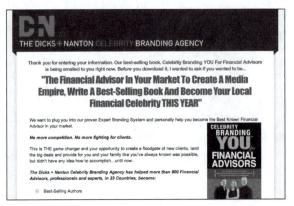

If you're familiar with online marketing, this series of ads follows a tried-and-true path: offer something substantial for free and then make a sales offer to the prospect after they show interest in your free content. In this case, however, we were able to structure the entire campaign through Facebook - and that's a big advantage for reasons we'll reveal a little later in this chapter.

For now, however, you may be wondering - how did we do? Did the financial advisors take the free book and run? Or did they actually invest in our services?

Here are the numbers: we spent about $2200 this test campaign and brought in $28,000 in new sales over the next six weeks. In other words, we made over ten times our initial investment in the ad campaign. We regard that as an awesome ROI.

THE MANY MEDIA CHANNELS

In today's world, there are 22 primary media channels you could be using to promote your business, all with their different advantages and disadvantages. Some are uniquely positioned to sell your services in an incredibly powerful way, others simply won't be right for what you have to say.

But you won't really know how effective they are for *your* business until you test them and compare your numbers to your control campaign that is working for you. The idea, obviously, is to spend "x" amount of dollars on using a particular media channel – and get "y" amount of dollars back in sales. Naturally, you want "y" to be a lot bigger than "x." The good news is, for many of these media channels, your initial investment is not going to be all that costly.

Let's back up to our Facebook campaign. We're willing to bet that nearly everyone you know is now on this premier social media site. What's more, nearly everyone lists their occupation, because they're using it to some extent to promote themselves. That means that, if you want to target a specific niche as we did, you can rest assured you're going to get your business exposed to a high-quality group within that niche. There are just too many Facebook users for that not to happen. Putting out $2200 to reach that high-quality niche group is actually an amazing price. Think about what you'd pay to do a national ad campaign in any of the "old media," such as TV, radio and magazines. Also think about the fact that those particular media channels don't allow you to niche-market and they also don't afford your prospects the opportunity to instantly click through and make an impulse purchase if they're so inclined. Instead, after they see the ad in question, they have to go *find* you to buy from you.

That's not to say there isn't a place for those "old media" channels – as a matter of fact, we ourselves use them quite a bit for our clients, but their cost to test market a campaign is outside the practical reach of most entrepreneurs and professionals.

The point is to think beyond your current 'marketing box' of media channels – the box in which you've nailed yourself over the years – and check out all the other ones you've either been ignoring or telling yourself they just wouldn't work for you.

It could be a simple matter of cost that's putting you off. That is why you should select marketing channels that allow you to test your results. For instance, if you were going to test a professional magazine, you wouldn't start off with a national run, but would use a regional test. You might also want to test the difference in size and color. All of these variables and more have an effect on your results. As you test, only change one variable at a time. If you do more, you won't know which change was the one that altered your ads performance for better or worse.

As test your various marketing channels, apply the ROI rule to anything you do. If you put a dollar towards a campaign, you should expect to get at least that dollar back in return. When you put that rule to work, you can spend an unlimited amount on your marketing – as long as you're successfully getting at least your investment back through sales that result from that marketing campaign. The reason that math works is because your ad is bring you a customer without a cost and that customer properly cared for will buy more from you than the first sale and increase your return on the ad cost. Some businesses who know their numbers very well are actually willing to go negative in return on the first sale, because they know they will sell more to a person who is happy with their products and service, so they try them out. This is a cash flow risk, so don't do it in your beginning marketing unless you know the results of what typically happens to a customer all the way through your marketing process.

Now that you understand the marketing math, you can see why we certainly wouldn't mind shelling that $2200 out month after month, if we kept getting ten times more back each time!

The more you experiment with different channels and different campaigns, the more sophisticated (and profitable) your marketing will become. And remember, in many cases, you're getting new customers at zero cost – because, if you're going by the ROI Rule, you're making money on your ads.

In other words, it may seem like your cash flow is taking a big hit by paying for these campaigns – but that money comes back to you when the ads start working. That means that, ultimately, that expense isn't a drain on your cash flow, it's actually helping it increase. That allows you to market more, pick up more new prospects and make more sales. And that's how a business grows!

About J W

JW Dicks, Esq. is an attorney, best-selling author, entrepreneur and business advisor to top Celebrity Experts. He has spent his entire 35-year career building successful businesses for himself and clients by creating business development and marketing campaigns that have produced sales of over a billion dollars in products and services. His professional versatility gives him a unique insight into his clients' businesses to see untapped opportunities to capitalize on, allowing him to use his knowledge of how to structure and position their business to take advantage of them.

He is the Senior Partner of Dicks & Nanton P.A., a unique membership-based, legal and business consulting firm representing clients who want to expand their business. JW helps his clients position their business and personal brand to take advantage of new vertical income streams they haven't tapped into, and shows them how to use associations, franchises, area-exclusive licensing, coaching programs, info-marketing, joint ventures, and multi-channel marketing to take advantage of them.

In addition to consulting and mentoring clients, JW is also a successful entrepreneur and America's leading expert on personal branding for business development. He is co-founder of the Celebrity Branding Agency, representing clients who want to get major media coverage, marketing and PR, and position themselves as the leading expert in their field. His Best-Selling book, *Celebrity Branding You!*, is in its third edition and new editions are currently being published for specific industries. He also writes a monthly column for Fast Company Magazine's Expert Blogg on personal branding, and has written hundreds of articles, blogs and special reports on the subject.

JW has led national conferences and conventions and has spoken to over 160,000 business leaders on branding, business joint ventures, capital formation, investing, and legal and business growth strategies. He is the Best Selling author of 22 business and legal books – including *How to Start a Corporation and Operate in Any State (a 50 Volume set), Celebrity Branding You!, Power Principles for Success, Moonlight Investing, The Florida Investor, Mutual Fund Investing Strategies, The Small Business Legal Kit, The 100 Best Investments For Your Retirement, Financial CPR, Operation Financial Freedom, Game Changers, How to Buy and Sell Real Estate, Ignite Your Business Transform Your World,* and more.

JW is the editor and publisher of The Celebrity Experts® Insider, delivered to clients in over 15 countries, and serves as the guide for entrepreneurs and professionals who are leading experts in their field. He has been called the "Expert to the Experts" and has appeared in USA Today, The Wall Street Journal, Newsweek, Inc. Magazine, The New York Times, Entrepreneur Magazine, and on ABC, NBC, CBS, and FOX television affiliates. Recently, JW was honored with an Emmy nomination as Executive Producer for the film, Jacob's Turn.

JW's business address is Orlando, FL and his play address is at his beach house where he spends as much time as he can with Linda, his wife of 39 years, their family, and two Yorkies. His major hobby is fishing, although the fish are rumored to be safe.

About Lindsay

Lindsay Dicks helps her clients tell their stories in the online world. Being brought up around a family of marketers, but a product of Generation Y, Lindsay naturally gravitated to the new world of on-line marketing. Lindsay began freelance writing in 2000 and soon after launched her own PR firm that thrived by offering an in-your-face "Guaranteed PR" that was one of the first of its type in the nation.

Lindsay's new media career is centered on her philosophy that "people buy people." Her goal is to help her clients build a relationship with their prospects and customers. Once that relationship is built and they learn to trust them as the expert in their field then they will do business with them. Lindsay also built a patent-pending process called "circular marketing" that utilizes social media marketing, content marketing and search engine optimization to create online "buzz" for her clients that helps them to convey their business and personal story. Lindsay's clientele span the entire business map and range from doctors and small business owners to Inc 500 CEOs.

Lindsay is a graduate of the University of Florida. She is the CEO of CelebritySites™, an online marketing company specializing in social media and online personal branding. Lindsay is also a multi-best-selling author including the best-selling book *"Power Principles for Success"* which she co-authored with Brian Tracy. She was also selected as one of America's PremierExperts™ and has been quoted in *Newsweek, the Wall Street Journal, USA Today, Inc Magazine* as well as featured on NBC, ABC, and CBS television affiliates speaking on social media, search engine optimization and making more money online. Lindsay was also recently brought on FOX 35 News as their Online Marketing Expert.

Lindsay, a national speaker, has shared the stage with some of the top speakers in the world such as Brian Tracy, Lee Milteer, Ron LeGrand, Arielle Ford, David Bullock, Brian Horn, Peter Shankman and many others. Lindsay was also an Executive Producer on the Emmy nominated film *Jacob's Turn*.

You can connect with Lindsay at:
Lindsay@CelebritySites.com
www.twitter.com/LindsayMDicks
www.facebook.com/LindsayDicks

About Nick

An Emmy Award-Winning Director and Producer, Nick Nanton, Esq., is known as the Top Agent to Celebrity Experts around the world for his role in developing and marketing business and professional experts, through personal branding, media, marketing and PR to help them gain credibility and recognition for their accomplishments. Nick is recognized as the nation's leading expert on personal branding as Fast Company Magazine's Expert Blogger on the subject and lectures regularly on the topic at major universities. His book *Celebrity Branding You®* has been selected as the textbook on personal branding at the University of Central Florida.

The CEO of The Dicks + Nanton Celebrity Branding Agency, an international agency with more than 800 clients in 23 countries, Nick is an award winning director, producer and songwriter who has worked on everything from large scale events to television shows with the likes of Bill Cosby, President George H.W. Bush, Brian Tracy, Michael Gerber and many more.

Nick is recognized as one of the top thought-leaders in the business world and has co-authored 15 best-selling books alongside Brian Tracy, Dr. Ivan Misner (Founder of BNI), Jay Conrad Levinson (Author of the Guerilla Marketing Series), Leigh Steinberg and many others, including the breakthrough hit *Celebrity Branding You!®*.

Nick serves as publisher of CelebrityPress™, a publishing company that produces and releases books by top Business and Professional Experts. CelebrityPress has published books by Brian Tracy, Mari Smith, Ron LeGrand and many other celebrity experts and Nick has led the marketing and PR campaigns that have driven more than 300 authors to Best-Seller status. Nick has been seen in USA Today, The Wall St. Journal, Newsweek, Inc. Magazine, The New York Times, Entrepreneur® Magazine, FastCompany.com. and has appeared on ABC, NBC, CBS, and FOX television affiliates around the country speaking on subjects ranging from branding, marketing and law, to American Idol.

Nick is a member of the Florida Bar, holds a JD from the University of Florida Levin College of Law, as well as a BSBA in Finance from the University of Florida's Warrington College of Business. Nick is a voting member of The National Academy of Recording Arts & Sciences (NARAS, Home to The Grammys), a member of The National Academy of Television Arts & Sciences (Home to the Emmy Awards). He is a co-founder of the National Academy of Best-Selling Authors, a 6-time Telly Award winner, and spends his spare time working with Young Life, Downtown Credo Orlando, Florida Hospital and rooting for the Florida Gators with his wife Kristina and their three children, Brock, Bowen and Addison.

CHAPTER 21

The Only Marketing System You Will Ever Need

By Greg Rollett

It's Sunday night, and for the past 23 seasons the Simpsons have taken over our TV's and our reality of all the craziness that goes on in the American household.

And for marketers, the characters in the Simpsons show us the uniqueness that everyone we try to get our message in front of, has. From their looks all the way down to the way they interact, where they hang-out, what they buy, where they work and how they vacation – everyone on the Simpsons has a different story, something that makes them just a little bit different from the neighbor, or the school teacher, the talk show host or the bartender.

I relate to this show often when speaking about marketing. And I do it for two reasons. The first is to teach the different needs that our prospects have – from their work and home responsibilities to how they spend their weekends.

The second is in our fascination we have with knowing everything about our favorite characters from TV world, but knowing little to nothing about the people that buy our products and services that keep the cable bill paid every month.

I want you to take out a piece of paper and draw a line down the middle vertically, top to bottom. On the left side, write down Homer Simpson (or insert your favorite character from your favorite TV Show here).

On the right side, write "my ideal customer."

Now put 60 seconds on the clock and write down everything that you know about Homer Simpson. Ok, go.

- He has 3 kids, Bart, Lisa and Maggie.
- He is married to Marge with the big, blue hair.
- He works at the Nuclear Power Plant and his boss is the ultra-rich Mr. Burns.
- He enjoys Duff Beer and frequents Moe's bar.
- His neighbor is Ned Flanders.
- He wears a white collared shirt with blue pants and has 2 strands of hair.
- And so on.

Now, put 60 seconds back on the clock and write down the characteristics of your ideal customer.

If you are like most business owners, your list is lopsided towards the yellow, beer-drinking cartoon character.

As a marketer, whose profile will help you grow your business? The answer is obvious.

CREATING THE ULTIMATE MARKETING SYSTEM

The epic battle between Homer Simpson and your prospects is the first step in creating your ultimate marketing plan. You simply cannot begin until you know what you are looking for; with the expenses of media buying, advertising and overall marketing increasing, you need to be able to identify exactly 'who' your message needs to be married to.

Another part of knowing the 'who' is knowing the 'what.' What is it that you are offering? What does it do? What are the features and benefits and more importantly how does it relieve the pain of your market? How does it build on your market's deepest dreams and desires, and how will it motivate them to take a break from their routine and give you a shot at fixing their lives?

Putting these two components together takes time, it takes thinking, and it takes an effort that only the truly successful will undertake – to ensure they have a winner on their hands.

Once you know your market and you know what you want to offer them, it is time to go out and find them. The quickest and easiest way to find them is to go where they already hang-out and spend their time. Go onto their turf.

This can be a magazine, a live event, a newsletter, a direct mail list or it can be through social media.

When you can break down your ideal customer like you can break down Homer Simpson, the quickest and fastest way to reach them on their home turf is through targeted placement – on online advertising networks that know more about people than the increasingly nosy government. Social networks like Facebook and LinkedIn.

It is vitally important that you understand the vast wealth of information that is shared on Facebook everyday, giving us more and more insight into the types of people that are going to be most interested in our business.

According to Facebook.com's Press Page, they mention that:
- There are over 900 million objects that people interact with (pages, groups, events and community pages)
- The average user is connected to 80 community pages, groups and events
- More than 2 billion posts are liked and commented on per day
- On average, more than 250 million photos are uploaded per day

Once you understand the volume of data that Facebook controls you can begin to understand the importance of knowing exactly who your ideal customer is and every characteristic about them.

When you combine your knowledge about your customer with the data behind Facebook's walls, you can literally pick your cream of the crop, everyday, 24/7, using the platform that Facebook has built for you and your business.

Place ads on Facebook's platform allow you to work with a combination of an image, a 25-character headline and a 135-character description. All three need to be designed to do multiple things.

First you must draw their attention away from their friends, the pictures and the activities on their News Feed, Timeline and Recent Stories. This is usually done through the image. Once you have moved their attention over to your image, your headline and description must match their needs and desires as it relates to what you are offering.

In Facebook's Advertising service, you are paying Facebook every time someone clicks on an ad, so it is vitally important that your message matches the person and that everything matches your offer so you are only paying for clicks that have the highest percentage of converting over to customers.

Once you have found your target market on Facebook and are placing relevant ads on their pages, getting their attention, it is time to capitalize on that attention.

WHAT IS THE ATTENTION SPAN OF THE AVERAGE INTERNET USER?

140 characters. This is the length of a message on Twitter and is also a very similar length given to the description field of a Facebook Ad as well as a headline on a landing page.

When you are competing for attention, especially when you are competing for attention of customers that are spending virtual time with their friends on Facebook, it is imperative to make the best use of your resources to ensure that you can keep that attention.

This is done with your landing page, the next piece of your marketing system.

When creating your landing page, your goal is to maximize attention. It should awaken the emotions, and focus the psychology and the mindset of the person that is visiting your landing page. If they clicked on an ad for a deal on green shoes, your landing page should focus on green shoes and what it means to be someone who is wearing that special pair of green shoes.

What many markets would do in this scenario is send someone to a page about shoes. Not green shoes. The prospect plays a very fast game in their heads that goes something like this: I wanted green shoes, I saw an ad for green shoes and now I am here, having to look again for green shoes. Where are the green shoes? Maybe I should go back to looking at pictures and talking to my friends.

In the above scenario you have lost them and their attention. And you have spent good money to get them to your site to look at your shoes, but you didn't go through the planning process necessary to deliver on what your prospect really needed.

A second element for your landing page and to keep the attention of your new web viewer is to schedule more attention. This usually comes in the form of delivering a free gift in exchange for their name, email address and potentially some other information. When this is done, the prospect is giving you permission to send them for information in the attempt to grab their attention.

This works well and is a great way to construct your marketing. In many cases, the free gift is in the form of education. The psychology of educating your client is immense as the more they know about a given subject the more rational they can make their purchase; if you are supplying the needed information they are likely to use you as a source of valid information and purchase product from you.

The downside to this type of marketing is that there is little to no way of knowing if they ever took the time to watch your video or read your special report.

SCHEDULING YOUR MARKET'S ATTENTION

Taking this concept of scheduling attention is having your new prospect commit to attending an event. I love events for many reasons, but the main one is the control of attention.

If you schedule an event, and this could be a live in-person event, or a webinar, live stream, teleseminar, call-in time or any other time of gathering that includes a specific date and time, you have a position of control for that given time slot.

If you can get them to commit to giving you 30 minutes, 60 minutes or longer, then you have an opportunity to really get them to know you, your ideas, your processes and how you can help them solve their burning problems and desires that they had when they were browsing on Facebook and clicked on your ad in the first place.

Think about a concert ticket. When your favorite band decided to hit the road, they booked a venue on a given day and time. They pre-sold tickets and marketed that event so all of their fans would show up.

When you bought your ticket, you got a confirmation of your purchase and you blocked out that date and time to anything else that might come up, because you have a commitment to that event. You don't want to miss it.

This is the same excitement and energy we are trying to convey when hosting our own events. We want our new prospects, our ideal customers, to block out a given chunk of time to join us, learn from us and hear about how we can change their lives.

If you can get someone to dedicate time to you, to your ideas and to the things that you have to say, you are setting yourself up in a great position to win.

Now, we still must go back to the initial thoughts of this process; the mindset and needs of your prospect. You have their attention, you found them where they hang out and you have crafted a message that hit them when they needed to see it. You have even gotten them to commit to a set date and time to listen to what you have to say.

Now it's time to deliver.

It is time to talk to them about their needs, their pain points, and how you, your products or your services can help them in their lives. Once you combine all of these features, you have an unstoppable marketing system. But it is still not yet the only marketing system you will ever need.

AUTOMATING YOUR MARKETING SYSTEM

The final step in this plan is designed to give you the ultimate value for being an entrepreneur: time freedom.

You see up to this point, you are doing a lot of work, and in the initial stages there will be much work. But once you have mastered the action plan above, you are able to leverage technology and run your marketing system every minute of everyday. You can reach people on their own grounds, on their own time and ultimately, when they need you the most.

Think about Facebook and social media advertising. People log on and use Facebook every minute of everyday and come from all over the world.

They can visit your site on their terms, when they need it. They can register for your event when it fits into their schedule and you can record the event in advance and use technology to play the event so it appears live whenever your prospect wants to watch it.

This is the value in the only marketing system you will ever need. Once you create it and master it, you can run it all day, everyday. And then you can scale it, change it, tweak it and move into new verticals on your own schedule.

All of this leads to more time on your couch watching the Simpsons, or doing whatever else you love to spend your time doing.

About Greg

Greg Rollett, the ProductPro, is a Best-Selling Author and online marketing expert who works with authors, experts, entertainers, entrepreneurs and business owners from all around the world to help them share their knowledge and change the lives and businesses of others. After creating a successful string of his own educational products, Greg began helping others in the production and marketing of their own products.

Greg is a front-runner in utilizing the power of social media, direct response marketing and customer education to drive new leads and convert those leads into long-standing customers and advocates.

Previous clients include Coca-Cola, Miller Lite, Warner Bros., and Cash Money Records as well as hundreds of entrepreneurs and small business owners. Greg's work has been featured on FOX News, ABC, NBC, CBS, the Daily Buzz and The Wall Street Journal. Greg has written for Mashable, the Huffington Post, AOL, AMEX's Open Forum and more.

Greg loves to challenge the current business environments that constrain people to working 12-hour days during the best portions of their lives. By teaching them to leverage technology and the power of information Greg loves helping others create freedom businesses that allow them to generate income, make the world a better place and live a radically ambitious lifestyle in the process.

A former touring musician, Greg is a highly sought-after speaker having appeared on stages with former Florida Gov. Charlie Crist, Chris Brogan, Brian Tracy, James Malinchak, Mike Koenigs and Nick Nanton, as well as at events such as Affiliate Summit, The Best-Seller's Summit, Putting America To Work and many other events across the country.

Download free information on creating more freedom in your life through information marketing and educational products at: http://productprosystems.com.

Contact Greg directly at: greg@productprosystems.com

CHAPTER 22

Make Your Wealth Your Business

Take control of your money by becoming CEO of YOUR investments in 30 minutes per week

By Andre Voskuil

You have worked hard to grow your business, make money, and achieve your life's goals. You have made some great decisions – and some scary ones – leading your company and your family to success and financial freedom. Your hard earned after-tax dollars are carefully invested with wealth managers, real estate, the stock market or other investment opportunities.

Your next task, ...possibly the most important one ever, is to preserve and grow your wealth and protect it for your piece of mind and for the next generation. With the world economy volatile and insecure, this is more challenging than ever before.

Perhaps your situation is similar to John's a couple of years ago. John had built and sold a profitable enterprise over the span of 35 years. His personal assets were diversified over real estate, stocks, mutual funds, and alternative investments. Many of these he had no knowledge of, it was to some degree a compilation of assets that had grown over the years. His assets were in part managed under the eye of three separate advisors – all focused on their piece of his portfolio. The economy turned and in less than a year his net worth was down well over 60% with some investments illiquid and highly uncertain. John is at retirement age and is having difficulty maintaining his lifestyle, because his personal wealth is under stress.

Could John have foreseen the economic recession? Should he have had better advisors? Can he just roll with the punches and wait for the tide to turn? No. Could John have handled his wealth better? Yes! With my recently implemented system and 30 minutes per week, John is now rebuilding his net worth. So can you!

The real key to preserving and growing your wealth is to increase your level of <u>personal involvement.</u> You must keep your finger on the pulse if you want to take charge of your financial future.

Like so many of us, John essentially abdicated his role in the process and wasn't able to maintain a bird's eye view of his wealth. It's not John's fault – he was overwhelmed by the seemingly complex world of money. He felt he didn't have enough time or knowledge to partake in the game. However, with the more pro-active, organized approach he's taking now, John could have surely avoided this unfortunate scenario. It is painful and unnecessary to lose a significant portion of your net worth regardless of economic circumstances. To avoid this you need to take matters into your own hands (with expert help), much like a CEO does. Nobody should be more invested in your money than you.

I will share with you the intimate knowledge and experience I gained as a professional portfolio manager, administering over half a billion dollars for captains of industry, celebrities and other high profile clients. In addition, I will share my insights gained as an international executive and consultant building and re-engineering both private and public companies. I guarantee you will have a better handle on your assets and business when you implement my ironclad roadmap in your decision making process. You'll be surprised how a small investment of time and best practices will increase your level of control, confidence and returns.

According to a report published by The Economist, the world's "rich" lost approximately 10 trillion dollars in the financial crisis. That represents an average of 25% of their total net worth and equals the economic output of Japan, Germany and China combined. Have you changed the way you go about managing your money after the turmoil? What systems do you have in place to prevent another catastrophic blow to your wealth? What are you doing to preserve and grow your family assets?

Most people have a hands-off approach when it comes to managing "My Investments, Inc." Ask yourself, could your business be successful if no one was invested in management and decision- making? It's fine to delegate and outsource to capable experts; I recommend seeking experienced, trusted experts and coaches to assist you. But you also need a foundation of skills and tools. You need a simple yet proven model that enables you to take control of your money.

FIRST, A DIFFERENT PERSPECTIVE

Most people do not realize that the biggest advantage they have over professional money managers and wealth advisors is the fact that they don't have to invest in anything. There are no sales targets, commission income minimums or other limitations. You have the luxury of patience and picking your investments carefully. Professional investors MUST invest every day. Good, bad or otherwise – they get paid to make investments – not to wait. Stack your deck for success. You can wait for the 'perfect' opportunity and then strike. Homework and patience are the key words.

The train rides every day ~ Andre Voskuil

This means every day there's another opportunity…you must determine which train to ride and what time to board and disembark. It's as simple (or complicated) as that.

THE MODEL – CREATING A FOUNDATION OUT OF BUILDING BRICKS

It is critically important you understand the general principles that determine the outcome of your money and business. When making major financial decisions like: analyzing your wealth, considering a company for potential investment, or the selling of your own business, you can use my template of the Building Bricks. Here's how it works: –

Make a 'Resource Diagram' and create two columns:

1. What resources do you have that you can work with? For example: skills, money, time, relationships and assets.

2. What resources do you require to achieve your desired outcome?

The model allows you to bridge the gap between the two columns in the diagram. Drawing pictures always helps with visualization.

The next step is very powerful and works like magic every time;

3. For every contact, option, resource, opportunity etcetera, you draw a brick. As more and more 'solutions' or 'problems' are discovered it builds a wall of bricks. It shows the foundation and walls of the company. You can color 'solution bricks' in green, and 'problem bricks' in red to easily detect where attention is needed. The key to discovering the bricks is asking quality questions.

You then have full clarity of the situation at hand and whether it makes sense to take action or not. Most companies have a hard time attracting investors because they're simply not built on a solid brick foundation.

ASK BETTER QUESTIONS

In order to use the Building Bricks system effectively, you have to ask razor sharp questions that can cut through any situation. You also have to be brutally honest with yourself (and others). A good CEO has a nose for business and a well-developed instinct for good deals (and bad ones). A brilliant CEO will ask astute questions to uncover what's not obvious.

Quality questions create a quality life ~ Anthony Robbins

In the days of the technology bubble, I worked with a high profile client who owned about 10% of a booming Internet company. His net worth in that company was over $400 million dollars. Locked up for two years through escrow agreements, he couldn't take the profit off the table. We engineered a complex strategy with derivatives to enable him to secure his wealth. The insurance premium due to high volatility was 48%. In other words he had to give up $192 million. Despite the professional advice, he declined. Within 9 months the entire $400 million literally vaporized – it was worth exactly zero. Do you agree that different questions would have led to a different, life-changing outcome for him? So, sometimes it's not the economy or the experts that are the problem; you can be your own worst enemy if you don't ask the right questions and be honest with yourself!

According to the World Wealth Report published by Capgemini and Merrill Lynch, between 7-10% of the financials assets held by wealthy individuals are invested in so-called alternative investments. This includes private equity and venture capital, meaning direct investments in private companies. This can range from your cousin starting up a new venture to the next Google. We have all been asked to participate in such ventures at one time. These investments are difficult and often result in a disappointing return or 100% loss of your money. Do you have a reliable template to screen these opportunities?

Examples of the basic questions everyone should be asking are: How many shares are outstanding? What is the debt versus assets ratio, monthly 'burn rate', working capital? What's my exit? The trick is to move on to relevant secondary questions based on the answers on the first set of questions. Go to my website: DutchOracle.com for my proven checklist of **"15 Must Ask Questions to Qualify an Investment."**

A recent study at the University of New Hampshire determined that in 2010 Angel Investors funded 61,900 ventures for a total of $20.1 billion. Do you know how to qualify each deal in no-time before you write a cheque? Is the corporate structure even accommodating profit for you when it is successful? Most wealth is destroyed by throwing good money after bad. Laser focused expert analysis can save you hundreds of thousands of dollars or even millions, by eliminating many bad investments you will be exposed to. Have you ever made a disastrous investment that could have been avoided in hindsight?

COCKPIT

A powerful instrument is what I call "the Cockpit." It helps to monitor and evaluate your portfolio. It can range from free Internet tools to sophisticated software or even a complete technology center. Without this tool, you're essentially driving your business by looking through the rearview mirror. In my personal Cockpit I have professional software which scans and filters the stock market through my proprietary investment system, but you can install your personal preferences. It doesn't have to cost much either. A client recently installed a high-end cockpit to help manage his business and personal life at-a-glance with everything at his fingertips. He said: "It's one of the best investments I ever made!"

"BUYING IS EASY, SELLING IS AN ART"

It's a saying among professional traders. Any fool can buy - just open your wallet. However, to successfully sell your investment proves to be much more difficult. When do you take your profits and more importantly, when do you cut your losses? Timing is everything!

I had the privilege to learn from one of the world's best commodity traders. He's the master at cutting losses. I remember one occasion when he had a significant position on the stock market index – betting it was going up. Instead the markets crashed at opening. The financial damage was so severe he lost almost half of his account in a matter of hours. He made a tough executive decision to cut the losses and regroup. Anyone else would have been paralyzed, called it a day, or simply hoped and prayed. Not him. At market close he nearly had it all back! Had he not taken the hard loss, the results would have been disastrous. I certainly don't recommend investing this aggressively, but the best decisions are often the ones where you pull a hard stop. Have you made investments you regret not cutting off? Are you still looking at assets on your statement that only frustrate you and do nothing but lose money?

Like in the game of golf…*"You don't have to improve your best shots, just work on eliminating the really bad ones."*

ADVANCED STRATEGIES

One of my favorite investment strategies is what I call a **"Renegade Account."** This concept is often used by institutional investors as it usually guarantees a minimum principal or return. You invest the majority of your capital in a safe or traditional holding to seek protection from market crashes or inflation. Then you allocate a small portion of your money; say 5%, to the Renegade Account, investing aggressively to seek ultra high returns between 200 and 1000%. Typically you use leveraged investments to amplify the returns, such as options or commodities. If you lose it…you lose it. The majority of your wealth (95% in this example) is preserved and can actually yield enough to replenish your Renegade Account in the event you need to. The overall average return can be spectacular and you can take realized profits and add them to your traditional account. Nowadays you can lose 5% in the stock market in just a few days anyway; you might as well set it aside in a high risk/high reward strategy.

Did you know you don't have to pick winners on the stock market to make healthy returns of 20% or more? There is a lucrative strategy that professional traders use and it's called **"Delta Neutral."** With a little tweak, you can apply the same technique in your portfolio (or have your wealth manager do it). Essentially it doesn't matter whether the markets go up or down. This strategy is based on selling time. You can quickly understand why that's a remarkable and profitable strategy!

Most financial institutions do not offer these strategies to their clients, because it's a potential liability and their mainstream funds and services provide enough income for them. These strategies require an advanced understanding of the markets if you "Do-It-Yourself." Or consult an expert who is experienced and knowledgeable and can execute my strategies for you.

KNOWLEDGE IS POWER

Invest in your personal knowledge and education about wealth and investments. There's lots of free and valuable information available on the Internet. You have virtual access to a basic university and even certain 'hot' picks. However, the Internet doesn't have specific knowledge of your situation and does not provide personal attention. I work closely with hand-selected clients that have considerable investable assets. In our one-on-one relationship, I help them by implementing my proven strategies and qualifying investments. With our combined knowledge and expertise, clients make financial decisions with confidence. Knowledge is a long-term investment that will greatly increase your returns for years to come.

PERFECT EXECUTION

Once you have the tools and knowledge, a strategy and a plan – it's time to execute. Whether you have a manager or you Do-It-Yourself, never invest without a pre-defined investment system. It creates measurable results, takes emotion out of every decision and works towards consistent returns. My proprietary system generates unbiased and predetermined parameters to buy or sell. Any system is 10 times better than reacting on emotions or opinions often predicated on daily market hype.

3-STEP ACTION PLAN

I have given you ideas and strategies how to "Make your Wealth your Business." Here are three steps you can do immediately to improve your wealth.

1. Review and filter every single investment and asset with this trusted system. Liquidate the two worst investments right away (cut your losses) and address one item that needs improvement.

2. Invest 1% of your net worth in tools or expertise that will improve your results and returns for many years to come.

3. Commit 30 minutes per week to monitor your holdings, find 'golden nuggets' and educate yourself.

MY GIFT TO YOU

I'm known as the "Dutch Oracle" for publicly predicting the 2008 debt crisis and the unprecedented rise of gold and oil. Clients consult me to receive an independent expert analysis on their business or investments combined with customized recommendations. I work closely with investors and entrepreneurs to help them preserve and grow their hard-earned wealth and achieve their financial goals.

I would like to help you as well. At: www.DutchOracle.com, you're welcome to download my special report revealing: **"The 3 Most Common Mistakes People Make That Erodes Their Wealth."** Gratis – my gift to you.

Discover what a positive difference having the 'Dutch Oracle' on your team can make.

About Andre

Born in the Netherlands, mentored by one of the world's best commodity traders, Andre Voskuil made a name for himself in Europe's financial industry. He managed a portfolio of over half a billion dollars for celebrities and high profile clients before reaching the age of 30. His professional career has spanned from institutional investments to senior executive positions in both public and private companies.

Andre is known as the "Dutch Oracle" for making accurate predictions in the markets and his uncanny ability to analyze companies and businesses. Among some of his foresights are publicly calling the 2008 debt crisis and the unprecedented rise of gold and oil. Business leaders and investors around the world consult with Andre to receive his independent expert analysis and practical advice. "Andre is the master at putting his finger on the right spot by asking astute questions with surgical precision and clarity," says accomplished serial entrepreneur Carman Adair.

Pursuing new opportunities, Andre and his family made the bold decision to leave the comfort of their established life and in 2005 moved to British Columbia, Canada. Andre founded a private oil and gas company, which is successfully listed on the Toronto Venture Exchange and he is intimately familiar with both private and public companies.

As a corporate executive and President of businesses, Andre has been through multiple ups-and-downs and gained extensive knowledge and experience in investments and finance. He has also raised millions of dollars and actively invests in companies with his inner circle of investors.

Andre is passionate about helping investors and entrepreneurs to preserve and grow their wealth. He works with high profile clients to help them manage their investments and businesses and acts as their trusted advisor and personal confidante. His style is professional, unique and brutally honest, yet, compassionate. "I have worked with thousands of professional investors from all over the world. Andre's ability to analyze investments is in a class of its own. You want him on your team," says Rob Plukker, senior executive manager with institutional market leader Reuters.

In his personal life, Andre is deeply committed to his family. Together with his wife Ineke and their two boys, he enjoys living in Canada's "playground" of the sunny Okanagan Valley. This is where he plays his favorite game of golf and embraces life to the fullest.

For more information visit: www.DutchOracle.com and receive Andre's Special Report revealing: "The 3 Most Common Mistakes People Make That Erodes Their Wealth."

CHAPTER 23

Control Your Future Financial Security

By Gregory Herlean

In life, the difference between happiness and distress, a good outcome or a bad outcome, is often due to an error of only a few degrees.

In 1979, a large jet with 257 passengers on board left New Zealand for a sightseeing flight to Antarctica. Before takeoff, someone had modified the flight coordinates by a mere two degrees, without the pilot's knowledge. This error placed the aircraft 28 miles to the east of where the pilots believed they were geographically.

Once the aircraft was approaching Antarctica, the pilots started to descend to a lower altitude in order to give the passengers a better look at the landscape. Although both pilots were experienced fliers, neither one of them had made this particular trip to Antarctica before. They had no way of knowing that the incorrect coordinates placed them directly in the path of Mount Erebus - an active volcano that rises from the frozen landscape to a height of more than 12,000 feet. The white of the snow and ice covering the volcano blended with the white of the clouds above, making it appear as though they were flying over flat ground. By the time the instruments started sounding off alerts to warn the pilots that the ground was rising fast toward them, it was too late.

That airplane crashed into the side of the volcano, killing everyone on

board. This was a terrible tragedy brought on by a minor error, a matter of only two degrees.
(Marcel, Arthur)

Let me start off by saying I am not an advisor, but an educated friend. While successfully planning for your retirement through investments is not a matter of life or death, it can often be the difference between your ability to enjoy or struggle through your retirement years. It can mean the difference between having the cash you need to live comfortably, or being forced to reduce your standard of living in order to "get by" with what you have available. Whether you're just starting out on a voyage to achieve financial freedom, or you are already on your way, this chapter is for you. As you embark on this journey, you'll find that financial freedom comes down to a basic principle:

You must take control of your financial future!

Now this can, and usually does, mean a different thing for every person. What is universally true, however, is that you must:

1. Understand the options that you have to grow YOUR money and

2. Be able to ensure that anyone managing your assets (i.e. an advisor) is really looking after your best interests.

I can tell you from much experience that no one cares more about your money then you do. Don't ever forget that. Make sure you treat your financial future and freedom that way. Taking control of part or all of your IRA (qualified) money is what you must do.

I am going to teach you about a subject you have never heard about, and specifically never heard about from your advisor. It is called self-directing. Self-directing is when you make investment decisions and investments on behalf of your own retirement plan. It is an option that is only very rarely offered by employers. When you self-direct you are able to keep your funds in tax deferred programs that IRAs are known for, but you have control of your retirement.

Most advisors will not support your decision to self-direct. Why you ask?! You could guess it. Money! They don't make money when they are not managing your money. Have you noticed that advisors make money regardless of you making or losing money?

An advisors common response to a client's request to self-direct part of their funds is "you shouldn't do this because you don't know what you're doing."

Though in some circumstances this may be true, it is less true than they want you to believe. If you truly understand self-directing this will not be the case. And, there are likely already investment methods that you are familiar with.

Have you ever read your prospectus with your financial group or advisor? If you do, you will find that you are paying a lot more then you thought every year. A typical customer on average is paying between 1.5 to 5 percent per year on your account value. When self-directing you still pay a fee but it is normally about a quarter of that every year and YOU are not only choosing your investments but you understand what your money is in.

Now take a deep breath. This is very important, I am by no means saying that you must self-direct and move all of your money from them. However, just changing a part of what you invest in, and allocating some of your retirement funds in what YOU know will make a huge difference. It's a matter of two degrees. Do not let your coordinates be off by two degrees. You may miss your mark because you are not paying attention to where your money is currently invested. You may miss your mark because you are currently paying more than you should in account fees. You may even miss your mark because you are spending more time on thinking about your vacations than you are your future.

You must first identify the issue and become knowledgeable about your options and how to self-direct. Then, you must set your goals and priorities according to what you plan to accomplish - including timelines and measurable targets. From there, you only need to repeat this task once a month. That's all!

I will tell you that I am sure that currently over 90 percent of you spend more time planning your next vacation, than you do your financial freedom. I will also guarantee you, that evaluating your IRA funds just once a month, will allow you 10 times more profit then you are currently making.

<u>What your advisor will not tell you.</u>

▸ They do not tell you what a mutual fund is.

▸ They do not tell you what all of your options are.

▸ Advisors do not want their clients to self-direct, because if you are self-directing they do not get paid.

▸ They also do not explain (and often hide) all of their fees.

The biggest secret advisors keep from their clients is that you can direct some or all of your funds into a self-directed IRA. You can roll over your funds from another IRA, or a 401 (k), into a self-directed account. You can purchase and sell securities on your own - using a self-directed IRA.

<u>You can buy Real Estate or businesses with your IRA.</u>

Over 72 million Americans have IRA's with $4 trillion invested. Of that $4 trillion, 4 percent of it is invested in self-directed IRA's. Why is that? The answer is, because people need to become educated about self-directing. Ninety-six percent of IRA money holders in the U.S. are not educated on self-directing. This tells you that although advisors tell you to diversify they do not mean it, or necessarily do it. It is time to start the education now!

<u>There are many reasons to self-direct, which include:</u>

▸ You invest in what you know.

▸ You have control of directing where your funds are invested. (i.e., not just mutual funds but Real Estate).

▸ Reducing your annual fees and expenses.

▸ Opportunities that typically only the wealthy can get.

A self-directed IRA is funded solely by you. As the account owner, you make investment decisions on behalf of your IRA account. Self-directed IRAs enable you to make alternative investments, such as:

1. Real Estate	5. Private Businesses
2. Trust Deeds	6. Limited Liability Partnerships
3. Tax Liens	7. Stocks
4. LLC's	8. Bonds

9. And many more......

Achieving your financial goals in life and getting your coordinates back on track requires you to follow these three principles: **Identify, Prioritize,** and enjoy the **Success.**

Identify

When you **identify** you need to:

1. Recognize the problem

2. Want to change

3. Learn how to self-direct

Self-directing is easy. It can be done in these simple steps:

➢ Choose your custodian (www.HorizonTrust.com)

➢ Open your new account

➢ Transfer your funds to a new custodian

➢ Choose where your money goes

Many Americans are not successful in achieving their financial goals because they have a lack of education, and knowledge of where and how to invest. They are not able to identify where exactly their money is invested, and why it is invested there. Remember that 96 percent of all IRAs and qualified money are invested through advisors or brokerage firms. As a client, you usually have little to no experience with, or knowledge about either your advisor or brokerage firms. Further, the things that they will recommend that you put your money into you will have very limited knowledge about. Knowing who you are working with and where your money is being invested in is crucial to achieving financial success.

Prioritize

When you prioritize you need to make educating yourself on your retirement funds a priority. You can educate yourself with: seminars, webinars, and semi-annual reviews. If you fail to plan your plan will fail. Make knowing your IRA and where it's being invested a monthly priority. Gain the knowledge of how to set up a successful self-directed IRA. Now that you have identified the problem, you must commit now to getting your statements out, reviewing them and opening up your self-directed account, this must be a priority within the next 7 days. If not, you will continue to be off 2 degrees. Further, you should commit to setting up an appointment with Horizon Trust in the next 30 days to set up a free one on one consultation.

Enjoy Success

Success means not losing a percentage of your earnings in fees every year. Saving in fees grows your retirement that much more. Success is investing in what you understand. After following the steps to identify and prioritize you will naturally become successful with your financial goals. The main ways to become successful are, first eliminate your annual brokerage fees, and then, earn double digit returns on your IRA funds. Becoming successful at one of those two things will increase your portfolio and your retirement direction by at least two degrees (2 percent), but by doing both, there is no reason why you will not be seeing as much as 4 to 6 percent changes in your retirement every year.

The wealthy are not the only ones who can use their investments to become richer. You can too. One way to become wealthy is to become your own bank. Being your own bank means having enough IRA funds to lend to your business as an opportunity or to others. When you have money to lend quickly to someone, as the bank you are in a position to make good solid returns. As the bank you are also in the position to repossess and take over an asset if the lender does not come through.

A lot of people choose to use funds from their IRA or old 401k accounts to lend out. A lot of people are cash poor; we either have used our savings at one point to get by, or want to keep our savings liquid or accessible in case of an emergency. If you want to use your IRA to become a bank, you must first self-direct that IRA by putting it with a custodian that can hold your account, but give you the flexibility you need to use your funds how you would like. My company, Horizon Trust, serves as a custodian. With Horizon Trust your annual services include help with filling out forms, and getting your funds set up in your first deal of your choice.

Once you have chosen your custodian you can now use your funds like a bank would. Becoming a bank is essential to allow you to become more flexible in life, but also allows you to get involved in opportunities when you want, without having to ask a bank for funds. Opportunities can include: buying a home, lending to Real Estate professionals, and lending to businesses. Being a bank allows you to close on deals that others cannot, because they cannot get bank financing fast enough.

I have seen many success stories throughout my career. A woman named Stanley, 63, from Reno, Nevada had over 500k invested with a financial planning firm before the market crashed in 2008. When the market crashed she lost a lot of money, her funds went down to 230k. She had no understanding of why her money was not coming back. My company educated her on what her money was doing. She learned her advisors were making money off of her money, but she was not. She had a major concern that she would not have enough money for retirement. We invested her money at a 10 percent fixed interest rate for 3 years. After 3 years her funds will reach 330k. this will enable her to collect 33k a year once she retires, which is what she needs to help her live comfortably during her retirement years.

Michelle, 71, from Indianapolis, Indiana was in a particularly frustrating position. She has an IRA worth 430k. Since she was over 70 she had reached the mandatory age where she was required to take out funds monthly. She was losing money with her investments in the market, while drawing $2500 a month from her funds. My company got her to invest 350k of her funds in a trust deed and rental property. She is now able to withdraw $2900 monthly solely on inter-est. She is now able to enjoy her retirement with her money protected. We made her very happy.

Growing up, I watched my Dad work 60-80 hours a week. Yes, although he worked hard to earn money, never took the time to focus on his retirement planning. My mom was the only one who even looked at his 401(k) statements. She would receive my Dad's quarterly 401(k) statements, open them, and then file them away. The only time financial planning was even discussed in my home was when my Dad would get a new advisor, who would call to make sure the account was intact and his commissions were secure. My parents did not pay attention to planning their financial future. If they had, they would be in a completely different position today. Once I learned how to successfully self-direct IRAs, I showed them how to take hold of their retirement account. I showed them what the wealthy do with their money, and how to self-direct their finances to grow rich.

My parents were able to trans-form their normal average 6 percent annual returns to 10 percent overnight! The power of taking control was huge for them. Now, years later, I am able to help over 100 new people a month learn the exact same process.

The time is now! Your success may only be a mere two degrees off. But, that two degree difference is the difference between having 200k in your account and having 300k. For those of you who learn this, and practice merely once a month, you will see things in your account you haven't seen in a long time – strong growth. Many of you have grown too comfortable allowing others to control your future financial security and have seen how devastating that can be.

Learn now. Grow now. Take back control.

Horizon Trust Company
4801 Lang Avenue NE, Suite 110
Albuquerque, NM 87109
888-205-6036
www.horizontrust.com

About Greg

Greg Herlean is a tenaciously self-determined businessman. His accomplishments in the financial industry are the result of his commitment to clearly defined goals, hard work, and his unstoppable determination. Greg is a man who defines his goals and then surpasses them.

Greg has spent the last 10 years focused on the growth opportunities and wealth accumulation through Real Estate vehicles. His aptitude for business has afforded him the opportunity to provide management direction, capital restructuring, investment research analysis, business projection analysis, and capital acquisition services which governed and impacted over $500 million in Real Estate transactions. His business acumen is complemented by his ability to cultivate and grow long lasting relationships. Greg prides himself on being a man of his word and in always holding himself to the highest delivery standards. This ethos allowed him to assemble a broad network of investment resources, brokers, and lending institutions worldwide who eagerly anticipate the opportunity to engage with him in business ventures.

His ability to bring about sustainable business growth was acutely illustrated when he co-founded and built his first Nevada trust custodial company in 2007. Through his efforts, the company went from inception to holding over $95 million in just over 24 months. The success was no accident. Mr. Herlean's financial expertise and insightful business design methodology coupled with his keen marketing strategies and grounded operational management conventions, to form the foundation for the company's success.

Today, Greg serves as the CEO of Horizon Trust Company, a New Mexico-based custodial company, where he is leading his latest team. At Horizon Trust, his experience and in-depth knowledge of the SDIRA industry market dynamics are frequently leveraged and employed. The vista for Horizon Trust is a bright one. There is no doubt that the sun is rising at Horizon Trust.

Greg is also a much sought-after platform speaker on the topics of capital development, investment growth through use of self-directed IRA vehicles, and estate planning. These speaking engagements allow him to share his experience and knowledge with others who are interested in obtaining greater financial security.

This University of Phoenix graduate (B.S. Business Administration) is an active member of the Las Vegas community, where he currently resides. Greg is devoted family man, who relishes the opportunity to enjoy his life with his wife of 10 years, Kristy, and their 4 beautiful children.

CHAPTER 24

Marketing 007

By Julie Guest,
Your Client Stampede Coach & Marketing Mentor

The **Top Secret**, Small Business Owner's Field Guide To Creating **A Stampede Of Ecstatic Customers** Through Your Front Door, Every Single Day…

WARNING: These strategies are not for the faint of heart, or anyone uncomfortable with astounding their competition and laughing all the way to the bank.

www.TheClientStampede.com

If I was taken into a small dimly lit room, placed under a searing spotlight and told to "spill the beans on how any small business could become massively profitable in the shortest amount of time, - "or else", – then here's exactly what I'd say. (And pretty quickly too, I might add!)

First of all, in order to be successful, you've got to understand the #1 reason why many small businesses fail. No, it's not due to a tough industry, cut-throat competition or a sagging economy, (although these 3 reasons usually take the blame).

The #1 reason why businesses fail is because their owners didn't understand the *real business they were in.*

They mistakenly thought they were in the business of selling real estate, fixing people's teeth, helping people get well, giving legal advice. When in fact, these were just their deliverables. As a small business owner, the real business you're in is the **marketing business!**

At the end of the day, it's NOT the best product that wins, IT'S THE BEST MARKETING! That's why you need to see Marketing as your chief job, not the fulfillment of your "deliverables."

Just think about your competition for a second.

Specifically think about who in your market is making a lot more money than you. I'd be willing to bet you're at *least* as smart as they are. You probably also offer a superior service.

Yet day after day, they're raking in more cash than you.

Why? Because **their marketing is better than yours.**

Seem unfair? I agree. In a perfect world the best product or service *should* make the most money, but that's not how the real world works.

Now it's time to level the playing field. In fact, it's time for you to learn how to dominate any market you choose to enter.

I'm about to share with you 5 Secret Strategies that, if you let them – will completely change your life. These are some of the very same strategies that I share with my private consulting clients and coaching students for very powerful results.

TOP SECRET STRATEGY #1
CHANGE YOUR FOCUS FROM TRADITIONAL BRAND ADVERTISING AND 'ME TOO' MARKETING, TO DIRECT RESPONSE MARKETING

If you insist on doing brand and image advertising to promote your business, unless you're Bill Gates or own a gigantic hundred million dollar company, you're likely wasting just about every advertising dollar you spend.

That's a horrifying thought I know.

Only big businesses can afford to do brand advertising. With their multi-million dollar ad budgets, *their marketing agendas are very different from yours.* They're concerned with looking good to the public, keeping their board of directors and their stockholders happy, winning advertising awards and looking good on Wall Street.

Your agenda? Much simpler: SELL something. NOW.

Brand advertising does not automatically translate into sales. Why? Because there's no real way of measuring actual results. You hope your ad is working. You pray your ad is working but you've got no way of *really* knowing how effective it is. All that guesswork means huge sums of money are being wasted.

So don't *ever* copy big business advertising. And don't copy what your competition is doing either.

Most industries are filled with businesses that all just copy each other. It's a terrible marketing strategy because it means your business just blends into oblivion along with everyone else's. And your prospects are getting bombarded with the same boring 'me too' marketing messages.

Instead, your marketing needs to stand out and its results need to be measurable down to the last penny. That way, you know almost instantly what's making you money and what isn't.

How can you achieve this?

By abandoning image and brand advertising and getting your business on a strict diet of **direct response marketing**. Starting today.

What exactly is direct response advertising? It's advertising that contains a compelling, benefit-laden headline, ALWAYS contains a special offer, and a deadline to respond by.

Its objective is to build desire and propel your prospects out of their la-z-boy armchairs, grabbing their wallets and tripping over the cat in the mad dash to the phone to place an order.

Here are The Client Stampede 7 Commandments for a powerfully effective direct response advertisement:

1. *A curiosity arousing, benefit-laden headline*

2. **An irresistible offer** *(or offers)*

3. *A deadline for response (or the creation of scarcity)*

4. *Clear instructions on what they need to do to respond (e.g., To place your order call our customer service department at xxx-xxx-xxxx or fax your order to...etc.)*

5. *A bold guarantee that reverses the risk for your prospects*

6. *Strong sales copy that talks about **benefits**, not **features** (e.g., Feature: This drill has 21 different speeds. Benefit: You can get your work done in half the time)*

7. *Testimonials from customers that overcome your prospect's main objections*

Photocopy this page and pin it up by your desk.

From today forward, let NOTHING (I repeat nothing), leave your office in the way of advertising without containing these essential requirements.

> *For an example of the biggest, most successful advertisement ever created (not surprisingly a direct response ad), visit my blog at: www.TheClientStampede.com and do a search for "WSJ billion dollar ad".*

TOP SECRET STRATEGY #2
CLIMB INSIDE YOUR CUSTOMER'S HEAD TO CONNECT WITH THEM, BOND WITH THEM AND BUILD TRUST

Get to know your target market intimately.

Creating highly effective marketing hinges on the successful marriage of three things – matching the **right market** with the **right message** and the **right media.**

The most important of these three is your market – WHO you're selling to. That's also your starting point.

Without a thorough, intimate understanding of WHO you're selling to – the rest of your marketing – the message and the media you choose, become irrelevant.

Here are some questions to ask to really get to know your target market intimately:

1) What are their chief concerns? What's keeping them up at night, hearts pounding, preventing them from sleeping?

2) What do they secretly want? (Often it's not what they tell you they want.)

3) Who are they mad at?

4) If they go out to dinner with a friend, what are they most likely to talk about?

5) Who else are they buying from?

6) Do they have a special language? (Every group or association does. To effectively sell to them and be included as an "insider," it's essential you get to know and use their language.)

Get a copy of every trade magazine, journal, magazine or book they're likely to read. Visit the other stores or order from the companies they do business with. Study their likes and dislikes.

Walk in their shoes.

In every sense of the word, get to know your customer inside and out. Then you can provide them with perfectly matched offers that they need and want. You can now communicate with them as a trusted friend who understands them, instead of an annoying pest trying to sell them something.

TOP SECRET STRATEGY #3
GET YOURSELF THE BEST LITTLE SALES FORCE YOUR MONEY CAN BUY: A GREAT SALES LETTER

An outstanding salesletter is THE most powerful 'employee' you could ever hire. For the price of a cup of coffee - it will relentlessly go out and deliver your message *perfectly*, every time. It will never call in sick. It will never complain. And it will never let you down. It will work 365 days a year around the clock, never taking a vacation or asking you for a promotion.

Simply put, a powerful salesletter is like having your very own army of sales pros, working for you tirelessly…day and night.

Think about this. How much is one good salesletter worth to your business? Suppose you could sit down, write a letter to your prospects and customers, mail it and then have your phone start ringing off the hook.

One great letter could bring you countless hot leads and new customers, buying from you over and over again. So anytime you need more business - you simply "turn the tap up" – and send out more letters… it's like having the goose that lays the golden egg in your own back yard.

There are two ways to get your hands on a great sales letter for your business. You can either immerse yourself in how to write great copy, look at proven examples of other great sales letters, and then set about writing one yourself. Or, you can hire the very best copywriter you can afford.

Remember that <u>great sales copy is the oxygen of your business,</u> and there's nothing more expensive than cheap copy. You might feel good about saving money at the front end, but it'll wind up being the most costly item you pay for because of the lost sales and missed opportunities.

Really good copywriters don't cost you money. They're a very smart investment that brings rapid returns. ***Hire the very best copywriter your can afford.***

> RESOURCE: If you're thinking about hiring a copywriter, don't do a thing until you've read a copy of my free special report: "The Small Business Owner's Guide To Choosing & Hiring A Top Notch Copywriter Without Breaking The Bank: 23 Insider Secrets That Will Save You Thousands."

Visit: www.BlazingCopy.com to download your free copy.

TOP SECRET STRATEGY #4
TREAT YOUR EXISTING CUSTOMERS EVEN
BETTER THAN YOUR PROSPECTS

Many businesses have this strategy backwards. They're so busy trying to get new customers through the front door, they forget about the ones they have. Meantime their customers who they've fought so hard to get, inevitably wind up making a beeline for the exit. They never buy from you again because they've been ignored or forgotten about.

Selling to someone you've already done business with is at least 5 times easier than making a new sale! So why expend five times the amount of time and money to find a new customer, when you're sitting on a goldmine with your own customer list?

The purpose of getting a customer is NOT to make a sale. *The purpose of making a sale is to get a customer.*

In your own business – what's the average lifetime value of one customer? What if you could double this value? *Without adding a single new client, just increasing the amount they spend with you could double the size of your business.*

TOP SECRET STRATEGY #5
GET A MARKETING SYSTEM IN PLACE TO PUT YOUR LEAD GENERATION ON AUTOPILOT AND AUTOMATE YOUR FOLLOW UP

Imagine going to bed every night, knowing exactly how many new clients are going to be marching through your front door the next day, and the volume of sales you'll make.

Imagine having a steady flow of cash you could depend on month after month and an automated system that enables you to turn the faucet up or down depending on whether you want more or less business. No more slow periods unless you decide you need the break.

I'm talking, of course, about having your own automated marketing *system.*

All the best businesses in the world use systems. It's no accident that McDonalds, the most successful franchise in history, is a 'systems junkie' – every action, every procedure is meticulously systematized, automated, and every sale maximized.

I'll give you a quick example of how you could apply this "McDonald's type system" to your business.

Let's say you're a plastic surgeon.

You've invested in a great sales letter that's been proven to work. The call to action in your sales letter could be to download or request a copy of your free special report: "Discover The Latest Advancements in Cosmetic Surgery To Look 10 Years Younger Without Needing Surgery."

The free report is itself a 'sales letter' promoting these latest advancements but also provides readers with very valuable information. At the end of the report, you could make your readers a special offer e.g., 50% off their first procedure plus a free teeth-whitening kit.

Having read the report, the prospect calls to book their initial consultation. Now the entire sales process is carefully scripted and choreographed, both by the admin staff, and by the doctor. This results in the first sale – the booking of a procedure.

Following this, a welcome package is mailed to the new client containing a special second offer or a maintenance plan and a second appointment made and so on.

You can think of your marketing system as a giant marketing conveyor belt that prospects ride through your business towards the first sale. Once the first sale is made they get transferred to a different conveyor belt. Now they're pampered and taken great care of, continually being offered much needed products or services by a trusted provider.

Every step, every communication is systematized and automated so it can be replicated again and again.

Based on how much marketing you have out at any one time, you know how many prospects will download your report, book consults and become a customer. It's money in the bank you can depend on each and every month, like clockwork!

So there you have it. 5 top secret marketing strategies to transform your business, bewilder your competition, attract a steady stream of qualified customers to your door and make you a lot more money.

Now I'd like to offer you a FREE add-on to this chapter. Get your copy of my FREE audio CD: "*The New Rules Of The New Economy: 10 Client Stampede Secret Strategies To Get More Customers, Make More Money And Prosper In The New Economy.*" The old way of doing business, the old rules are out. We're entering an entirely new era in business, and only the strong, enlightened business owners will survive. The rest will be left out in the cold. YOU need to know the NEW Economy's New Rules to attract all the business you need. Order your FREE copy of my audio CD today by visiting my website: www.theclientstampede.com

To your success!

Julie Guest – *Your Client Stampede Coach And Marketing Mentor*

www.TheClientStampede.com

About Julie

Julie Guest is an **expert** direct response copywriter and business coach to ***entrepreneurs and small business*** owners looking for proven, ingenious, easy ways to attract all the business they need in the new economy. Julie has been recently named as one of America's fast rising stars in the marketing industry and has studied marketing greats like Gary Halbert, Joe Sugarman, Robert Collier, Eugene Schwartz, Dan Kennedy, David Ogilvy, Victor Schwab, Gary Bencivenga and Joe Karbo. Using her proven, easy and fun 10 Step Ultimate Client Stampede Marketing System™ Julie has helped hundreds of entrepreneurs and business owners make dramatic transformations to their work and home lives.

Julie's private copywriting clients range from a handful of Fortune 500 clients to mostly self-made multi-millionaire entrepreneurs and business owners, in industries as diverse as plastic surgery, real estate, financial and legal services, dentistry, insurance, beauty and healthcare. More than 85% of Julie's private clients use her repeatedly because she does so much more than "just writes copy" - she delivers STRATEGY, uncovers hidden opportunities, creates new opportunities, repositions products and re-invents businesses.

Julie is founder of TheClientStampede.com – the most valuable marketing resource on the planet for solo-preneurs to attract all the business they need in the new economy. Request your copy of her free audio CD *"10 Client Stampede Secret Strategies To Get More Customers, Make More Money And Prosper In The New Economy."* by visiting: www.TheClientStampede.com

CHAPTER 25

Story Driven Brand Marketing

By Cindy Speaker

I will never forget the day that Anne Okelo came to my studio and told her story on camera. As I listened I could hardly believe what I was hearing. "Two strokes," she said. Every day she would receive two strokes for being late to school. Anne lived in a remote village in Kenya and because the village had no clean water, the young girls in the family would have to walk 8 miles every morning to bring a bucket of dirty water from the nearest river for their family to use. Often they would get to the river and have to wait in line. Or the river was dry and they would have to dig for water. More often than not Anne would return with the water, head to school and find that she was a few minutes late. So she was beaten virtually every day.

When I met Anne she was working on a project to raise $35,000 to build a well in her village. It was within this context that she had come to my studio to share her story on video. She spoke of being an outcast among her village because she refused to be married at 14 and chose rather to pursue her education. She told us about her life and that of her people, how they didn't even have basic needs met. No bathrooms, no water, no bed to sleep on and often no food. But what surprised me most was that although Anne had just received her graduate degree from the University in my home town, the only thing she wanted to do was to return to the very village where she was rejected and ostracized. More than anything, Anne wanted to go back and help her people. And getting them water was her starting point.

After knowing Anne for a few months, I asked her if I could make a documentary about her story. I told her that I thought a film would help give her greater visibility and a more public platform for doing her work and raising necessary funding. And so together Anne and I embarked on a journey. The film is called "Well of Dreams: The Journey of Anne Okelo."

In July of 2011, I took a small film crew to Kenya and we spent 10 days with Anne and it changed my life. I saw poverty that I never knew existed. I witnessed a male-dominated society where only men were educated and spoke English. The women we talked with, other than Anne, spoke only their native language. I observed schoolrooms housing 90 children in an area smaller than my living room where only the first third of the children that arrive at school in the morning get to sit on a bench. The other two thirds sit on a dirt floor. I saw a small shack where 11 children lived and I asked where they put the beds and I was told, there are no beds. The children simply lay their heads on a dirt floor at the end of the day. There is no electricity, no bathrooms, no toys, and often no food.

You may be asking how this story fits into a book entitled "The Only Business Book You'll Ever Need." How is this relevant to my business? Ultimately, Anne Okelo has a personal brand and that is her business. Just like other businesses, if she is able to successfully motivate others to join her cause, there is a greater opportunity for her to accomplish her goals and have a successful business. To do that she needs people with various resources to get onboard. Anne is doing that very effectively by using her story. If you can use a powerful, relevant and authentic story to tap into the passions of your audience, you will have unlocked the modern day holy grail of marketing.

When Anne told her story about the need for water in her village, she raised $35,000 in 3 months and a large group of people worked with her to get the well installed because they were drawn in by her story. Before we went to Kenya in July, Anne expressed that there was a great need for the girls in her village and other villages to have sanitary napkins, which are a luxury item for them. That story quickly reached the heart of over 90 women who pulled together one week before our trip to raise over $10,000 to purchase enough sanitary napkins to supply not only Anne's village but eight other villages for an entire year. It was the story that compelled so many to step out and make a difference.

The very first time I witnessed the power of what I call story-driven brand marketing, I was in a supermarket. The woman ahead of me was checking out and she had a certain brand of tissues. The woman had a friendly smile and I remember that she picked up the tissues before the employee placed them in her shopping bag, and she said loud enough for those of us close by to hear; "please buy this brand. They are a great company. My husband works for them and although they are struggling financially they are trying not to lay anybody off so I'd sure appreciate your support." And from that day until this day, that is the only brand of tissues that I ever buy. Why? Initially it was because her story touched my heart. However, when I buy that brand now it's because I believe that is the best brand. Why do I believe that? That's where the magic happens.

To fully understand the potential for story-driven brand marketing, we can start by understanding cognitive dissonance marketing. In 1956, a psychologist named Leon Festinger introduced the theory of cognitive dissonance. This theory states that if a person holds two cognitions that are inconsistent or contradictory, that person is likely to make a change in their beliefs to reduce the dissonance, which they find unpleasant. In cognitive dissonance marketing a person may see an advertisement for a new product or service that they find compelling. However, if they already use a competitive brand it creates a dissonance or uneasiness in their mind. To resolve that dissonance they may decide that the current brand they are using is outdated. Modifying their belief will give them the permission they need to try out the new brand.

For a brand to make use of cognitive dissonance marketing they need to first endeavor to establish that their product is superior. If they do that effectively, this is likely to cause a dissonance in the mind of prospects that currently use other brands. The next job of the self-proclaimed superior brand is to seek to create a distrust of competitive brands, which will give the prospect a way to resolve their dissonance and give them permission to choose the "superior" brand without feeling disloyal.

Let's return to the supermarket tissue story. As I stood in line waiting for my turn to check out, I had in my cart a box of tissues. They were the cheapest tissues on the shelf. I had no allegiance to any brand at the time and so I had chosen based only on price. However, once I heard the "tissue story" I was moved in my heart. I got out of line, went back to the tissue aisle and chose the "superior brand" caring little about price.

Because of the power of a story, I quickly catapulted beyond the normal obstacles created by the cognitive dissonance that arose in my mind, so that I could give myself permission to choose a different brand. You see, the story took me out of the rational realm and into the emotional realm where resolving dissonance is irrelevant.

Dale Carnegie, author of the classic book *"How to Win Friends and Influence People"* said this: "When dealing with people, remember you are not dealing with creatures of logic, but with creatures of emotion." What Dale Carnegie understood so well is that if you wish to persuade someone regarding a decision, you will have a much better likelihood of success if you can motivate an emotional decision rather than a rational one.

I commented earlier in this chapter that going to Kenya with my small film crew to shoot a documentary about Anne Okelo changed my life. Why? Because it brought me into a story that touched my heart. And that story was so compelling that I completely discounted logic and the rational thought that might have said "slow down Cindy, you don't have $250,000 to make this movie and you're a first time filmmaker with no real experience." You see story defies logic and it sidelines rational thought in favor of heart and emotion.

Whether you are a business owner or an employee you know that for your business to survive you must have a growing base of loyal customers/clients. We live in tough economic times. We also live in a world where we are bombarded all day long with messages and sales pitches and decisions and other noise. So the question that we all ask is this – how do I get heard? My answer to you is to find the compelling story in your brand and perfect telling it.

HOW TO FIND OR CREATE YOUR BRAND STORY

In order to develop your brand story, you must put yourself in the realm of the emotional. Your brand story will not be drawn up on a spreadsheet. It will not come from doing competitive intelligence. The starting point is to ask yourself these questions:

- What do I want to leave behind as a legacy

- What am I doing or what is happening in my business that will contribute to that legacy

- If the business you are in is not contributing to the legacy you hope to leave behind, I suggest you re-evaluate your career

YOUR BRAND STORY MUST BE AUTHENTIC

We live in a world where social media and new media technologies are the way we communicate. There is a demand for authenticity in the world we live in today. Nothing can be more damaging to your brand than to be discovered as a fraud. People are very intolerant of sales pitches and even minimal fabrication of facts, figures and capability. Do not create a slick marketing campaign that positions your brand purporting to be more than it is. I can almost guarantee you it will backfire. Instead, be authentic. Be honest.

YOUR BRAND STORY MUST COME FROM THE HEART

Suppose you work at a car dealership. If your town is like my town there are numerous car dealerships and for the most part they seek to differentiate themselves using price, facts and figures. When I have been in the market for a car, I will look on the Internet and look at what is out there and in most cases it's pretty hard to differentiate. I might try to find the lowest price for the car or cars that I'm interested in reviewing. I may be swayed by a coupon or a special offer but for the most part it tends to be a pretty level playing field out there.

But suppose I learn that one car dealership in town is committing a portion of profits one weekend to a local war hero that needs a handicapped van because he is now a quadriplegic. Or maybe they are running a weekend campaign where part of the proceeds of car sales will go to fund a program in high schools that provides education regarding underage drinking in the name of a student that died as a result of being hit by a drunk driver.

In the past it was enough for a brand to give money to causes. We call it cause-related marketing. But that is no longer something that makes a brand special. That is demanded of a brand so it simply puts you on a level playing field with everyone else. However, when you make it personal by connecting with a story – then you go right to the head of the class. Story-driven brand marketing reaches the heart so fast it's like an adrenaline rush.

If you don't have a brand story yet, it's ok. You can develop one. Your brand story needs to meet the following criteria:

• Be relevant to your brand

• Be relevant to at least some of your target audience

• Involve a personal story of someone who is either part of your brand or closely related to your brand in some way. This could be through the mother of a secretary.

YOUR BRAND STORY MUST BE CONVEYED USING THE TOOLS AND TECHNOLOGIES OF TODAY

Once you flesh out your brand story, you need to convey it. Sharing your story must be done in as many different ways as possible. I work with attorneys and I have some attorneys that prefer that I send them all information in written format. Others like to listen to an audio CD in the car. Still others want to watch an online video. My recommendation is that you capture your story initially with a professionally produced video. You can then repurpose it in just about every way imaginable including but not limited to:

• Audio CD

• iTunes podcast – either audio or video

• Ebook

• White paper

• Special Report

• DVD

• Online video

You see, ultimately, just as my friend Anne Okelo has a personal brand, so do you and so do I. Because of Anne and the way she has almost unknowingly used story driven brand marketing, she is impacting a whole generation of girls and women in Kenya. But she has also impacted at least 90 women here in the US that took action to contribute $10,000 in a week to purchase basic supplies for young women that live 12,000 miles away. Her story motivated an elementary school to start a campaign to gather 50 soccer balls to be sent to Kenya. That story was picked up by NBC which disseminated it even further. A film has grown out of Anne's story and that film is touching the hearts of everyone that sees it. Many are motivated to give money to Anne's work. Can we call that a business? I think so. Hundreds of thousands of dollars are likely to exchange hands in the coming years to facilitate very positive efforts because of Anne's story.

Some of you have a great story within your brand. If so embrace it, flesh it out, and use it to do great things and leave a lasting legacy. Others don't have a big story to build upon. So for you, my recommendation is that you find a great story that is relevant to your brand and adopt it. Stories touch the heart and that's where magic happens. If you can compel your customers/clients and prospects to see your brand through a story that touches their heart, you will be light years ahead of your competitors that are competing in the realm of facts, figures and price.

About Cindy

Cindy Speaker is a filmmaker, story teller and marketing consultant. She is passionate about helping brands find their story and then telling it through the medium of film. According to Speaker, her method of story-driven brand marketing is helping brands transition purchase decisions from the realm of rational thought and price shopping into the realm of the emotional, where they can tap into the passions, hopes and dreams of individuals. "Stories touch the heart and that's where magic happens," says Speaker.

Her first film, *Well of Dreams*, has been lauded by film industry insiders as "breathtaking," "powerful" and "the best first-time film I have even seen." Well of Dreams is Speaker's maiden voyage into documentary productions and she has said that the experience changed her life. "I quickly realized that a great story told through film has tremendous power not only to promote a cause, but also to be used as a brand building tool for small businesses." Speaker states that she is already in pre-production on several short independent films being produced for small business owners and law firms in the coming year.

As president of Speaker Media and Marketing (S/M2), and now Speaker Films, Cindy has been a professional marketing coach and consultant for law firms since 1994. She has focused primarily on marketing strategies aimed at growing relationships, leveraging technology and building systems. Her ultimate goal for her clients is to help position them as thought leaders and experts in their market and to generate a consistent stream of referrals.

As a result of her efforts Speaker Media and Marketing has been called the secret weapon of some of the top plaintiff's law firms and trial lawyers in the US. S/M2 works with law firms on a market-exclusive basis, and Cindy's vision for her clients is for them to be on the cutting edge of marketing and technology and to have a dominant position in their respective markets.

Cindy travels and speaks to attorney groups and marketing groups nationwide.

To learn more about Cindy Speaker, you can visit: www.cindyspeaker.com.

CHAPTER 26

HAPPINESS.
THE ULTIMATE CURRENCY.

By Olga Rickards

"Happiness has a strange arithmetic – the more you divide it, the more it multiplies." ~ Unknown

Let me ask you - how happy are you? Most importantly, why are you not as happy as you could be? Especially when cutting-edge scientific research has proven that happy people are more creative and more productive; happy people make more money compared to their peers; happy people have better health and live longer; they attract better friends, enjoy better marriages and even have a better sex life. After all, happiness is really good for you and your bottom line.

What if I told you that lasting happiness is real and showed you a practical, scientifically proven system to get there? What if I told you that lasting happiness is a learnable skill, just like learning how to build a business? Actually, what if I told you that building your happiness is very similar to building your successful business?

Slow down and think about this for a moment. What is it in life we all want the most? What is the ultimate reason behind everything we do? If you repeatedly ask yourself the question "Why?", you'll come to the same conclusion as most people – whatever we pursue, we believe it will ultimately make us happy. We get married because we want to be happy. We get divorced because we are not happy. We work hard because one day we want to be happy. We sacrifice because we want our children to be happy. We are all in the pursuit of happiness, whether we are conscious of it or not. Harvard's most popular lecturer Tal Ben Shahar, Ph.D. calls happiness "the ultimate currency - the end toward which all other ends lead."

What is really sad though is that most people think about their happiness and take a hard honest look at their lives when it's often too late – after an unexpected heart attack or stroke, death of their close friend or some other tragedy.

Do you know what even the most successful people regret on their deathbed? World-renowned psychiatrist Elisabeth Kubler-Ross studied dying people for over 40 years. Her near-death studies and related research revealed that dying people regret things they never did. They almost all say they wish they had taken the time to love more and work less. They regret making money at the expense of relationships. Many say they never knew their true selves and were not clear on what they really wanted in life. Many say they had not really lived. Most regret postponing their happiness until the day they could "afford" it. That day never came.

Do you postpone your happiness? Or, perhaps, you are like some of my clients that have chased ever-elusive happiness for years, but ultimately accepted their unhappiness as the inevitable price of their success.

A nurse I know well once told me about her patients in the "heart tower" of a regional hospital. Cardiac Progressive Care is the place they take you after you've had open-heart surgery. She's had many patients over the years, but the ones who affect her most are middle-aged businessmen with extensive heart failure. Before surgery, the nurse refers to most of these patients as "cold and impatient." When they wake from anesthesia after a long surgery, some of them experience what she can only describe as an epiphany: a sudden knowing of deep emotional wisdom. They would not live forever, perhaps not much longer and certainly not in the same way.

Bill Morris laid in his hospital bed staring at the walls, at the leaves shaking outside in the wind, at the kind eyes of the nurse changing his IV bag. He stared through tears, sobbing, holding a stranger's hand. Bill's dominance and detachment had transformed into wonder: being alive now and yet so near death, gave him a strange sense of grace and vulnerability. Heart surgery forced this powerful business man, used to giving orders and making the outside world conform to his view, to truly depend on others to live. This strong, independent and creative business dynamo was stopped in his tracks. It was devastating and liberating at the same time.

Bill felt each thump of his heart; he smiled gently with each gift of new breath. He felt something new – the space between his heartbeats, the depth of true presence in the moment. Doctors gave Bill one year to live. Gratitude for life was not an abstract concept anymore – Bill Morris had become gratitude. He knew that pain and regret would flood him later, but it didn't matter in this moment. In this moment he was free. Ironically, in this moment he experienced something he had not felt in a very long time – deep comforting contentment. Somehow, he had reunited with his true self, with that vulnerable little boy inside; he returned to the healing intimacy of human connection. It was something he had been missing. He just did not know how much. No wonder they call it open-heart surgery.

You know what's ironic? Even though pursuit of happiness is the #1 underlying reason behind everything we do in life, few people consciously, intentionally, actively create it. Over the years, I've had many heart-to-heart conversations with millionaires and billionaires. In my professional experience, the top critical mistake even the most successful people make is they leave their happiness to chance. Sadly, many of them do not even realize how much they are missing out on.

Why do we invest so much time, energy, and money into our businesses – but not into our happiness? Well, most of us simply do not know how to create a happy, fulfilled, truly successful life.

We are led to believe that lasting happiness is beyond our control. Happiness is something that comes and goes; sometimes we have it, most times we don't. It seems that lasting happiness is almost a myth.

We are led to believe that happiness is not a journey, but a destination: just think about the "I-will-be-happy-when-I..." syndrome (lose weight, meet my soul mate, earn enough money – fill in the blank).

The primary reason is we are led to believe that if we choose money, power and prestige for the main course, happiness will automatically come as a side dish. This belief is so deeply programmed in our subconscious by the media and society that we don't even question it. Sadly, many people work very hard to get rich and then, when they "get there", they often discover that happiness is nowhere to be found. "I had it all, yet I had nothing. My success cost me two marriages and my happiness. Olga is brilliant at what she does. I wish I had met her 20 years ago," says one of my clients Ed Alfke, serial entrepreneur, Director of the National Angel Organization.

Don't get me wrong, wealth is a wonderful thing. I am all for making a fortune, enjoying privileged lifestyles, pushing boundaries and playing the game of business full out. What gets under my skin though, is pursuing success at the expense of our own happiness and the happiness of those we love. It breaks my heart to see so many smart, talented and driven people miss out at the end of the day. They miss their kids' school plays and sport games, they miss on a deep connection with their partner, they miss out on their own lives until one day they wake up too late - when the Universe hits them over the head with a cosmic two-by-four and they find themselves in a hospital bed or divorce court. It does not have to be this way!

Did you know that happiness has been scientifically studied for decades? Previously, psychology focused almost entirely on treating pathology, analyzing misery and repairing bad experiences. The new research field called Positive Psychology is just over a decade old, and is focused on developing human strengths, nurturing talent and making our lives more fulfilling. We now have tangible proof why it pays to be happy and what the "how-to"s of lasting happiness really are. Unfortunately, most people have no idea about the profound recent discoveries and their practical applications. For example, did you know that we are all born with a genetically pre-determined happiness set-point? Did you know that happiness has an actual proven formula? Did you know that our brain is not designed to make us happy?

At some point I realized - if I keep doing the same things expecting different results, I certainly won't get to where I want to be. I started with the end in mind and reverse-engineered my life, which turned out to be an amazing shortcut to finding fulfillment and joy. I now use this approach with my clients and find that this process is very similar to creating a successful business. See, anyone who wants to build a thriving business knows they have to take action. They have a vision, written business plan and clearly defined goals. They have weekly, monthly, quarterly and annual meetings to monitor their progress and make necessary adjustments along the way. They have legal counsel and trusted advisors in place. Smart business people know - if they want to be successful, they have to be proactive.

However, when it comes to their own happiness, often even the most successful people do not take action. They do not have a clear vision, concrete plan and written goals to build a truly happy, fulfilled life. They do not apply a systematic approach to monitor their progress and adjust accordingly. They don't have happiness mentors. Ask yourself honestly - if you treated your businesses like you treat your happiness, where would your business be right now?

I strongly believe the best thing you can do for yourself and everyone around you is to treat your personal happiness like a serious business matter, starting right now. Because if not now, when? At the end of the day, what is it all for?

Take a hard honest look at your life and your level of happiness (or unhappiness). If you were hit by a truck tomorrow, did you live enough? Did you love enough? Did you make a difference? You must "get real" about where you are currently at if you are serious about wanting something better.

Stop compromising your happiness. I bet on your deathbed you won't be thinking, "Oh, I wish I'd have spent more time working." Start with the end in mind and create your long-term happiness plan – your life's Grand Plan – reflecting all important areas of your life. Like some of my clients – highly successful people that make important business decisions in a blink of an eye – you might find that you don't really know what would bring you lasting happiness, freedom and peace of mind. Trust yourself and write your plan anyway – treat this process as an exciting adventure into your ideal future. If you are completely honest with yourself, dig deep and dream big, you'll be amazed with what will show up. Revisit this plan often and make necessary adjustments along the way.

Figure out what your purpose is, what really feeds your soul. Life is too short to only do the things we have to do; it's barely long enough to do the things we want to do. The happiest people I know are those who are passionate about what they do, those who dared to make their deepest dreams come true. What is your legacy?

The hardest, but the most rewarding part of all is dealing with negative subconscious programming and the limiting beliefs getting in your way. However, this is where real freedom begins. You see, our conscious mind is not that powerful. Up to 96% of our actions, thoughts, beliefs and feelings are automatically controlled by our subconscious mind. Imagine our subconscious mind as an elephant and our conscious mind as a rider – the man on top of the elephant. The rider can manage the elephant for as long as the elephant does not have an agenda of its own. But if the rider wants to go in a new direction, and the elephant wants to take a well-known path, guess where you are going? To travel the road of lasting happiness you need to "retrain your elephant." Re-programming our subconscious and letting go of limiting beliefs is a delicate process that, if done properly, pays huge dividends. Look for help and guidance of an experienced mentor you trust and respect. It's time to invest in your happiness and live life on your terms.

My signature system, *The Business Approach to Personal Happiness*, is designed to help you go through these steps in record time. Learn more at: www.OlgaRickards.com.

The ripple effect is remarkable. Happy people create happy businesses that in turn create happy communities. *Zappos*, the largest online shoe store acquired by *Amazon.com* for $1.2 billion, is a great example of a happy business devoted to outstanding customer service. Next time you are in Vegas, take a tour of *Zappos* – you'll feel happiness in the air. It's contagious!

Ted Leonsis, former AOL Vice Chairman, calls it "double bottom line – great financial result and positive impact on people and society." He believes that "happiness can be achieved by approaching it with the same degree of discipline and rigor that's needed to built a successful business." Ted knows it firsthand. After selling his company for $60 million, Ted, a perfect example of "the American dream" at the age of 28, got on the wrong plane. A routine flight from Melbourne, Florida to Atlanta, Georgia, ended with an emergency landing. In the 25 minutes Ted spent unsure if he was going to survive, he faced something he did not like: if the plane crashed, he would not die happy. Thanks to this unwanted "wake-up call," Ted committed to pursuing happiness and living his life without regret. Twenty-five glorious years later the Internet pioneer, sports team owner, venture capitalist, author, filmmaker, philanthropist and family man, whose net worth is estimated by Forbes at $1 billion dollars, reflects on his life, "Money did not make me happy. I believe with all my heart that my pursuit of happiness has made me a better businessman than I would have been otherwise. Happiness is a driver of success, not the other way around."

There are proven strategies to building successful companies and creating wealth; they require commitment and discipline. Success does not happen overnight. If you choose to master the skill of happiness and approach it with the same commitment and discipline you approach building a successful business, you'll be amazed with the outcome. Darren Hardy, the publisher of "Success" magazine for achievers, puts it this way, "Happiness is a choice. Your life is the product of moment-to-moment choices. In essence, you make your choices, and then your choices make you."

Choose happiness – it will result in an exceptional payoff. After all, the more you invest in the ultimate currency, the more it multiplies.

References

1 Seligman, Martin E.P. (2002). *Authentic Happiness: Using the New Positive Psychology to Realize Your Potential for Lasting Fulfillment. Free Press*

2 Ben-Shahar, Tal (2007). *Happier: Learn the Secrets to Daily Joy and Lasting Fulfillment. McGraw-Hills*

3 Haidt, Jonathan (2006). *The Happiness Hypothesis: Finding Modern Truth in Ancient Wisdom. Basic Books*

4 Gilbert, Daniele (2006). *Stumbling on Happiness. Knopf*

5 Lambert, Craig. *The Science of Happiness: Psychology Explores Humans at Their Best. Harvard Magazine, Jan-Feb 2007*

6 Hanson, Rick with Mendius, Richard (2009). *Buddha's Brain: The Practical Neuroscience of Happiness, Love and Wisdom. New Harbinger*

7 Leonsis, Ted with Buckley, John (2010). *The Business of Happiness: 6 Secrets to Extraordinary Success in Work and Life. Regnery*

About Olga

Olga Rickards has been referred to as "one of the most insightful and effective coaches and thought leaders in America today" by world-renowned business mentor Brian Tracy. Known as *America's Premier Happiness Expert,* she has appeared on FOX, ABC, CBS, NBC and is a regular guest speaker on positive psychology at the University of British Columbia.

Olga is a trusted advisor to her clients - highly successful people who, despite their achievements in the business world, still find themselves unfulfilled and want more out of life. "My success was robbing me of happiness my whole life, until I met Olga. Her practical, scientifically proven system - The Business Approach to Personal Happiness - delivers transformational results", says Andrea Lucas, former Director of the World Bank.

Olga learned the hard way that success without fulfillment is failure. She grew up in Siberia, Russia - one of the unhappiest countries in the world. In her pursuit of a better life Olga immigrated to Canada, where she had to start over with poor English and only $200 in her pocket. Olga's drive and determination earned her a privileged lifestyle, but even when she seemed to have it all, deep down she wasn't happy. Determined to find that ever-elusive happiness, Olga spent six figures personally studying with some of the world's leading experts. By interviewing millionaires and billionaires – those who are happy and not so happy - she pieced together the formula to creating financial freedom while also living a truly happy, purpose-driven life. This quest has completely transformed Olga's life and is now transforming the lives of her clients.

Many of Olga's clients learned the hard way that extraordinary achievements do not guarantee extraordinary love, peace of mind or sense of purpose. "My success cost me two marriages and my happiness. Olga is brilliant at what she does. I wish I'd met her 20 years ago", says Ed Alfke, Director of the National Angel Capital Organization.

"If, despite your success, something essential is still missing, it's time to get brutally honest with yourself and do a P&L on your own life", says Olga. "It's time to fill that hole deep inside and stop postponing your happiness to a day that may never come."

If you are ready for a breakthrough, Olga's direct and compassionate approach will empower you to create life on your terms. "Olga's unique set of skills in psychology, business and marketing sets her apart from anyone I've ever met", says Andre Voskuil, former manager of over half-a-billion dollars in the European markets. "She helped me connect with what really makes me tick, then effortlessly set the vision and marketing in motion. Now I do what I love!" Mark Victor Hansen, co-author of the *"Chicken Soup for the Soul"* series, puts it this way: "Allow my friend Olga to help you manifest total happiness in your life."

Visit www.OlgaRickards.com to receive Olga's complimentary special report *"7 Critical Mistakes Wealthy People Make that Cost Them Their Happiness and Freedom and How to Fix Them Once and For All"*.

CHAPTER 27

There's A Treasure In Your Mailbox (And More)!

By Meny Hoffman

As he deposited a few checks into an ATM machine in San Francisco, Patrick Combs had a strange idea.

He had received an envelope containing what looked like a real check – an obvious piece of junk mail – from a company claiming he could make big money and receive checks just like the one enclosed if he'd sign up for their offer.

The check looked authentic and had a signature on it. It was written out to Patrick Combs in the amount of $95,093.35. With nothing to lose, Patrick decided to deposit the check as a joke and see what would happen.

A week later he walked into the bank and looked at his account balance – it read $100,000. Patrick began laughing in disbelief at what happened and decided to tell the bank teller about the prank he pulled, hoping the incident would just wash over.

But after reviewing the facts, the teller refused to take the money back, as the check had technically cleared within the bank's computer system. Although the bank had made an obvious error and the funds in Patrick's account actually came from the bank's own coffers, it appeared the money legally belonged to Mr. Combs – all thanks to a simple junk mail envelope.

The moral of this seemingly unbelievable story? Those ubiquitous junk mail envelopes are obviously worth a lot more than most people realize.

Now before you close this book and run to your mailbox to find junk mail packets with mock checks, do realize that the banking industry has created rules to prevent this scenario from occurring again.

But it doesn't mean that junk mail is now worthless – quite the contrary!

ONE MAN'S JUNK IS ANOTHER MAN'S TREASURE

The fact is, companies across North America spend millions of dollars each year hiring professional marketing agencies to create campaigns ranging from direct mailings to online contests to customer loyalty programs.

Every single component you come across in a junk mail envelope – or any other external element for that matter – results from the decision made by a group of experts who've chosen to incorporate that particular concept and create a solid corporate image.

The fonts used in their logo.

The way their employees are dressed.

The size and design of their brochures.

The choice of greeting employees use when welcoming you.

Whether it's a holiday sale circular, the on-hold greeting you hear when calling by phone, or the creative design of a window display, there are so many valuable marketing tactics that you run into on a daily basis which cost others thousands of dollars to implement.

Now the average business owner probably can't compete with those giant, oversized Fortune 500 companies who spend big money on hi-tech, low-balling marketing campaigns.

That's why I would suggest you do the next best thing: take all the marketing money those companies spent on developing ideas for their campaigns and borrow it to benefit your business.

For example, those junk mail envelopes mentioned earlier generate tremendous revenues. Some of the world's most skilled marketing and business experts spent hours poring over every little detail before the mailing was sent out, from the colorful headline on the envelope right down to the font size on the reply card.

So why not take a moment to sit down and benefit?

By reading, analyzing and dissecting the headlines, sales pitch and tone of a single direct mail piece, you can develop a wealth of marketing ideas which can be implemented into your own business – without having to hire a pricey marketing consultant.

NEVER COPY IDEAS – JUST ADAPT THEM

Before we go further, allow me to set things straight.

My goal here is not to have you go around copying ideas from other companies. Aside from the moral and legal issues that may be involved, copying a concept used by another company can easily backfire if you don't fully understand the mechanisms behind it.

To successfully utilize the ideas conceived by others, you must adapt the idea's core concept and tweak it to meet your specific needs.

Let's begin this process by studying the inner workings of a typical company or business. There are three distinctive elements that help make up the corporate foundation of every successful entity:

- Marketing
- Sales
- Systemization

While the three are closely related and often intertwined, they all possess unique elements that can help make or break the success of your company.

IT'S A FACT: MARKETING REALLY WORKS

There's a reason why brands like Coca Cola, American Express and Macy's are so popular. And part of that reason is because of their marketing tactics.

Beyond their high-profile elements of being official sponsors of the International Olympics or featuring hot air balloons at New York City parades, they incorporate a variety of low-profile marketing strategies into their everyday operations.

Things like customer loyalty programs that offer rewards and incentives to keep their client-base from going to the competition.

Or utilizing colorful, in-store signage with persuasive messages to convince shoppers to buy and use the product.

Or inserting offers along with invoices asking customers to sign up for additional protection plans or purchase exclusively discounted gifts.

But it doesn't end there.

Marketing can come in the form of press releases to local newspapers announcing upcoming sales or events; postcards mailed to homes in specific zip codes which are redeemable for discounts; or even simple pens and paper pads emblazoned with your brand logo for customers to use.

Techniques such as these can really go a long way to help better promote your company or product and create a professional image.

LET'S MAKE THE SALE HAPPEN

Chances are, you can't afford to spend thousands of dollars to hire a professional sales coach to train you and your staff – but the seasoned saleswoman calling you from that big, brand-name company can.

So why not listen to her sales pitch?

You may have no interest in the product or service she is pushing – but her sales process and techniques are definitely worthy of your attention.

Listen closely at how she strategically raises and lowers her tone of voice during the conversation to add emphasis or convey a point.

See how she fields your questions with specific responses that are meant to steer the conversation in a certain way.

Carefully hear how she repeats your comments and attempts to gain your favor by cleverly weaving them into the sales pitch.

Every single word, expression, pause and sigh of that conversation has been carefully planned and crafted by some of the world's leading sales experts before you even received a telephone call.

So don't instruct your secretary to say that you're in a meeting and hang up the phone. Rather, hang on to every single word of the sales call and benefit from valuable techniques that cost large corporations hundreds of thousands of dollars to develop.

It's practically guaranteed to help make the sale happen.

GROW BIGGER BY ACTING BIGGER

Big companies often do things in a big way.

When a sales representative places an order, it isn't just scribbled on the back of a paper scrap and stuffed inside a filing cabinet.

Rather, the employee will enter the information into a CRM (Customer Relationship Management) software system which will systemize every detail of the transaction and store it for future access.

More than just a repository for factual information, a CRM system can implement strategies for managing a company's interactions with customers and sales prospects, allowing the organization's client-base and profits to steadily grow larger.

But that's only the beginning of what the benefits of systemization can do for your company.

When a person calls a company and is greeted by a professional-sounding, automated telephone system that offers options from hearing office hours to leaving voicemails, the caller will reasonably assume the company is a successful and well-run corporation – even if it's simply a one-man shop operating in a dusty garage.

By utilizing modern technology to perform the systemization tasks that you can't always do, you're setting yourself up for success.

Get a phone system that will give off a sharp image. Create an auto-response email form that customers will get as soon as they contact you. Link your bookkeeping software to a program that spits out invoices the moment a sale happens.

Because you don't have to be big to look big; you just have to act big.

THE SMALL GUY ALWAYS HAS AN ADVANTAGE

If you own a small business, you're going to have a hard time competing head-to-head with large companies and retail chain-stores.

You don't have the same purchasing power with suppliers.

You don't have the same brand recognition.

And you most certainly don't have the same budget to launch effective marketing ideas or tactics.

But as a small business owner, you do have one valuable advantage – you're small and nimble.

Because of your diminutive size, you can develop and implement ideas much faster than big, stodgy corporations. All you need to do is let your employees know about the new idea and let them know what tasks they must accomplish to execute it.

Not long ago, I met an associate of mine who works as a marketing consultant for numerous Fortune 500 companies. During the course of our conversation, we began discussing the typical challenges large companies face when launching marketing campaigns and he made a casual remark that shocked me.

He commented that in the majority of companies he's consulted with, it usually took between 8-12 months just to get a marketing campaign approved by the Board of Directors.

When I heard that, I was absolutely floored.

It took him almost an entire year just to get a simple marketing campaign approved? You would think that a company with extensive money and manpower could easily roll out a campaign in a matter of weeks.

Why the long wait?

He explained that coming up with ideas and concepts were easy for him; it was the bureaucratic process that slowed everything down and hindered the potential success of his campaigns.

There were always lengthy board meetings to attend.

And confusing internal memos jammed with lots of corporate jargon.

And lots of other time-wasters that would always threaten to compromise the success of his campaigns.

As a small business owner, you don't have to put up with those distracting shenanigans. In fact, you possess a serious advantage that large companies can only dream about. The time-frames behind any campaign you seek to launch are dictated only by the amount of time you want it to take.

Be sure to take advantage of this benefit – by taking it all the way.

IT'S TIME TO CHANGE THE WAY YOU THINK

Everything you've read in this chapter up until now was to prepare you for the message I'm looking to convey.

I want you to adjust your mindset.

I want you to change your perceptions.

I want you to open your eyes.

When you open the mailbox and see a piece of junk mail, take a moment to look it over and see the clever sales tactics woven within. Perhaps you can use some of those valuable ideas for promoting your own business.

From now on, don't just go to the mall and shop for clothing – shop around for ideas, too. Look at the signage, banners, store displays and lighting techniques that are used to appeal to customers and generate sales.

The next time you see a large company roll out a customer referral program, study it carefully and see how you can adapt the concept to swiftly grow your own client-base.

Keep your eyes open to all the different marketing, sales and systemization strategies that large companies spend thousands of dollars to create – from tiny paper coupons to huge cardboard delivery boxes – and swiftly adapt those ideas into your own business.

Change your mindset and begin viewing everything you see as a way to help grow and expand your business, bank account and future.

And just like the aforementioned Patrick Combs found out, your journey to success can begin with a simple envelope in the mailbox.

About Meny

Meny Hoffman is the Chief Executive Officer of Ptex Group, an Inc. 500/5000-ranked marketing and business services firm headquartered in Brooklyn, NY.

Renowned for his ability to provide clients with advanced business-boosting tactics and strategic marketing solutions for achieving success, Meny has worked to elevate the status and popularity of prominent brands spanning a variety of industries including corporate, not-for-profit and institutional.

Mr. Hoffman has been honored with multiple legislative awards for his work in encouraging entrepreneurism amongst New York businesses and is a member of the Brooklyn Chamber of Commerce. He is also the founder of Let's Talk Business, a popular email series that is sent to thousands of online followers each week, which discusses powerful strategies that can be used by companies and organizations to help sustain further growth.

A longtime entrepreneur himself, Mr. Hoffman has been featured in Crain's Magazine, The Daily News, The New York Enterprise Report and the American Express OPEN Forum.

To learn more about the unique business strategies that have earned Mr. Hoffman and his firm widespread recognition, visit: www.ptexgroup.com or call him directly at 718.407.1818.

CHAPTER 28

BRAND. PLAN. IGNITE YOUR BUSINESS™:
TRANSFORMING FROM A MARKET PLAYER TO AN INDUSTRY LEADER

by Kelly Borth, Chief Strategy Officer
of GREENCREST

BRAND

Our clients are small and mid-market sized privately-held businesses. They engage us to guide them in establishing a reputation as a market leader in their industry. Establishing a business as an industry leader begins with uncovering its brand. Then, based on systematic research, we identify a marketing strategy that will allow them to occupy a leadership position and develop a tactical plan to get them known, heard and recognized. And, undoubtedly, time and again, these companies emerge an industry leader. In this chapter, I share a few trade secrets in the hope that you gain insight into how you can help your business achieve similar results.

Define market differentiation
The first step toward achieving market penetration is establishing market differentiation. CEOs take the lead in defining market differentiation. Yet, as a specialist in brand development, it is disheartening to listen to all the brand-speak. There is much confusion in the marketplace as to what a *brand* is. Brand is not a logo, an advertising tag line

255

or design elements (or graphic "look"). It is, by my definition, "an undisputable evidence of distinction" and something that can be proved. A *brand* defines a company's market differentiation. It is important not to confuse "brand" with "branding." So while "branding" is what is turned over to the marketing director, *brand* development must be led by the CEO. A *brand's* distinction is what separates it from its competitors, makes it stand out as extraordinary or different, or better yet, more valuable to the end user.

Uncover your BRAND

Brand development is the internal discovery of *brand* distinction. Surprisingly, it is not discovered by talking with your customers or believing that you can become something your organization is not capable of being. *Brand* is the essence of what your organization already is and always has been. It is what you are. Remember your company mission is to "be…," your vision is to "become…," and your *brand* is "what you are and what you do differently."

The process starts with fact finding until you have a prioritized list of absolutely unique, provable selling points. Don't underestimate the power of *brand* discovery—the deeper you dig and the more thorough the analysis, the more obvious the essence of the *brand* and its leadership capabilities will become. And, the easier it will be to assume a long term *brand* leadership position going forward.

From this process, you can establish the foundation for an undisputable statement of differentiation and a leadership position you are capable of controlling. It will provide a lens through which all company strategic direction should be viewed. It is your corporate values, reputation capital, name equity and social capital which encompasses your relational and cognitive beliefs and values. Your company *brand* is your market driver and as such, must get incorporated into the company's mission, strategies and operations. It must align with the overall business plan.

Align business strategy and brand strategy

Your business strategy should encompass your customers, strategic partners, distributors, employees, marketing and sales. So, too must your *brand* strategy. And when the two are aligned they form your overall corporate strategy, infusing your organization with the momentum it needs to take over the leadership position.

Brand leadership is the vital, added value good brand positioning offers. It allows customers to adopt your *brand* as their own and allows for better brand management, internal adoption and crystal clear communication.

Once successfully differentiated, a company separates itself from competitors, and thus, is positioned for industry leadership. Once aligned with the company's business strategy, it is positioned to succeed. If there is a downside to brand leadership, it would be living up to your company's claim and having the guts to posture the company as a leader, not a follower. Are you ready?

PLAN

After the *brand* development process, it is vital to your organization to regularly survey the market landscape to develop and execute a leadership strategy in order to maximize market potential.

Keep your business focused and relevant

As lead strategy officers of our organizations, we need to pull ourselves and our key reports away from the day-to-day minutiae to re-evaluate the business playing field and how we competitively fit into that landscape.

Listen to the voice of the customer

A great place to start the strategic process is to reach out to customers—active, inactive and prospective. How you get customer feedback is less important than obtaining it and doing something with it. Effective customer feedback will provide input on needs, impressions of your business, how your company performs against expectations, what matters most to customers in the selection process, and other important information. Listening to our customers can result in tremendous strategic opportunities.

Engage the team in a strategic discussion

More than just a SWOT analysis, business leaders need to look deeper to identify how business, industry and consumer norms have shifted, and how those changes impact the business. Some business leaders may be comfortable leading these discussions while others may need to hire a professional facilitator. The best results involve the key players in your business—sales, marketing, operations, production, human resources, corporate finance, engineering, etc.

Start with a thorough evaluation of your company today. Define your core competencies, what it takes to be a "good" player in your niche and how well you measure against that mark. Talk about your sales and service delivery processes and identify opportunity gaps. Incorporate important findings from the customer feedback into your discussions.

Next, thoroughly evaluate the marketplace. Define your customer, the markets you serve, your share and growth potential of those markets. Explore the potential of new product or service opportunities based on customer feedback and identify any barriers, operational or market, to adding them to your offering. It is not as important to know the answers as it is to capture what you do know so that you can find the answers to what you don't know.

Also identify current and future trends: market, political, economic, social, and technological and analyze their impact on your company's mission and goals. Identify and analyze your top competition, and in doing so, make note of each competitor's strengths, weaknesses, and mindshare of prospects.

Define the company's goals

In defining the company's goals, break it down until everyone in the room realizes how the goal can be achieved. Will the company's growth be organic or will an acquisition strategy come into play? Identify the percentage of business that will come from current customers versus new customers, and how that goal breaks down by product line, market, geographic location, etc. Define your company's goals for the next three years and talk about what you need to change in order to achieve those goals. Also talk about how these changes will impact company operations, facilities, personnel, delivery, marketing and sales structure.

Leading your team through strategic exercises such as these will keep your business focused and relevant today and in the future.

IGNITE YOUR BUSINESS

With a *brand* and a plan in place, you ready to hit the ground running. Driving market impact requires communicating the right message to the right people—in other words, driving market impact requires the implementation of your marketing plan.

Driving market impact doesn't happen by accident. Quite the contrary. Leading companies attribute market strategy as the reason they are in the number 1, 2 or 3 position in the marketplace. As CEOs, driving market impact is one of your top responsibilities.

Create a strategic marketing foundation

Your chosen strategic position is your company's *brand* foundation. So to drive market strategy you need to know what is required to do better than average in your industry and know the sustaining sources of competitive advantage. Industry leaders regularly analyze their market position and keep the company's competitive advantages focused, clear and sustainable.

A company will emerge with a huge market advantage if a *brand* foundation exists. Now take that advantage and create a well-defined, well-executed *brand* message backed by a strategic marketing plan that leads you toward penetrating the industry and you will reach market domination.

Overwhelmingly, the weakness of otherwise knowledgeable business leaders to reach market domination resides in their ability to be a good player. They may have product superiority, but they are seriously *brand* or marketing handicapped. Sometimes this is lack of *brand* clarity, lack of strategy, lack of execution and/or lack of a dedicated marketing budget—all of which are required to achieve and sustain a lead position.

Use the right marketing mix

Today there are more choices in the marketplace to reach customers and it continues to multiply daily. I believe it is better to do one thing well than to do three things in a mediocre way, and never reach a level of meaningful market penetration. And even though the communication choices have grown, the same marketing science of reach and frequency applies—you just need to listen and participate differently than in the past. It's still important to reach your target audience, just through a different mix of mediums, including social media. You also need to make sure your marketing program is reaching every essential audience—new customer acquisition, retention and growth of current customer revenue and generating overall industry awareness of your *brand*.

Manage sales effectively

Every company needs to have someone managing the sales process—too often this does not happen. The CEO needs to oversee the management of the process to realize the results. It is about holding people accountable, which I know is easier said than done.

Companies I have worked with tend to have a sales force comprised of customer relationship management people rather than new business development people—companies need both. It is difficult, but possible, to manage your salespeople to do both.

Recognizing that CEOs need help overseeing the sales process, the development of an Accountable New Business Program accomplishes five important steps for success. First, it identifies for the CEO how much new business activity is needed based on the company's sales metrics to ensure the company will meet its year-end sales goal. Second, it lays the foundation for a new business development process and implementation milestones. Third, it establishes a target list of prospects to pursue. Fourth, it provides tools like a script, prequalification survey and sample prospecting letters. Fifth, it includes prospect profiles and contact reports so the CEO can verify and manage progress-to-goal and make adjustments as needed. Even armed with this information, most CEOs have a difficult time managing accountability.

Use marketing and sales in tandem
Most CEOs have heard of the sales funnel process that uses AIDA (Awareness, Interest, Desire, Action). Marketing's job is to increase *brand* awareness—the first quotient of the formula. Research has proven that when *brand* awareness is high, new customer acquisition is high. If the *brand* is not known, a prospect cannot give it purchase consideration.

Marketing can also assist with the second quotient by maintaining and growing interest through frequent and meaningful messages or touches with prospects. Marketing can equally assist the sales team with the third quotient to transition interest into *brand* preference. Lastly, marketing can help the sales process by presenting the marketplace with offers that elicit action.

Here's the catch. Marketing works in tandem with new business development efforts. They both need to be performing at a high level. One without the other will have less success—research has proven that when the two work together, sales success is exponential.

SUMMARY

Transforming your company from just another market player to an industry leader requires effective, strategic brand management. From brand discovery through tactical implementation, all business efforts should reflect the integration of your brand. Only then will you develop the brand leadership necessary to move from good to great. I wish you the best of luck as you pursue this lofty goal.

About Kelly

Kelly Borth is a visionary with an intense pioneering spirit, an unfaltering commitment to achieving excellence, and a firm belief in the value of helping others. She is a strategic advisor to CEOs, a best selling author, speaker, and a columnist for *Smart Business* magazine.

In 1990, Kelly was inspired to launch GREENCREST, a strategic marketing, advertising, public relations and interactive firm that provides direction for small- and mid-market privately-held companies. As a certified business consultant, an accredited public relations specialist and a certified brand strategist, Kelly leads her team as chief strategy officer, in propelling businesses from market players to distinguished market leaders within a remarkably short period of time. Kelly understands what it takes to define a brand and turn that into an increase in market share and solid results. Her company specializes in brilliantly executed communications programs that begin with a solid marketing foundation and result in increased market penetration and awareness.

Kelly is a sought-after business advisor and sits on numerous community and business advisory boards. She has been recognized extensively for her business savvy and philanthropic involvement.

To learn more about Kelly Borth and GREENCREST, visit: www.greencrest.com or www.brandproblog.com or call 614-885-7921.

You can also follow Kelly Borth on Twitter@brandpro

www.greencrest.com

CHAPTER 29

Get Naked First

By Erin T. Botsford, CFP®, CEO,
The Botsford Group

What an odd title for a chapter but none could be a better description for the true recipe for business success. Despite what you might think, all business comes down to one thing: relationship. Whether you are buying from Amazon, Nordstroms, Zappos or Apple, or even if you are buying services from your accountant, attorney or financial advisor, what people want is something real and authentic. They don't want to buy a fake. It can be a tangible product or an intangible service but people want something genuine they can count on to deliver what is promised. The quickest way to get the sale done is to be real, to tell the truth and ultimately do or deliver what you say you are going to do.

I am in the business of giving financial advice, as are another hundred thousand people. So what has catapulted me to the top echelons of the financial services industry? Why do I have an unusually high closing ratio? Because I get naked first, not in a literal sense of course, but in a metaphorical sense and it works. I'll explain.

In the financial services business, if I am going to help people, I first have to get to know them. I must identify their dreams and more importantly, their fears. Are they afraid of running out of money before they die, of entrusting money to an unscrupulous financial advisor, of potential health issues or lawsuits filed against them? If I am going to help them navigate the potential financial minefields, I need to know intricate details about their lives. Eventually I need to see their balance sheets, but ultimately, I will ask them to reveal very real, raw, intimate details about their lives, things that might otherwise only be discussed under extreme duress and only with their physician or pastor. Interestingly enough, I do get all of this information and without much trouble at all. Why? Because I get naked first! In our first meeting, I reveal the intimate details of my life and tell my story first. I have found when I do tell my story and share intimate details of my personal trials, tribulations, mistakes and triumphs, all of the walls and the barriers they walked in with come tumbling down, never to be reconstructed….at least not with me nor my team. They may walk out of the door and put up those walls with others but in my office we are going to get real and stay real, which is actually a very safe place for both of us to be.

How did I learn this and what has it meant for my business? For the first ten years of my practice, I never told my personal story. I was far too ashamed of my background and I wanted my prospects and clients to see me as the sophisticated woman with the shiny diamond ring and perfectly manicured nails, the world traveler who drove the new car. It's not that I wanted to deceive them; in fact it was quite the opposite. I wanted to relate to them. I thought the 'them' that sat in front of me was the real *them*. But I learned it wasn't. They were putting on the same front as me; we just had different roles in this charade of being self-assured and ultimately, extremely successful.

I'm not sure of the exact appointment when I first told my story, but I remember the prospect's reaction was clearly visible. They had likely come in, like so many others, with arms folded and distinct body language that told me there wasn't anything I was going to discuss with them that they hadn't heard a thousand times before. I was probably the last stop in a long line of interviews. I'm not sure what prompted me to "get naked" with them, but my guess is that they said something leading me to believe telling my story might have some relevance to their situation. In any case, I took a deep breath, as I still do, and started unpeeling the onion of my story, metaphorically removing one layer of clothing after another until I laid naked with the truth of who I was, where I came from, what happened to me and why that should matter to them.

I told them about growing up in a loving, Irish Catholic family, the 5th of 6 children in a small town south of Chicago. My father was a teacher, a school superintendant and even a professor at Northwestern University at one point in time. When I was eleven, my father decided to pursue his lifelong dream, to open a clinic for early childhood education in San Diego, California, a place he had visited during the war. He borrowed against his teacher's pension, wrote a book and we moved to San Diego in August of 1969. While my father waited for his teaching certificate to be transferred to the State of California, he sold cars, albeit not very successfully. At one point, we had our only car repossessed as dad waited for the day he could finally open his clinic. But that day never came. Six months after we moved to California, my father died of a massive heart attack. He was only fifty.

Life immediately changed for our family. Dad only had a $10,000 life insurance policy and because he had borrowed from his teacher's pension plan, there was no benefit available. While my mother had never worked outside the home, we all had to go to work to put food on the table and keep a roof over our heads. I babysat, raked leaves and did whatever I could to contribute, as did all my siblings. None of us regrets that; we all developed a good work ethic as a result. Realistically, that part of my story is not unlike the stories of many in the 'baby boomer' generation.

Unfortunately, we were barely scraping by when tragedy struck again. I was sixteen, driving to my first "real" job at McDonald's, when I was involved in a terrible accident with a motorcyclist. The driver of the motorcycle was killed, and I was charged with involuntary manslaughter by the State of California. My mother and I met with an attorney and were honest about our family's financial situation. After hearing our story, he spoke to my mother as if I were not there. "Mrs. McGowan," he said, "this is purely a matter of economics. If your daughter will plead guilty to these charges, I will be happy to enter the plea at no cost to you. As a result, your daughter will get the appropriate sentence prescribed by the State of California. However, if she wants to defend herself it will cost you a lot of money."

Since we had no money, my mother instantly realized our choices were limited. She thanked the attorney and agreed that I had no option other than to plead guilty. To say I was horrified would be an understatement. I begged and pleaded with my mother. That's when she looked at me and said the ten words I will never forget, "Honey, we have no money; therefore, we have no choice." That was the day I learned that money can buy you choices. Fortunately, the case wasn't closed. My older brother had just begun his real estate career; he suggested we take a second mortgage on our home to pay for my defense. With the money from the mortgage, our attorney was able to bring in expert witnesses who proved that the motorcyclist was driving well over the speed limit, and that he had hit me, not the other way around. The judge dropped the charges. At the end of the court proceeding, he said, "Take this little girl home. She's been through enough."

I wish the story had ended there, but it didn't. Shortly after the criminal proceeding, the family of the motorcyclist sued my mother and me for a substantial sum of money. My mother was terrified that we would lose the only asset she possessed, our family home. She lived with this fear for many years until the case was finally settled at the eleventh hour by our auto insurance company, which came to my defense.

I usually take a brief pause in telling my story at this point, because there is a point to be made. I want the person sitting across from me to make a clear and definite connection to my story. I want him or her to realize this car accident and its myriad ramifications happens to people every day. What would it mean if it happened to them or one of their children? I often tell them it is a direct result of this accident that I came to be in the business I am in. When I begin asking them questions (which I tell them I am going to do right after I finish "getting naked" in front of them), I am going to ask them about their personal and professional vulnerabilities. I am going to ask them to reveal very personal and private information about themselves. Why? Because I am looking for the answer to this question: If something like this happened to you, Mr. or Mrs. Client, which of the assets on your balance sheet could be used to satisfy a judgment? How exposed are you? I want the clients to see their entire life's work could be at risk for failing to address things such as market meltdowns and legal issues which threaten people every day.

I want them to also know the end of my story. Through my diligent saving and a fortuitous winning appearance on Wheel of Fortune (ironically winning by solving the puzzle "Down in the Dumps"), I accumulated a nest egg of about $22,000, no small sum in 1979. Shortly before I married, I invested $3,000 to buy a townhouse in San Diego County with a friend. This investment worked out well. However, soon after we married, my husband, Bob, and I entrusted the balance of our savings to a stockbroker, assuming we were being smart by investing our "wealth" for future growth. The stockbroker divided our money among four investments, none of which were appropriate for us. All four went belly-up in a very short period of time, and we lost every cent we had entrusted to him.

I was devastated. While it may not have been much money to our broker, it was everything to us, and it represented years of hard work and sacrifice. I felt stupid, betrayed, and embarrassed. From that day forward, I made it my personal mission to learn everything I could about money and investing. I was determined never to let what happened to us happen to anyone I cared about.

Do you think sharing my story changes the dynamic in the room? You bet it does. In effect, I realized by sharing my story the people in the room can share in my vulnerability. They can share in what was a horrific time in my life, and we can relate on an entirely new level. More importantly, through having exposed my experiences, I have found everyone has had their share of suffering or at least severe disappointment somewhere along the line......everyone. It is in this sharing that people can be people. They can take off the façade of success, prestige, persona, or whatever they walked in with and just be real. And it is in this realness business is done, because ultimately we all want to work with real people with whom we can connect and with whom we can share our lives, our hopes, our dreams and our fears. We want to relate. In this world of twitter and texts, how successful is the man or woman who can get naked first and take a chance on authentic relationships that are deep, profound and lasting. That's the business I want to be in; I'll bet it's the business you want to be in too!

So if you want to be successful in business, my advice is to "get naked first." Relate to the people you meet. If it's the Vice President of a company, realize his or her decisions leave them vulnerable to the outcome. They might lose their job or their position as a result of their decision. Relate to that. If you are trying to sell the services of your company, relate to the time you made a decision you regretted, learning the lesson of how important it is to work with people who do what they say they are going to do. Assure them if they work with you, you will do everything in your power to be sure they receive what they are buying because you've been down the alternate road. And if you are in the personal services business as I am, relate to your buyers as if they were your best friend, because it is very likely they will become close confidantes; it all depends upon how deep you go with them and how closely you can relate to that person. Good luck and remember, get naked first!

About Erin

Erin Botsford, CFP® is the founder and CEO of The Botsford Group, a boutique financial planning firm with offices in Frisco, Texas and Atlanta, Georgia.

Erin's firm specializes in retirement and asset protection planning for business owners and senior executives of Fortune 500 companies. Having trademarked an investment philosophy called "Lifestyle Driven Investing™, she is considered a thought leader on 21st century investing, risk management and retirement. Among the top echelon of financial advisors, she is often asked to share her views on investing and the economy in the media and in keynote addresses across the country. As a top-producing business owner in an industry dominated by men, Erin is frequently asked to speak to her success at industry conferences. Her key note, "Get Naked First" is always an industry show stopper as she addresses the true power in authentic business relationships.

In addition to *The Only Business Book You'll Ever Need,* Erin recently published *The Big Retirement Risk: Running out of Money Before You Run out of Time.*

Erin's personal story of overcoming poverty and adversity in her early life to becoming one of the top financial planners in the country has been featured in numerous articles and publications. Her business success has been recognized by publications such as *Barron's* magazine, *D Magazine, Success Magazine* and *Investment News,* along with television appearances on CNBC, Fox News and Bloomberg Television.

CHAPTER 30

The One Thing That Changes Everything

By Greg Link

*The world is changing very fast. Big will not beat small anymore.
It will be the fast beating the slow.*

~ Rupert Murdoch, Chairman and CEO, News Corporation

There is one thing that is common to every individual, relationship, team, family, organization, nation, economy, and civilization throughout the world—one thing which, if removed, will destroy the most powerful government, the most successful business, the most thriving economy, the most influential leadership, the greatest friendship, the strongest character, the deepest love.

On the other hand, if developed and leveraged, that one thing has the potential to create unparalleled success and prosperity in every dimension of life. Yet, it is the least understood, most neglected, and most underestimated possibility of our time.

That one thing is trust.

Trust impacts us 24/7, 365 days a year. It undergirds and affects the quality of every relationship, every communication, every work project, every business venture, every effort in which we are engaged. It changes the quality of every present moment and alters the trajectory and outcome of every future moment of our lives—both personally and professionally.

So it is that Stephen M. R. Covey began his #1 *Wall Street Journal* best-selling book, *The Speed of Trust.* As we did the research for that book, tempered by our 25+ years of experience teaching leadership and advising business owners and executives around the world, it became very clear to us that trust did in fact change everything. Repeatedly, as people over the years rehearsed their version of their success story, whether they used the same wording or not, there were always threads of evidence that trust is the common denominator to success in virtually all cases. This transcended industry, generation, gender, business culture, ethnicity, and even country.

When I was asked to contribute to a book entitled *The Only Business Book You'll Ever Need*, I felt strongly that trust deserved a prominent and primary position in the discourse. Saying trust is the one thing that changes everything may seem like a bold statement, but I have come to believe that not only is it true, but even more so today than ever before. The ability to grow trust in a progressively 'low trust' world gives you a significant competitive advantage. More and more business leaders today are "rediscovering" trust and are experiencing a paradigm shift of perspective as to its importance in business. Historically, hardened business people have viewed trust as some soft, intangible, and illusive social virtue that you either had or didn't have. It was "nice to have" but didn't determine success. Business was run more like the military – in a command and control style. Today's enlightened and informed work-force demands meaningful engagement in their work as never before. You can hire their hands and back, but they must *volunteer* their hearts and minds.

I intend to make the business case for trust and how it is now the career critical skill and ultimately the currency of this emerging global economy. I challenge the age-old assumption that trust is merely a soft, social virtue and demonstrate that trust is a hard-edged, economic driver—a learnable and measurable skill that makes businesses more profitable, people more promotable, and relationships more energizing. I will show why business leaders around the globe are seeing trust as a critical, highly relevant and tangible asset; that trust affects—and changes—everything within a business…literally every dimension, every project, every decision, every relationship. Trust is the single most powerful and influential lever for leaders and business owners today, and it is desperately underutilized.

> *You cannot prevent a major catastrophe, but you can build an organization that is battle-ready, that has high morale, that knows how to behave, that trusts itself, and where people trust one another. In military training, the first rule is to instill soldiers with trust in their officers, because without trust they won't fight.*
> ~ Peter Drucker

After making the business case for trust, I will conclude by showing that trust is not an intangible mystery, but a tangible and learnable skill. In fact, we assert that the ability to establish, grow, extend and, when necessary, restore trust with all stakeholders—customers, business partners, investors, and co-workers—is the key leadership competency of the new 21st century global economy. The good news is that because trust is a skill, you can get better at it—and even faster than you think. More importantly, you can learn to extend smart trust to others, increase your influence, and grow your enterprise.

Let's begin with the business case for trust. No one argues against trust. They sense it is nice to have. But few recognize the significance of both internal and external trust to the bottom line of business.

Again, trust is the most underestimated possibility in business—a hidden variable that changes everything. Let's take the classic business school formula of strategy times execution equals results:

S x E = R
(STRATEGY TIMES EXECUTION EQUALS RESULTS)

If it were only that simple! As failed business strategists repeatedly discover, it is more complex. Many well-thought-out business plans and strategies crash on the rocks of a missing factor in their assumptions when they ultimately try to execute in the real world. There is a hidden variable that changes the outcome of even the most well planned strategy. This hidden variable modifies the traditional formula with a significant filter:

(S x E) T = R
(STRATEGY TIMES EXECUTION)
MULTIPLIED BY TRUST = RESULTS

In other words trust can positively or negatively change the outcome of the execution of your strategy.

The reality is trust has a measurable impact on the bottom line result. Why? Trust always impacts two outcomes—speed and cost. The business case is simple: when trust goes down in a relationship, on a team, in a company, or in a government, speed goes down and cost goes up. This creates a low trust tax. When trust goes up, speed goes up and cost goes down. This creates a high trust dividend. It's that simple, that predictable.

Business owners or leaders can devise a "grade 10" strategy on a scale of one to ten, but if they try to execute this strategy with a low trust team or workforce, they pay a low trust tax. This results in a 7 execution and costs a 30% low trust tax, which slows things down and costs more. Now these taxes won't show up on the business' income statement as "low trust taxes," but they are charged just the same, disguised as bureaucracy, politics, redundancy, disengagement, employee turnover, customer churn, and even fraud. The financial hit of this low trust tax on a startup or seasoned business can tip the profit scales from black to red faster than you think.

On the flip side—and this is the strongest case for trust—a 10 strategy executed by a high trust, high performance team or workforce generates an exponential return as speed goes up and costs go down. Consider a 20% trust dividend and do the math. The spread of the difference of a low trust tax of 30% and a high trust dividend of 20% is almost 50% – or close to double the effectiveness. In fact, a study analyzing *Fortune Magazine's* 100 Best Companies to Work for in America, which acknowledges trust as two-thirds of the criteria, showed that these high trust organizations have outperformed the market over the 13 years of the study (from 1998 to 2010) by 288 % or almost three times.

Interestingly, Harvard Business School and others are now beginning to recognize the business significance of this hidden variable of trust. When I filled out a recommendation for a candidate for Harvard recently, they asked for input in three fundamental areas; one of the three was this:

The Harvard Business School is committed to developing outstanding leaders who can inspire trust and confidence in others. Please comment on the applicant's behavior (e.g., respect for others, honesty, integrity, accountability for personal behavior, etc.) within your organization or within the community. [Emphasis added]

Ask yourself…mercilessly: Do I exude trust? E–x–u–d–e.
Big word. Do I smack of "trust"? Think about it. Carefully.
~ Tom Peters

In conclusion, let's look at trust as a business critical skill. Many business owners and leaders are a little jaded and cynical about skill training. However, now that we have made the business case for trust, I would expect you can see that the potential return is worth the risk. This reminds me of a story from years ago at Covey Leadership Center. One of my colleagues told me of a director on the board of a mid-sized business who asked the CEO, "What if we spend money to train people who then turnaround and leave?" The CEO, who was proposing leadership training as part of the budget, thought for a moment and then replied, "What if we don't train them and they stay?" Clearly, the right skill training increases the chances for a profitable, high-performance enterprise.

Unfortunately, that board member's cynical sentiment is not uncommon among many business managers today. But I completely disagree with it. I believe trust is a skill we can learn and teach others, and as we do, it becomes a performance multiplier. We can get better at trust. We can increase trust—and much faster than you think. And doing so will have direct impact on your bottom line. Getting good at trust is a performance multiplier because high trust makes every other skill you have better. This positively changes the trajectory of every other skill, every other strength, every other asset, every other strategy. Research shows specifically how trust increases value, accelerates growth, enhances innovation, improves collaboration, strengthens partnering, speeds up execution, and heightens loyalty. Trust also has a profound impact on joy in teams and organizations in terms of employee satisfaction and the ability of companies to attract and retain talent. Remarkably, a 2008 Helliwell Huang study showed that a 10% increase in trust inside an organization had the equivalent effect on employee satisfaction as a 30% increase in pay!

In contrast, research also shows how low trust siphons value from every other competency, skill, strength, and asset. As an illustration, only 46% of disengaged employees trust their leaders, compared to 96% of engaged employees. There's also a cost to organizations in terms of attracting and retaining talent. The vast majority of people, both managers and workers, want to be trusted, and they want the autonomy of a high trust environment. When they're not trusted, they become disengaged (i.e., they "quit but stay"), or they leave—especially the top performers. Turnover in a low trust environment is substantially higher than in a high trust culture. For example, compare the average turnover rate in the supermarket industry—47%—to the mere 3% in high-trust Wegmans Food Markets. Or consider the fact that 25 of the 2011 "100 Best Companies to Work for in America"—for which trust is two-thirds of the criteria—had turnover of 3% or less! The cost of turnover can be enormous, ranging from 25% to 250% of pay.

There is no leadership without trust. There may be management. There may be administration. But, as Warren Bennis said, "Leadership without mutual trust is a contradiction in terms." Our definition of leadership, and the first job of any leader, is to get results in a way that inspires trust. It's increasing both your current influence and your ability to influence in the future by growing the trust that makes it possible. We have identified 13 behaviors common to high trust leaders throughout the world. Leaders that model these behaviors consistently find they have significantly more influence and are much more trusted by all stakeholders. (Get the list of behaviors at speedoftrust.com/13.)

The means are as important as the ends. How you go about achieving results is as important as the results themselves. When you grow trust, you increase your ability to get results the next time. And there's always a next time.

Trusted employees engender more trust from customers. We all know that it costs several times as much to create a new customer than to get a referral. Referral sales are one of the reasons we call it the "speed" of trust. Customers buy more, buy more frequently, stay longer, and refer more with businesses and people they trust. Plus, these businesses grow faster and outperform their competitors with less cost. The net result is not just higher growth, but higher profitable growth. To get things done in ways that destroy trust is not only shortsighted and counterproductive; it is ultimately unsustainable.

Finally, a caveat and a challenge. The caveat is that we are not advocating *blind* trust. Two of the 13 behaviors of high trust leaders are accountability and clarifying expectations. We acknowledge that there is risk in trusting. Just know there's a solution—a third alternative to the blind trust that gets us burned and the distrust that cheats us out of growth and possibilities. We advocate Smart Trust. Our short definition of Smart Trust is *judgment*. It's a competency and a process that enables us to operate with high trust in a low-trust world by minimizing risk and maximizing possibilities. Smart Trust optimizes two key factors: 1) our propensity to trust, and 2) our analysis. We find that the pendulum has swung too far in the direction of analysis—the paralysis of analysis in too many businesses. One example is quoting policies and procedures to your best customers because a rare, bad customer cheated you. Another is employees who are disengaged and afraid to present their best ideas for fear of criticism or making a mistake. We propose that the fastest way to grow your business is by mastering and extending smart trust. It sure worked for Tony Hsieh of Zappos, as he grew an online shoe store from $0 to a billion dollars in sales during one of the worst economic times in history this past 10 years. Tony told me he attributed his success to trusting his employees and his customers. Go figure. Consider the possibility that trust is reciprocal and that, by trusting your people, they will rise to the occasion.

I know trust changed my career. During my teenage years, I was a regular hellion—somewhat of a juvenile delinquent in fact. Thankfully, by 18, I had straightened up a little—enough to manage to get into college and land a job at a local grocery store to help pay my tuition.

I hadn't been working there for more than a few months when Ralph, the store manager, unexpectedly tossed me the store keys one afternoon and told me to lock up when we closed in four hours. This included putting the tills in the safe. Obviously, I hadn't elaborated on my dubious background when I applied for the job. I can distinctly remember (after recovering from the shock of the situation) the unfamiliar feeling of responsibility that rose up in me, and the gratitude and loyalty I suddenly felt towards this good man. I desperately wanted to prove worthy of his trust in me and absolutely did *not* want to let him down. It was a turning point in my career.

Now, the challenge—test this from your own experience. Think of a person in your business career that extended trust to you, gave you the benefit of the doubt, or maybe believed in you even more than you believed in yourself. In our work, we often ask business leaders and executives around the world to reflect on their lives or careers and to identify a time when someone took a chance on them. Whenever we do this, without exception, the feeling in the room changes. People become deeply touched and inspired as they recall these experiences and acknowledge with gratitude the impact the experiences had on their lives. And they become even more inspired when we invite them to share, and they "take in" each other's experiences.

We encourage you to take a minute now and do the same thing. Think of someone who extended trust to you. Who was it? What was the situation? What difference has it made in your life?

A second challenge is to look for opportunities to increase your propensity to extend trust to someone. Smart Trust that is; don't suspend your analysis, just subordinate it more than usual to the possibility that they might respond like *you* did. Remember the words of Albert Schweitzer, *"In everybody's life, at some time, our inner fire goes out. It is then burst into flame by an encounter with another human being. We should all be thankful for those people who rekindle the inner spirit."*

ACKNOWLEDGMENTS

"Greg Link is my 'make it happen' friend and affirming creative genius. He was crucially instrumental in the success of my book, *The 7 Habits of Highly Effective People*, and the Covey Leadership Center."

-Dr. Stephen R. Covey

"Greg Link delivered his keynote presentation with confidence and enthusiasm and engaged the audience. Greg had our audience laughing, while also providing them with information they could take back and put into practice immediately at their own organizations. His keynote on 'Leading at the Speed of Trust' shares the importance of how to take an organization to the next level by cultivating trust. It was a compelling presentation, not just because the content was excellent but because Greg is an excellent presenter. If you want your conference to be a success, hire Greg Link!"

-Catherine Upton, Group Publisher/CEO, Elearning! Media Group

"My team is a different team. If you ask the people in PepsiCo when they come down here to visit Frito Lay, they'll say something's changed. It's the Speed of Trust. It's the most exciting change in the culture I've seen in the 28 years I've been at PepsiCo, most of which were at Frito Lay. They'll say there's a buzz in this building. And I think they'd say the team works as a team better than they've ever seen before."

-Al Carey, CEO, Frito Lay

"The SPEED of Trust is red-hot relevant."

-William G. Parrett, CEO, Deloitte Touche Tohmatsu

About Greg

Greg Link is co-founder of the former Covey Leadership Center, CoveyLink, and The Global Speed of Trust Practice, a fast-growing global consultancy committed to influencing influencers to grow their careers and their organizations at The Speed of Trust.

A recognized authority on leadership, trust, sales, marketing, and high performance, Link is a sought-after advisor and speaker. His authentic and engaging style endears him to audiences at all levels – from senior executives to the front lines. He is a "business expert who speaks" not a "speaker that theorizes."

Link, his business partner Stephen M. R. Covey, and the team at The Speed of Trust Practice equip people and organizations to transform toxic relationships, teams, and organizational cultures and to harness high trust as a performance multiplier. Link convincingly challenges the age-old assumption that trust is merely a soft, social virtue and demonstrates that trust is a hard-edged, economic driver—a learnable and measurable skill that makes organizations more profitable, people more promotable, and relationships more energizing.

As co-founder of the Covey Leadership Center, he orchestrated the strategy that led Dr. Stephen R. Covey's book, *The 7 Habits of Highly Effective People*, to one of the two bestselling business books of the 20th century according to CEO Magazine, selling over 20 million copies in 38 languages. He created the marketing momentum that helped propel Covey Leadership Center from a start-up company to a $110+ million-dollar enterprise with offices in 40 countries before merging with Franklin Quest to form FranklinCovey.

He also led the Center's international publishing success resulting in partnerships with over 30 publishers worldwide. This included making publishing history in Japan, leading the strategy that sold over one million copies of a foreign language translation, non-fiction business book, *The 7 Habits of Highly Effective People*, in Japanese. He was also instrumental in formulating and executing one of the world's largest international business satellite broadcasts with partners Lessons in Leadership and *Fortune Magazine*.

Link has taught The Seven Habits, Principle Centered Leadership, and The Speed of Trust and advised executives at numerous leading enterprises, including Hewlett Packard, the U.S. Navy, Sony, Chevron, IBM, Microsoft, Boeing, and many other well-known organizations. He is a trusted confidant.

His business acumen and experience as a successful, real-world executive inform his presentations and make them uniquely relevant to clients and convention audiences alike. Link and business partner Stephen M. R. Covey are currently co-authoring a new book titled *Smart Trust: Creating Prosperity, Energy and Joy in a Low-Trust World* to be published in January 2012.

Link resides with his wife, Annie, on a quiet stream in the shadows of the Utah Rockies in Alpine, Utah.

CHAPTER 31

PATTERNS OF SUCCESS
A Guide for Mapping Your Success Blueprint

By Karl R. Wolfe

Are you just starting your career? Are you a business professional who wants to accelerate your performance, double, triple or add a zero to your income? Do you want to get your career on track? Well, you are about to learn a foolproof method to do that. You may have noticed that any complex system begins with either a blueprint, a schematic, or a map. A design and specification is necessary before construction of the project begins. It's the same in life: you need a vision, a blueprint or a map. You need to know where you are and where you're going before you start anything. And then you take action and implement! Action is the bridge to success.

I've always been curious by nature. At two, I began taking apart everything I could find – clocks, motors, toys, appliances, bugs, …you name it. At first, I had loads of parts left over, and a few dead bugs. Eventually, I understood system design, the relationship of diverse components, and reverse engineering. Soon, I learned to reassemble everything I had taken apart - except the bugs!

By the age of seven, I felt anything was possible. I spent hours in the basement designing and building complex electronic systems from obscure parts. Every failure (and there were hundreds) – was an opportunity for another solution. It was a constant correct-and-continue. As soon as I discovered something that worked, I implemented it in every area of my life, as fast as I could. Taking immediate action became fun!

I never gave up and I got results.

Whatever my vision, it became real in the world. If I wanted something, I didn't wait for permission or someone else to do it - I took action and made it happen.

Fast-forward a few years. Visualize 16 years old, à la-*American Graffiti*, summer of 1962. I was as a carhop at the A&W Root Beer drive-in restaurant. On breaks, while my co-workers were paralyzed by whining and complaining, I asked about the business: *"Could I cook the burgers? ...How do you make the root beer? ...May I clean the grill? ...Is it okay if I wash the dishes?"* When I learned something new that made things easier, I immediately implemented it in my life. Each carhop had a spike, their orders stacked for tallying at the end of the night. Mine always had two or three times more than anyone else. This wasn't about competing – it was about *speed of implementation*. While others dithered, I took action, had fun, enjoyed the customers, the conversations, and gave great service! I loved the results, the relationships and the adding of value to every interaction.

One day the owner of the restaurant said, "Karl, how would you like to run an A&W?" He was serious! He saw what my father had seen when I was young: that there was a certain way of taking action and being in the world. I was unstoppable, filled with passion for anything and everything. As a result, at the end of summer, when my boss wanted to go off to Australia to open another shop, for some reason he wanted *me* to run his business, at 16.

When I left home at seventeen, I effectively had 14 years of electrical engineering and problem-solving experience under my belt. And a pattern of success that just kept repeating and getting better as my life unfolded. No matter what I did, I ended up running things. It happened when I was in the Air Force. At the age of 28 that attitude of action and curiosity led me to running a company with 2000 employees. When I first walked in the door, I dressed and felt like I owned the business. I immediately began identifying and solving problems with an attitude of immediate action that saved the company $80,000 in the first month. Two months later, management doubled my salary. Three months later, they doubled it again and gave me the responsibility for running the company on the evening shift. What an amazing training experience that was.

Two years later, all those who called me *smart ass* and *hot shot* ended up working for me. As I took on more and more responsibility, my life became easier and easier, because for me this was a big technological playground – an extension of my childhood in the basement. I could barely wait for the next day. I was having a blast, while most everyone else was busy trying to avoid work.

Running a company with 2000 employees at the age of 28 is not an accident. At an early age, I chose this path. I was on a mission with a connection to an inner map: always a dream, a vision, always picturing myself as an electronics engineer running a large company. The 'feeling' and the 'knowing' of that picture was always alive within. It was like a taste or smell I was always in touch with. It was always there.

Without realizing it, I had learned to solve diverse technical problems while creating internal blue prints that allowed me to build devices of ever-greater complexity. I found that these internal maps were consistent and transportable from situation to situation, allowing me to build one success upon another. It was soon clear that these pattern- making skills were applicable to solving any problem.

And, most important, I learned self-respect and self-trust. My parents gave me an amazing gift: the opportunity to experience freedom, failure, success, responsibility, and how to deal with it all.

It became clear that what you focus on becomes reality. There are no victims. We create our reality from moment to moment. If you are waiting for things to get better or someone to do it for you, you will always be waiting and wanting. Only that which changes and grows, lives.

DEVELOP YOUR OWN SUCCESS PATTERNS

1. See every failure as an opportunity for another solution. If something does not work, try another solution. Simply correct and continue.

2. Be unstoppable.

3. If you want something, take action. Don't wait for permission or for someone else to do it for you.

4. Implement immediately. *You* make it happen.

5. Create relationships and add value to every interaction.

6. Always be curious.

7. Identify and connect with your inner map, blueprint and vision. Know, feel and live your dream and vision.

8. Find a way to make everything you do *fun*.

CREATE A MAP FOR YOUR LIFE

How you do anything is how you do everything. I have watched hundreds of clients, no matter their level of income, follow these map-making instructions. Some begin to double, triple or add zeros to their income – *within days*.

How you approach this is how you do everything. Will you let it be easy? If you're lying to yourself about where you are, nothing will change. If you have no sense of your starting point you cannot reach your destination. If you don't know where you want to go, you'll wander aimlessly through life. We make up our lives from moment to moment from an unseen mythic structure. Your thoughts produce a matching reality in every situation, whether you are aware of what you're thinking or not! The universe is completely unemotional. It will give you exactly what you ask for.

Begin your map-making with an empty circle on a blank page. In the emptiness awaits all possibility. This map is an energy blueprint for your life. You may download a blank map and full instructions at: www.karlrwolfe.com/map/map.pdf

1. On a line at the top write your name.

2. Then where one o'clock would appear on the face of a clock, place your present age.

3. At two o'clock write *one week*.

4. At three o'clock write *one month*.

5. At four o'clock write *one year*.

6. At five o'clock write *two years*.

7. At six o'clock write *five years*.

8. At seven o'clock write ten years and fill in the rest of the numbers up until eleven o'clock

9. At eleven o'clock, put down the maximum age that you would like to attain, plus a few years for an extra measure of quality life.

For each daily, weekly, monthly or yearly increment, make an entry relating to each of the five areas below. When completed, this circle is an energy-mapping tool for your conscious and unconscious mind, a blue print from which to begin creating your future. As you read the questions below, give yourself permission to visualize the ideal for each. Release all sense of limitation and imagine that you can have whatever you choose.

This is the big secret: if you do not know what you want, just make it up. That is what creative people do. They live as if they were already there, …in the vision. Then, as if by magic, the vision begins to show up. This isn't about believing. A belief is a fantasy, a form of addiction, a longing or desire. Usually what you believe isn't true. When you desire something, energetically you push it away. A belief is external, in the future, while a choice is an internal experience in the now. Choice is an action that manages energy; you only need to make this choice once, and then let the feeling run all the time in the background. Once you are open to outcome – rather than attached to it, things begin to show up.

Choice is more than a belief. You make a choice and then take immediate supporting action. Pay attention to the results you get, because - unconscious mythic structures may invisibly misdirect the energy and your outcome. If the results you get vary from the choice, make corrections in your actions until the outcome matches the choice. Creative people see any mismatch as an opportunity for self-inquiry and refining the action. Without hesitation they make a correction and make another choice.

MAKE MONEY DOING WHAT YOU LOVE

What you love to do will ultimately make money for you. Let go of all the stories that bind you to your past. Stories that limit and hinder – *I'm too old or I don't have the right education* – whatever! Just let it all go. If you don't know you have limitations, you won't have any! You have nothing to lose and everything to gain. Every time you write something on the map, listen inside for any negative voice that is shouting you down. Acknowledge the voice, thank it for sharing, release the story and make your new choice.

The negative voice is an automatic choice, a survival strategy from your past, a mythic structure that is trying to help. However, the negative voice of the mythic structure blocks forward progress. That is its purpose: *to keep you safe and limited.* Thank the negative voice and move on.

If there were no limitations and you could walk out the door tomorrow – to a new life, what would you choose? What was it that you used to do as a child – where you lost all sense of time? *This is where your true passion lives.* What do you really have passion for that you ignore?

Below are examples of questions to ask yourself to help focus your vision more clearly. If there are other questions – which come to mind, use those as well. For each of these questions, take a look at what you would like to achieve in the next week, month, year, five years, ten years etc., … *as if there were no limitations,* and then enter that on your life map.

1. What level of income do you choose for the next month, the next year? In five years? In ten years?

2. What living conditions would you like? A new apartment? A new house? A new location? Include how much you'll pay for the apartment or house. Where it is located? Visualize a similar house and when you will purchase the house.

3. What about your relationships with friends, family, lovers? What would each relationship look like?

4. What about your career, your business, your job? What does it look like in one year, two years, three years, when, where, how much? Take a moment and go inside to check this all out.

Whenever you make a new choice, you create, sustain or release a mythic structure. Commit it to writing. This helps focus and bring what otherwise might be mythic fantasy into reality. Begin to feel the possibility in your body. Listen inside for all the mythic stories of what you need to have, do or be, …first – before you can have what you choose. Acknowledge and face this inner dialogue. Go to the center of each voice and feeling and penetrate them, and watch as the power of the story dissolves its hold. The energy released when you penetrate the story is the natural resource from which you create the new vision.

Desire and wanting actually push what you want away from you. You can desire something, long for it, and it will not manifest until you choose it and allow yourself to become the *energetic experience* of the choice. Begin living in your vision as if it has already happened, as if it is the experience that it is already manifest and present in your life. Step into it now, in the present moment. Taste, feel, smell, and become your vision.

Allow yourself to project into the future to see what it feels like to be living in your vision. If you like what you feel, then choose it and write it down – add it to the map. If you are uncomfortable with or unable to accept the outcome of the new place, this will block the flow of energy. If you can see yourself and feel comfortable in the experience, in the future, then the energy is free to create the vision.

Refer back to the map on a regular basis. Feel free to change your mind and update the map at any time. The key is to make choices. You can always make another choice, if you find you don't like where you are going. It is easy to make a correction in your course. If it does not feel like the right direction, just change the map.

Years from now, when you look back at this map, you will be astounded at how fast some things happened. You will see that the choices you held in fantasy did not happen because on some level, they were beliefs rather than choices; you did not really *feel* they were possible. *You* have all the power. Just choose!

Your mind is your personal Google for vision and goals. Get clear on what you want, and your mind produces the result. If you don't know it's impossible, then it's possible. Almost everything you see around you was once considered impossible.

About Karl

Karl R. Wolfe mentors Executives and projects in every industry including top studios such as Warner Brothers, MGM, Paramount, Universal, the major Television Networks, also, record companies and their recording artists such as DreamWorks, Sony, Michael Jackson Productions and major law firms and medical institutions.

Karl was Manager of Engineering with a subsidiary of the Atlantic Richfield Company in New York, administering an annual capital budget of more than $300 million. He then accepted the position of Director of Marketing and Design, with a high technology company in San Francisco; specializing in Industrial Automation. Then with more than $500 Million in successful design projects completed; he established a Counseling and Consulting practice in San Francisco, where he also lectured and was research associate in the Graduate School for the Study of Human Consciousness, at John F. Kennedy University, in Orinda, California. With more than 30 patents, his accomplishments brought honorable mention in *Who's Who* in Technology and many other publications. Several other *Who's Who* publications document more recent achievements as Creative Consultant and Mentor.

Karl uncovers the one thing that prevents you form achieving everything you want in life. He developed a video technology that helps everyone see the invisible and unconscious narratives and myths that hold them back and at the same time, what works. The diagnostic process is equivalent to 5 or 10 years of traditional therapy, it is illuminating, revealing, unusual, enjoyable and it works. In less than two hours, the client sees how their inner conflicts inhibit their ability to manifest their vision. A step beyond therapy, this process is known for getting immediate, practical and ongoing results. Often within, in a few days, everything changes for the better.

His process has been mentioned in *Vanity Fair, Newsweek* and *Time*. Barbara Walters, with ABC's 20/20 and the Oprah Winfrey Show featured these seminars and how they transform his clients' lives from average to outstanding. Dr. Stanley Krippner documents Karl's work in the recent book, *Spiritual Dimensions of Healing;* first published in German and more recently in English. The book chronicles the practices of ten practitioners in North America; from native healers to contemporary health care providers.

Karl edited the recent best sellers: *The Lazy Man's Way to Riches*, by Joe Karbo, revised and expanded by Richard G. Nixon, and the companion workbook *Roadmap to Riches*, by Richard G. Nixon, which has now sold more than 4.2 million copies. He is currently finishing two new books dealing with the topics of personal growth and organizational transformation: *Millionaire Body-Millionaire Mind-How to Get Everything in Your Life Moving* and *Fingers Pointing at the Moon— A Journey to the Authentic-Self.*

As Creative Consultant to United Paramount Television Network News KCOP TV 13, in Los Angeles, and as Consulting Producer and Creative Consultant, he developed an award-winning and highly rated series of Feature News, Science and Technology Documentaries.

Visit the website: www.truesilence.com to take that next big step, find out more about consultations and seminars, to read articles, and receive his recent eBook. Or you may call 888-296-0084.

CHAPTER 32

How to Make Millions as an Info-Preneur

By Robert G. Allen

You have probably thought "I know what I know" to yourself many times in your life. We chalk things up to experience and use them to guide our future moves. Sometimes those experiences become the advice we give others but, more times than not, we keep that information to ourselves.

It's time to pull out that information YOU know and dust it off. Then, put it on the market. What you know is worth millions!

I call it Info-Preneuring!

An info-preneur is an entrepreneur who sells information. It is truly the most exciting business in the world. And . . . if you do this business right, within a few months, total strangers will be sending you money for your ideas. This will happen even if you think your ideas are worthless! I will show you how Your Ideas Are Profit Empires!

Why do I think I can teach you to become a profitable info-preneur? Because since the 1980's I have written TEN best-selling books about what I know, and have further taught seminars nationwide on the subjects of real estate and creating wealth – the subjects I know best!

In case you haven't noticed, the world is experiencing an information explosion. The majority of the households in North American have access to hundreds of channels of interactive television – giving every customer instant, unlimited access to information, communications, and entertainment. In addition, there are soon to be billions of computer screens hooked up to the net — yours included. The Internet is exploding. People are communicating and sharing information like never before.

Who is going to provide all of the programming for the 500 channels, the on-line databases, and the hungry airwaves? You are! You are the source of the ideas, information, data, and entertainment to fill the voracious appetite of millions of info-maniacs.

PROFIT FROM THE SHIFT FROM THE INFORMATION AGE TO THE COMMUNICATION AGE

The serious money in the future will not be made from information alone – we are already information drunk; we are bombarded with information all day. The problem is not a lack of information or ideas but a lack of information that is packaged properly. Your job in the future is to convert the mountains of raw data into specialized knowledge presented in a way the consumer can assimilate and use quickly.

Time is the currency of this new millennium. Time is our most valuable asset. Since all of us are already on information overload, with too much information to absorb and too little time to absorb it, we all will be looking for information that is "time friendly."

We don't want to waste valuable time to reorganize general data to fit our unique circumstances and problems. We'll want information we can use NOW that is fast and easy. Your information must be simple and easy to use and must provide fast results. Your advertising should emphasize this.

BE WELL-INFORMED IN THE AGE OF INFORMATION "HAVES AND HAVE-NOTS"

Information is coming at us rapid-fire and at point blank range. We'll need to react in lightening quick time. Those who react slowly will find themselves amongst the "information have-nots."

To be prepared to understand how to deliver your information the fastest and easiest way, you must be technologically up to speed or you will be left in the dust. The information business is moving at Mach 2. If you're not computer literate, if your employees are not computer literate, you're missing the boat.

HOW TO TURN YOUR EXPERTISE AND PASSION (YOUR HOBBY OR FAVORITE PAST-TIME) INTO LIFETIME STREAMS OF CASH FLOW

With all the talk about the billions being spent on this information super highway, you might be a little bit intimidated. How can you compete with the big boys and girls; how can you sell your ideas, your life's expertise in the face of the media moguls? Anyone with a good idea, persistence, and some savvy can make millions selling information. You don't need a six-figure advertising budget and the staff to spend it!

What you really need is an interesting story, an expertise that people want, and a powerful marketing plan. It is my belief that everyone – including you – has at least one good book idea floating around in his or her head. By the end of this chapter I think you will realize that you have enough information and expertise inside your head right now to turn into a lifetime stream of income. You have a book in you that is waiting to be released. With some proper positioning, your book can become the cornerstone of an information empire!

Need proof?

Let me tell you the story of Walter Swann from Arizona. A few years ago he wrote a book about growing up in Arizona with his brother Henry. He called his book, *Me and Henry*. Sounds like a moneymaking title, doesn't it? However, no publisher would publish it. So, he published it himself. No bookstore would buy it. So he opened his own bookstore. His bookstore was unique: It carried only one title — that's right —*Me and Henry*. He called it the One Book, Book Store. The only book you could buy in his bookstore was *Me and Henry*. Dumb idea right? Wrong.

He sold tens of thousands of books worldwide. And he made thousands of dollars a month from this one simple idea. In fact, his business was so good that he wrote another book. This one was called, *Me and Mama*. It was also for sale in a special room in the One Book, Book Store. It's called the Other Book, Book Store. He became such a hit that David Letterman invited him on his show. What I want you to realize is that you, your life story or your life's expertise have market value. It may have enough market value to support you for life.

YOU CAN TURN YOUR LIFE STORY INTO MONEY EVEN IF YOU'RE A MISERABLE FAILURE

Nearly all success books start off with a miserable failure. The author tells how he or she used to be too fat, too thin, too poor, too ugly, too lonely, too unhappy, too addicted and through some miracle, will- power, or newfound knowledge, they were able to overcome failure and rise to newfound heights of success.

Let me give you some pretty impressive examples:

Author	Title	Subject
Tony Robbins	*Unlimited Power*	Success
Susan Powter	*Stop the Insanity*	Diet
John Bradshaw	*Homeward Bound*	Self-esteem

And the list goes on and on. Each of these info-preneurs used the story of their rise from the ashes of failure to create an information empire. Each of them now produces books, seminars, newsletters, tape programs, video courses, speeches, consulting relationships, and infomercials. They turned their failure-to-success story into millions of dollars.

Everything that has happened to you, good or bad, has cash value.

Do you ever wonder how those famous stars on those diet commercials are able to take the weight off and keep it off? How do they do it? Where do they get the will power to lose all that weight and keep it off?

Think! If someone offered you a half-a-million dollars to do a diet commercial, wouldn't you be able to find the motivation somehow? Now take this to the next logical conclusion. What if someone offered you ten-million dollars to turn your life around right now? How much would it take for you to be motivated to perfect your relationships, to get in shape, to get your financial act together, to be a top salesperson, etc.? What if you decided that YOU ARE THE BEFORE AND AFTER STORY? Fix yourself, then you, too, can market the new-found "know how."

You don't even need a unique, new system. It can be old knowledge, repackaged and remarketed in new ways. Look at all the diets out there. There are only three variables in the diet game: food, exercise and mental attitude.

Several years ago, Susan Powter, in her hugely successful diet infomercial and book, *"Stop the Insanity!"* didn't teach anything new. She taught old stuff in a unique way. And MADE TENS OF MILLIONS OF DOLLARS DOING IT!

The formula is pretty simple:

- Identify a Core Human Desire/Need
- Find new technology for solving this Core Desire/Need
- Find a new way to market to this Core Desire/Need

Once you have indentified these things, the sky's the limit to your fortune. You simply need to work your info-preneur business from the inside out – think of this as a series of concentric circles.

FIVE RINGS OF RICHES: THE VAST OPPORTUNITIES THAT AWAIT ALL INFO-PRENEURS

One of the least understood concepts, even by successful info-preneurs, is how vast the opportunities are for making money from just one good idea. I'll explain this to you by teaching you what I call the Five Rings of Information Riches.

Ring One: Succeeding in your core expertise

You must have a core expertise that is either a revolutionary new technology or is an old expertise that has a new marketing strategy. My core expertise was real estate investing. I became very good at it, therefore, I could teach it to others. You don't have to be the expert yourself, but you do need to borrow, license or acquire the expertise from someone. You are looking for an expertise with a hungry marketplace, in other words, think of your market as a school of fish.

Does your market contain enough fish?

Is it a growing or declining school of fish?

Is it easy to find where they are and what their feeding pattern is?

Are they really hungry?

Is the weather/climate cooperating for ideal fishing conditions?

Is there certain bait that makes them "bite like crazy?"

Are they willing to come out of the safe, dark depths of the bottom to fight for this new bait?

Once you have identified your market and your expertise, then you must begin to "crack the code" as to how to offer your expertise in such a way that the fish rise to bite.

Ring Two: teaching others know-how to succeed in your core expertise

First, I made money by investing in real estate (Ring One) then; I taught others how to succeed in real estate just like me (RingTwo). There are about twenty ways to sell this Ring Two information. In other words, there are twenty separate $100,000 + a year businesses that result from having cracked the code.

Some of the successful businesses that grow from your core expertise are: Author, Desktop publisher, seminar promoter, public speaker, newsletter editor, personal consultant, freelance writer, calendar creator, and online expert. Most successful info-preneurs have only tapped into a few of the above businesses. They are leaving millions of dollars on the table. Once they see the big picture, they are more able to capitalize on the opportunities around them. Then they are ready to expand into the third concentric circle, or what I call, the Third Ring.

Ring Three: Using your specific experience to teach general success skills in your market place.

For example, one of the greatest salesmen in the world, Zig Ziglar, honed his sales skills selling pots and pans. But there wasn't a large and growing market of hungry pots and pans salespeople to market his expertise to. Therefore, he became a general expert in the broad field of sales training. He went from specific expertise to general expertise and made millions of dollars.

There are literally thousands of successful Third Ring info-preneurs nationwide. Harvey MacKay (with his best-selling book, *How to swim with the Sharks* and a host of other books) is one example. He made his fortune in the envelope business in Minnesota. What do envelopes have to do with you?

Nothing.

But he claims that his great success in the envelope business has given him the right to teach us all kinds of general success principles in the areas of sales, management, and positive attitude. And he makes millions turning his specific "know how" into general how-to information.

Ring Four: Marketing other products to your database

Once you have attracted a growing satisfied customer database, you may approach your database with other products and services. For example, my original database is comprised of people who have attended my real estate and wealth creation seminars. But in reality these people are entrepreneurs who like to explore other moneymaking opportunities. I can mine money from my database by pursuing four separate routes – mailing list rental, lead generator for other businesses, joint venture partner or direct marketer.

Ring Five: Support services for info-preneurs in the other four rings

At the outer edge of the five concentric circles is Ring Five. Some info-preneurs don't service the general market. They focus on other info-preneurs. Once you get good at marketing information, building databases, taking care of your customers, and the like, you may also wish to share your new expertise with other info-preneurs.

If you were an especially gifted copywriter, you may want to hire out your copywriting services to other info-preneurs. You see, whatever your experience in life, there is always a market for it. So keep all your ads, your tracking procedures, keep everything that relates to creating your successful business. Eventually, you may want to use it again in teaching others how to do what you did.

Whether you're selling widgets or information, you must create a relationship with your clients whereby they feel that you are their ultimate source for everything they want in life. If you are in the information business, proclaim yourself as their information source – as their data detective. You can follow your customers for life and refine and adapt your database to their changing lifestyle needs.

But you cannot start earning customers' trust and business until you have packaged your information to share. So get writing! Write 1000 words today! That is my mantra. I have calculated that whenever I write a word on a page, I eventually make $20 per word. As an info-preneur, everytime I share a word of knowledge, I make money. Your book will be a lead generator for the many other avenues of income in the Five Circles we talked about.

So, why are you still reading? Get out there and figure out what information or which of your life experiences are valuable. Write that book you have trapped inside of you. Unleash your inner INFO-PRENEUR!

About Robert

Robert Allen's colossal best-seller *Nothing Down* established **Robert Allen** as one of the most influential investment advisors of all time. **Robert Allen** has followed that success with several other best-selling books including *Creating Wealth, Multiple Streams of Income* and *The One Minute Millionaire*; as well as the audiocassette programs *"The Road to Wealth"* and *"Multiple Streams of Income"* from Nightingale-Conant.

A popular talk-show guest, **Robert Allen** has appeared on dozens of programs, including "Good Morning America" and "Larry King." **Robert Allen** has also been featured in the *Wall Street Journal, Newsweek, Barron's, Money Magazine*, and *Reader's Digest*.

Thousands of people have attended **Robert Allen's** cutting edge investment seminars during the past 20 years!

And now he wants to work with you. But he can only help you if you will let him.

Please enjoy his website and don't forget the two most important steps to YOUR success.

1. Remember To Register For His FREE Webinar at: www.robertallen.com.

2. Remember To Join His FREE Newsletter and

3. Remember To Check Out His Free Special Reports

CHAPTER 33

Discovering Your Unique Contribution

By Janet Bray Attwood and Chris Attwood

Money and profits.

That's what business is all about right?

Of course, read any management book and it'll tell you that profits are a by-product of providing value.

But money's siren song is too hard to resist—for most people and most companies.

In the decades leading up to the crash of 2008, money became the predominant decision-making tool for both most people and most companies. That's why Harris Interactive found that only 20% of working Americans were passionate about what they were doing in 2005. That's why 45% of Harvard business grads chose finance as a career in 2008 (MBA Recruiting – Data and Statistics, 2010) compared to 5% in 1970 (Gudras, 2008).

In the years leading up to 2008, we saw the creation of more, new and "better" ways to make money in the financial sector. From leveraged buy-outs, to subprime mortgages, to mortgage-backed securities to the aggregation of those securities, global financial institutions built a house of cards. Unfortunately, money-based decisions are not sustainable.

It doesn't matter if you're an individual or a global conglomerate, if your primary basis for decision-making is how much money will it make, sooner or later collapse is inevitable. Money is a marker, a scorecard, measuring the amount of value you are providing to others. It just doesn't work as a decision-making tool.

PERCEIVED VALUE VS. REAL VALUE

There are two kinds of value. Perceived value and real value. Real value serves others in living fuller, richer, more fulfilling lives. Perceived value is the appearance of serving others. Providing great perceived value may generate lots of money in the short run, but sooner or later, perceived value alone will result in collapse.

Want an example? Bernie Madoff. Great perceived value. He promised, and appeared to deliver, above average returns. But there was no underlying value to his offer. Eventually, his house of cards collapsed.

Lehman Brothers and Merrill Lynch and other companies that were struck by the foreclosure tidal waves in 2006, 2007 and 2008, were providing real value in some parts of their business, but when the gap between perceived value and real value becomes too great, even long-standing institutions will collapse. Bad loans lack real value. Securities backed by bad loans magnify that lack of value. Like a "hot potato," the last one holding those financial instruments loses. Not unlike Bernie's scenario.

On the other hand, real value without perceived value serves no one. To a man who has no idea of its value, the diamond in his backpack is simply a heavy rock he has to lug around.

The true task of business is to:

1) Discover the real, unique contribution it has the ability to deliver to the world;

2) Find the ways and means to help others perceive the value of that contribution; and

3) Deliver that value to raise the quality of life, both for those who purchase its products and services, and in its community, nation and the world as a whole.

DISCOVERING YOUR UNIQUE CONTRIBUTION

Passion-based decisions are sustainable decisions. For individuals, those decisions lead to uncovering the purpose of your life, the unique value you have to provide to those around you. For businesses, passion-based decisions are the secret key to lasting success.

Your passions are the things you love and care about most. They are the things that matter most to you in your life. When you are connected to your passions, you feel passionate, turned on, excited and lit up. You'll do whatever it takes to follow that passion. When you feel miserable or unhappy, or just without any motivation, it's because you are disconnected from your passions. You feel disconnected from the things you care most about. The purpose of The Passion Test is to help you identify your passions because those will lead you naturally and inevitably to discovering your Unique Contribution.

Years ago, Janet was invited to join a company that recruited disk drive engineers in Silicon Valley. The owners of the company were friends who had made millions of dollars in this business.

After watching them driving around in their Mercedes' and Jaguars, they approached her and said, "Janet, you're so good at connecting with people, we want you to join our company. You'll be able to make *millions* of dollars." What do you think Janet heard? That's right, "*millions of dollars.*" She didn't stop for a moment to think about whether this work was something she was passionate about. She was just thinking about all the things she could do with those millions.

Janet started her new job with great enthusiasm, but it wasn't long before she realized that disk drive engineers were very left-brain thinkers and she was not. There was a bell in the office that the recruiters would ring whenever they made a placement. That bell rang many times a day, but never for Janet. As the weeks dragged on, Janet found her work becoming more and more trying. She had to drag herself into work every day.

Finally, when she saw a poster advertising a seminar called, *Yes to Success,* she said, "That's what I need!" On the appointed day, she called in sick and made the hour drive to the seminar. Taking her seat in the front row, she wasn't sure what to expect. When the seminar leader came out, Janet was blown away by the poise, the wisdom and the power of this woman.

All could she think was, "That's what I want!!"

It was during that seminar, The Passion Test was born. The seminar leader explained that in a study of the most successful people in America, the one thing they all had in common was that they were living the five things they considered to be most important. Immediately, light bulbs went off in Janet's head.

She thought, "If I can just get clear on the five things that are most important to me, that will be the first step in creating my own success."

At the same time, Janet was consumed with the desire to become a speaker like the woman leading the seminar. "How can I convince her to teach me?" Janet thought. When the seminar leader asked if anyone would like to give her a ride to the airport, Janet practically leaped out of her seat to volunteer.

On the way to the airport, all she could think of was, "How can I get this woman to teach me?" Finally, when they arrived at the gate, the seminar leader turned to Janet and asked, "What's your dream?"

Janet knew this was her chance, but what popped out of her mouth was, "I'm going to be a top transformational speaker, so you better hire me, or move over because I'll become your next competition!" Right at that moment, they called the speaker's plane, she gave Janet a hug, and she was gone.

All the way home, Janet was groaning. "How could I have blown it so badly?" But she had discovered her passion and nothing was going to stop her. She created a plan to travel from city to city following this speaker to each of her events, thinking, "Sooner or later, she'll just HAVE to hire me."

That evening, Janet went to her local meditation center for group meditation. Afterwards one of her friends asked her what was new. "What's new?!! Let me tell you …" and Janet laid out her plan. She told her friend, "The only thing I haven't figured out is how to get the money for the travel since right now I'm minus money."

The next day, Janet again went to the meditation center and while she was sitting with her eyes closed, she felt paper falling on her head. She opened her eyes and there was her friend, dropping $100 bills on her head, laughing and saying, "Merry Christmas! Go live your dream."

After thanking her profusely, Janet made the arrangements and was soon sitting in the front row of the *Yes to Success* seminar in New York, then in Boston, then Chicago, and then Iowa. In each location, the seminar leader looked at her with a quizzical expression on her face. Finally, in Los Angeles, when the speaker came in and again saw Janet sitting in the front row, she said, "Alright already, you're hired!"

Of course, today Janet is a celebrated transformational leader, with a New York Times bestselling book and having shared the stage with people like the Dalai Lama, Sir Richard Branson, Stephen R. Covey, Nobel Peace Prize winner F. W. de Klerk, Tony Hsieh, CEO of Zappos.com, Jack Canfield, and many others.

But it all started when she chose in favor of her passions... as scary as it was.

PASSION AND WORK

Your work passions are the things you love to do and get paid for. They are the things about your work that matter most, the things about your work you care most deeply about. They are the things that make work fun, exciting and engaging. Your passions will inevitably lead you to the ways you can serve others and serve yourself at the same time.

As our friend Steve Farber, author of *The Radical Leap*, says, fulfillment in work comes from... *"Doing what you love, serving people who love what you do."* Yes, it's time for love to take its place as the essential element of business success.

One of the most common questions we hear is, "How do I make a living following my passions?" There are a number of false beliefs embedded in this question. First and foremost among them is that whatever you are doing right now to make a living is not connected to your passions. This couldn't be farther from the truth. Every moment in your life is purposeful. Every experience you have is for the purpose of helping you connect more deeply with who you are and why you are here.

As we said in *The Passion Test: Every moment is a gift, when you are open to what is appearing now.*

Whatever work you are doing right now, that work is the stepping-stone to the fulfillment of your passions. Want to start living your passions immediately?

Here are the steps:

Step #1: Complete The Passion Test process to discover your top five Work Passions: (www.thepassiontest.com).

Step #2: Share your Work Passions with your current employer so they know what will make you a happy, engaged, committed employee.

Step #3: Do the very best you possibly can at your current job. This job is your stepping-stone to the next opportunity along your journey. When you do this job well, you will attract new opportunities like bees to honey. You will also gain the appreciation and gratitude of your current boss or employer so they will want to recommend you for your next position.

Step #4: Be open to new opportunities that are aligned with your passions. But passion alone is not enough to create financial success. You have to be able to fulfill a need that others are willing to pay for.

Fundamentally, every single one of us is here to serve the rest of us. That's our purpose, in the biggest sense. We serve others by providing them with products or services they find valuable.

The key to your fulfillment, and the secret to creating wealth for yourself, involves combining three elements to serve a need that others are willing to pay for:

- **Passion** – While not sufficient by itself, it is the foundation and essential element to create an income that brings joy.

- **Skills** – These are the things that you do well as a result of your training or education.

- **Talents** – These are the things that come easily to you, that others find difficult. If you don't know what your talents are, pay attention when someone says something is difficult, yet to you it's a piece of cake. Often our talents come so effortlessly and naturally to us that we don't even realize they are talents. We assume it's as easy for everyone as it is for us.

Because we all enjoy doing things we do well, many people get jobs that use their skills and talents. Unfortunately, sometimes we discover later in life that the things we studied were not the things we are passionate about.

Years ago, Chris took a position selling consulting and training services to Fortune 500 companies. Chris had gotten an MBA and he has a natural talent for communication, both speaking and writing. His new job required both. As a result, he enjoyed his work—for the first eighteen months. He performed well and became one of the top producers at his company.

But there came a point when Chris had mastered his job. It was no longer a challenge, and while he was good at it, it didn't light him up. While the work he was doing fulfilled a useful need for companies, and he was paid well for his part in fulfilling that need, the work was not connected to things he was passionate about, so eventually he left that job.

Companies that don't make sure their employees are doing work that connects them to their Work Passions, will see their staff leaving as well. Sometimes companies can inspire a sense of purpose among their employees by creating a shared purpose that allows the company's team to connect with something deeper and more meaningful.

That's what Peggy Pelosi did when she was brought on as VP of Network Management for USANA Health Sciences, a nutriceutical company. Peggy introduced one single new element that profoundly changed the company's results. She created a partnership with the Children's Hunger Fund that created a new sense of purpose, engaging the passion of the company's staff to provide nutrition to children in developing countries.

Within three years the company's sales had increased so dramatically that its share price rose from $1.70 per share to over $70.00 per share, a 3000% increase. At the same time, the company's distributors began supporting the Children's Hunger Fund with their own donations, $120,000 in the first year to over $1.2 million after three years. Company staff traveled with the CEO to visit orphanages benefitting from the company's contributions, saw directly the impact they were making and reported it to the whole company.

Passion and purpose are closely connected.

The secret key to living a passionate life requires following this rule from The Passion Test:

Whenever you are faced with a choice, a decision, or an opportunity, choose in favor of your passions.

When you consistently choose in favor of your passions, even if you don't feel like you know what your "purpose" in life is, over time you will notice that your life feels increasingly purposeful. You will discover that you are making a unique and important contribution to those around you. Before long, you will realize that you are living your life's purpose, without any lightning bolts from the heavens. That feeling of purposefulness comes naturally from living life aligned with your passions.

About Janet

From her own remarkable experiences, Janet created the profoundly impactful *Passion Test* process. This simple, yet effective process has transformed thousands of lives all over the world and is the basis of the NY Times bestseller she co-authored with Chris Attwood, *The Passion Test: The Effortless Path to Discovering Your Life Purpose.* Janet is a living example of what it means to live a passionate, fully-engaged life.

A celebrated transformational leader, Janet has shared the stage with people like His Holiness the Dalai Lama, Sir Richard Branson, Nobel Prize winner, F.W. de Klerk, Stephen Covey, Jack Canfield, and many others.

She is also known as one of the top marketers in America. In 2000, Mark Victor Hansen and Robert G. Allen paid for 40 of the top marketing experts in the country to come to Newport Beach, CA to consult with them on marketing their book, *The One Minute Millionaire.* Janet was one of the very first they invited. As a result of that meeting, Robert G. Allen and Mark Victor Hansen asked Janet to partner with them in their Enlightened Millionaire Program.

Her personal stories of following her passions, of the transformations which people like *Chicken Soup for the Soul* author Jack Canfield have experienced with The Passion Test, and the practical, simple exercises she takes people through to discover their own passions are a few of the reasons she gets standing ovations wherever she presents.

Janet has given hundreds of presentations and taken thousands of people through The Passion Test process in the U.S., Canada, India, Nepal, and Europe. Janet is also the founder of The Passion Test for Business, The Passion Test for Coaches, The Passion Test for Kids and Teens, The Passion Test for Kids in Lockdown, and The Reclaim Your Power program for the homeless.

Janet is a golden connector. She has always had the gift of connecting with people, no matter what their status or position. From the influential and powerful, to the rich and famous, to lepers and AIDS patients, to the Saints of India, Nepal, the Philippines and elsewhere—to anyone who is seeking to live their destiny, Janet bonds with every single person, and the stories she shares are inspiring, mind-boggling, uplifting and very real.

A co-founder of top online transformational magazine, *Healthy Wealthy n Wise*, Janet has interviewed some of the most successful people in the world about the role of passion in living a fulfilling life. Her guests have included Stephen Covey, Denis Waitley, Robert Kiyosaki, Neale Donald Walsch, Paula Abdul, Director David Lynch, Richard Paul Evans, Barbara DeAngelis, marketing guru Jay Abraham, singer Willie Nelson, Byron Katie, Wayne Dyer, Nobel Prize winner Muhammad Yunus, Tony Robbins, Rhonda Byrne and many others. These live teleconference interviews have attracted listeners from all parts of the globe. Edited versions of these interviews are made available to over 150,000 subscribers.

Janet served as Director of the Marketing Division at Books are Fun, at the time the third largest book buyer in the U.S., with annual sales in excess of $190 million. Under her direction, the division performed at record levels, laying the groundwork for its purchase the following year by Reader's Digest for $380 million.

An engaging, dynamic, and impassioned presenter, Janet has been a professional speaker, trainer, entrepreneur and coach for more than 30 years. Starting in 1974 when she worked with *Yes to Success* seminars, to her current work leading The *Passion Test* seminars, *Discover Your Destiny* seminars and Passion Test Certification programs, she has had the gift of inspiring and uplifting participants from wherever they are. Her Passion Test process has impacted people worldwide, and The Passion Test phenomenon has resulted in requests from schools to build a passion curriculum, from teachers, trainers and speakers to use the process, and from organizations like NASA to incorporate it in their staff development programs.

It was as a result of taking *The Passion Test* with Janet that Jack Canfield recognized his passion to be part of a spiritual leaders' network, and out of that came the Transformational Leadership Council. Janet and Chris are both founding members of that organization whose 100+ members serve over 10 million people in the self-development world.

Janet Attwood makes magic happen. Her presentations hold audiences spellbound. Her programs attract people from all over the globe. Through her magnetic charisma she is touching the lives of millions of people around the world.

To find out more about Janet go to:

www.janetattwood.com or www.thepassiontest.com

About Chris

Chris Attwood is co-author of the New York Times bestseller, *The Passion Test – The Effortless Path to Discovering Your Life Purpose*. He is an expert in the field of human consciousness and is also deeply grounded in the practical world of business.

Over the past 30 years, Chris has been CEO or senior executive of fifteen companies including a secondary dealer in government securities, a software developer, several magazines, and one of the leading consulting and training companies in the world. He has sold millions of dollars in consulting and training services to companies like Ford Motor Company, Dell Computer, Sprint, Royal Bank of Canada, Mellon Bank and others.

Over the past ten years, he has become one of the leading trainers and authors in the transformational industry, having created programs such as the Enlightened Millionaire Program, co-founded *The Passion Test Daily* magazine and the Transformational Magazine Network, and putting together some of the major strategic alliances in this industry. He is a founding member of the Transformational Leadership Council, which includes over 100 of the top speakers, trainers and authors in the world and of the Expert's Industry Association.

Chris is an expert in creating "enlightened alliances," having played a key role, with his business partner, Janet Bray Attwood, in arranging 70% of the interviews for the movie phenomenon, *The Secret,* and in creating the alliance relationships that launched #1 NY Times bestselling author, T. Harv Eker, in the United States.

Chris is committed to the experience and expression of the unlimited potential of the heart and mind. It is this commitment that weaves throughout his courses and workshops.

CHAPTER 34

Whatever Happened to Hustle?

By Ron LeGrand

A great deal of my time is devoted to teaching and I'm always confronted almost everywhere I appear with three different types of people in my audience.

The first type are those who are hearing me for the first time and just beginning their awareness stage of their training. They never knew so much opportunity was available or how to get at it so easily. Their lives are catered to conventional wisdom, listening to broke people tell them how to get rich.

Then they get a dose of Ron and you can see their faces change expression, their seating posture changes, and an aura of hope and prosperity lights them up like a Christmas tree.

The second group within the audience is repeat visitors who are doing well and for the first time in their lives feel in control and on fire with possibilities and excitement. They can't wait to share their success with me and others, and once their recent achievements become public knowledge, they become the stars and the focal point for people in the room who want to hear how they're winning the game.

These are the same folks who sat in the room a few weeks or a few months earlier in the awareness stage looking for answers. They are the group that's fun to be around and light up the room with energy because they took action and made something happen with information they willingly sought and paid for.

They are the winners, the success stories, the reason I still do what I do and the by-product of a system that works. This group also consists of many who are doing well, but would rather I not tell the class about them and/or afraid to approach me with their success.

Then there is the third group, which unfortunately is way too large. It's the group who live a life of complacency. They know what to do or at least think they do, but never get around to doing it or they make a feeble attempt and quickly give up or await a miracle to change their life.

Unfortunately........

MIRACLES HAPPEN MOSTLY IN THE MOVIES

This group is fully aware of their possibilities. They've attended seminars, boot camps, listened to countless CD's and made a positive movement toward a quantum leap by investing both time and money in an education.

But, then reality sets in. That great big, ugly fact of life called:

MOVEMENT

I wish I could train folks and as they leave the room, make them pass through a success scanner that instills all the qualities of a winner into their brain to eliminate failure and complacency and ensure success. Actually, that's not true. I really don't wish that because then they'd miss the biggest reward of success.......

THE ABILITY TO FAIL AND RECOVER AND GROW STRONG FROM ADVERSITY AND ACTION

The biggest key to success is constant and decisive action. Many people have succeeded in real estate with no boot camps, books, or tapes to learn from. They just kept moving until they figured it out. Of course, it took years, failure, pain, and constant peer pressure, but in the end they succeeded.

Why then, with all the systems and training available to people today doesn't everyone succeed beyond their wildest expectations.

A big, ugly answer is... BY AND LARGE MOST AMERICANS ARE SPOILED ROTTEN AND FORGOTTEN OR NEVER LEARNED WHAT IT'S LIKE TO <u>HUSTLE.</u>

We have it too easy. There's really no external forces making us do everything, but survive. It all must come from within. Complacency is easy. Just getting by is the norm. Succeeding wildly is the exception, although, gaining popularity and the number of rich people is growing rapidly. Did you know the wealthiest 5% of all households have over 21% of all income while the poorest 20% have only 3.4% of all the income? That's a staggering ratio which I'm sure has never been duplicated in our history so I guess it means more and more people are....

GETTING OFF THEIR DEAD ASS AND MAKING IT HAPPEN

And I truly believe our members are among that group. Adversity creates grit and the strongest people I know are those who've faced the demons and survived. Ask any elderly person who's survived the depression what they think of our lazy society. Ask any immigrant who comes here with nothing and gets rich what their secret to success is, and you'll get the same answer....

THEY WORKED THEIR ASS OFF.
GOOD OLD FASHIONED HUSTLE, DAY IN AND DAY OUT UNTIL THE STRUGGLE WAS PAST.

A lot of people who have not experienced adversity and truly developed a winner's attitude will be in for rough times when the economy changes and things aren't so easy anymore. They won't be prepared because they have no memories of hard times. They confuse minutiae with hustle, and live under the illusion that making money will always be as easy as it is now and the cash flow spigot never gets turned off. Yes, I'm aware we're in a recession, but we still have it easy and we're still a "What can you do for me?" society.

I'd suggest you not become one of these ill-prepared folks who take so much for granted and live life on the edge of bankruptcy because things will change, they always do, they can get worse and.......

THE TIME TO HUSTLE IS WHEN THINGS ARE GOING WELL. IT WILL REQUIRE A FRACTION OF THE ENERGY THAT IT WILL WHEN THINGS SLOW DOWN.

When I started in real estate in 1982 the prime rate was 18%. If you were a Realtor selling houses you had to hustle to survive. Many didn't. I did! I didn't know any better. I bought 23 houses my first six months and sold every one for a profit.

When the 1986 tax law changed the rules, chaos was rampant in the industry and you had to hustle to stay ahead of the game if you owned any real estate you bought for tax reasons.

Then came the early 90's, when inflation was high, the economy was in poor condition and commercial property owners really had to hustle, including Donald Trump.

The winners survived. The losers left the scene. Some folks went bankrupt, others got filthy rich and life goes on. The big difference between the winners and the losers is...... HUSTLE.

If I were you, I'd turn on the juice right now and grab all the gusto you can, while you can. No one knows what's coming, but if you're prepared, it really doesn't matter. In fact, you may even silently be hoping for chaos just because you know you can handle it and....

WEALTH COMES FROM CHAOS.

Here are a few things I'm working on in my businesses that perhaps you may want to consider:

1. Get Liquid- No business asset is more important than cash or cash equivalent. It's the thing that causes peace of mind in crisis and gives you the power to make intelligent decisions from strength, not chaos management. It also opens up lots of opportunities created by those without it. So simply stated, having cash leads to more cash. Not having cash means you're a slave to those who do.

   I'm working toward getting very liquid, but don't confuse that with not creating a lot of free equity. In real estate, it's hard to get to the cash without the equity to convert. Of course, this means you shouldn't tie up your cash in real estate long term. Use it to get to equity you can turn into cash short term or let me teach you how to buy all you want without using your cash or credit.

2. <u>Be Wary of Personally Guaranteed Debt</u>- Nothing new here, but you'll be a whole lot stronger if your financial statement isn't overloaded with debt that takes you out of control. Guaranteed debt does just that. "Subject to" debt will always give you the upper hand and puts the lender at your mercy, not the other way around. You'd be surprised what lenders will do in tough times to get problem properties off the books. I've been there. So have many of our readers. When all your assets are at risk, you have no leverage.

Each time you sign a note you risk three things…

1. Your credit

2. Your assets

3. Your marriage

Make sure the reward is worth the risk and you have one or more short term exits in mind before you guarantee debt or simply don't do it. It's not necessary to buy real estate.

Cash>Equity>Cash

Debt>Equity>Cash

3. <u>Develop Multiple Income Streams</u>- Income is a safety factor in tough times and I've never met anyone with too much of it. Last count I had over ten income streams. Some large and some small, but income none the less. <u>Focus on the large ones.</u>

A strong income makes you feel and act like a multi-millionaire even if your bank account doesn't show it yet. When you're not struggling to pay the bills opportunity just seems to find its way to you, even if you're not actively looking.

4. <u>Work Toward Putting Yourself Out of a Job</u>- That means you should be building income and assets that don't depend on you every day. This is the only way you'll ever become truly financially independent. <u>I continue to seek these kinds of opportunities and good people to make them happen.</u> It's amazing how fast you can grow if you quit trying to do it all yourself.

Consider this…..

CASH FLOW FREES YOU UP TO ALLOW OTHERS TO MAKE THE REQUIRED MISTAKES TO BUILD A FORTUNE FOR YOU AND THEM

You should always be training your replacement and expect some little things to go wrong until it just doesn't matter anymore.

That should give you something to think about, but it will always come back to a simple truth about wealth….

YOU MUST STAY IN THE GAME

Which is a synonym for Keep Hustling.

TO YOUR QUANTUM LEAP!!

About Ron

Ron LeGrand's real estate experience spans 30 years in both residential and commercial as an investor, developer, trainer and author of three books, including over 2000 single family homes he's personally bought and sold and multiple commercial projects in eight states.

Ron LeGrand has trained thousands of ordinary people to take their lives back and start their own home-based business. If you'd like Ron's new book and a CD on how he makes money in real estate without banks, credit or money, go to:

www.recessionproofron.com.

As an educator, he's been on numerous radio and TV shows all over North America and currently works with clients from all professions, numbering in the hundreds of thousands on real estate and business-related matters and marketing.

He's 65 years old and lives in Jacksonville, Florida with his wife Beverly of 46 years. He has 4 children, 9 grandchildren and 5 great-grandchildren.

If you'd like his number one best seller book free and a free CD called *"Foreclosure Fortunes,"* go to: www.recessionproofron.com. If you want information on his live, four day training for real estate investors go to: www.RonsQuickStart.com.

CHAPTER 35

Plan For Success

By Mikkel Pitzner

By failing to prepare, you are preparing to fail
~ Benjamin Franklin

Why, exactly, do you run your own business or are thinking of starting your own business? Do you crave the feeling of achievement of doing something on your own and creating your own future? Are you looking for a better, more flexible lifestyle? Are you tired of working for someone else? Are you finding it difficult to get a new job? Are you disillusioned with the job you've got or simply can't stand your boss? Do you have a passion that you'd like to turn into a profession and an income stream?

Running your own business can be a wonderful thing. It can provide you with freedom to do things your way, to do the activities of your choice and take something you are passionate about and turn it into an income and even possibly build it up – creating wealth for you and your family.

A business can provide a great income for you and your family and of-tentimes for many other families by providing jobs and opportunities for others to be able to share in. But a business can also rip the carpet away from under you and place you in great debt that will burden you for a long time. That is why planning for your success is so important.

So how do you plan for your success in business? Well, besides figuring out your business proposition, i.e., what you are selling or going to sell, and making certain there is a clientele for it, you estimate the viability of your scheme, then you plan your business by making your budget.

A budget is simply your estimated or projected numbers based on qualified guesses, estimations, experience, past results achieved and research for your projected sales and other revenues in the business, along with the associated costs of running the business.

I know this may sound boring for some, but it really isn't so bad after all, and it does not have to be such an overwhelming task. But it is critical and super important.

As one of the great mentors, Jim Rohn, said; *"Ten years from now you will surely arrive. The question is, where?"*

You need to know where you are going. I have seen businesses small and large that do not work with a budget. That means they are basically running their businesses not knowing where they are going.

When addressing this issue with the business owners or even the CEOs of these companies, the responses I get often go like this: "Well, we just need more sales, then we will have the right numbers and make profits".

But they are running blindfolded. What if the real numbers would in fact prove that their matrix is faulty, so that costs of achieving their sales along with the costs associated with producing their product or service are higher than the price at which they sell? Well, then their approach simply spells disaster.

And maybe the costs and sale prices are not as badly compiled as the scenario put forth above; and yes, …maybe just more sales would provide enough cash infusion and profits to the business to produce the right numbers, but what if you cannot afford to run long enough for those sales figures to be achieved? What if your liquidity will not sustain your business long enough for it to be able to reap the rewards?

I have seen many business owners who chased the next cash infusion over and over again − so that they could keep the business alive, and thinking: "if only I had some more money, then…" thinking that the additional money would bring about an avenue of more revenues (which potentially could be purchased), while never bothering to look at the fundamentals of the business they are running right now, and without addressing the difficulties which were killing their businesses in the first place.

In the process, they are really just accruing even more debt and even greater costs to the financing, and possibly diluting their ownership and certainly the value of their company and business even further.

You see, running a business is really very fundamental. You need your costs of producing, providing and selling your product or service, including all your costs of personnel, location, utilities, financing, etc., etc., to be less than the revenues you accrue from selling your product or service. But you also need the liquidity in place to keep you afloat along the way.

When you start up a business you very often have to bring money to the table by funding its start up. Setting up the business and producing your first product or service and marketing it will probably give you some expenses that will have to be paid for before you get the sale. But even with established businesses, you often have the income stream delayed or spread out over some time from each sale. So in other words, you need to know and arrange for that so you can sustain the business long enough while you deliver your products or services – while waiting to get paid.

So plan for success. Analyze every area of your business from A-Z, possibly having budgets of parts of the business that are subsequently worked into the entire overall budget for the entire business. As an example, you may have a sub-budget showing all of your employee expenses and then incorporate it into the overall budget for the business. Put these numbers on paper. A budget should show your futures estimates for your business over a time period of your choice, but should project for at least a full year, with projections preferably into the subsequent 1-5 years thereafter. The budget should be built up so you can see the numbers at least on a month-by-month basis.

For a start up, you know your numbers may well be just estimated guesses, but even these can be fairly accurate if you have done your research well. And if you learn things along the way that changes certain parts of the calculations significantly, then you may want to revisit and adjust your budget with these changes. For businesses that already have run a year or more, calculating your budget can produce a very precise picture of your future business.

Make sure you take a look at your business numbers by looking at your profits and losses at least monthly, i.e., your P/L statement and then compare with your budget. That means you need to have solid book-keeping in place that keeps all of your numbers up to date at all times.

Continuously monitor your sales and your margins and check how it compares with your budget. Adjust your formula and margins if you do not meet or better your expectations and make such adjustments with a sense of urgency. Stay on top of your market and know that markets can evolve and what you are able to sell today may not necessarily be saleable tomorrow. Look for improvements for every area of your business and push yourself a little harder. Make it a habit and it often will not seem like work.

Think of your budget as your autopilot too. By reviewing your profit and loss statement every month and comparing it with your budget, you can see if you are on track. If you are off your numbers if will help you see where you are not doing the right things and you will be better able to see where you need to make some adjustments in your business.

I recently learned that an auto-pilot does not set you on course from Point A to Point B and then leaves it there, but in fact adjusts your course ever so often, in order for you to arrive at your chosen Point B.

I know that budgets can sound very boring and a tedious task, and perhaps with your entrepreneurial mindset you are more focused on the next project or the excitement you have for your product or service, or the thrill of engagement with your customer, but I am sure we all enjoy when our businesses are thriving and when we can reap the rewards or know that we are doing quite well in terms of our income. Not for the sake of the money or riches, but for what the money can provide us with such as our homes, livelihood, food and security, and well, perhaps all the toys, experiences, travels and not least of all the freedom – and perhaps for what you can contribute to the world with your abundance.

Once you have the budget and you follow up every month, you are able to engage your business and fine tune it even further, cutting unnecessary costs, building and expanding it and growing it all together.

Your budget may tell you to adjust your expenses in a few places. Be willing to make swift adjustments. Sometimes you may need to adjust in the area of employees. We have all probably heard the sentence "Hire Slow, Fire Fast" ...and I urge you to keep this valuable point in mind. If you are a new start-up business, you will need to try to keep your expenses and overhead as low as possible until you have achieved some traction and can get the sales to support your organization. Firing anybody is not fun to do, and certainly no fun for the employee being let go – but remember it is not personal, and that in saving one employee from drowning you may risk sinking the ship. I meet many businesses and I often see that they are employing 'way too many heads' for their business to have a chance of survival when the economy has changed.

Learn from your own mistakes and even more brilliantly, learn from other people's mistakes, so that you do not have to go and repeat them in your own business.

This brings up the point of learning from others, which I will always recommend to everyone. Again in quoting one of my mentors, Jim Rohn, "Work harder on yourself than you do on your job." Seek out mentors and learn from them. You will be inspired and you will arm yourself with knowledge that has been acquired over many years of experience by many professionals, and been deciphered and assimilated into great lessons for us all.

Working closely with your budget and your monthly profit and loss statements will lead you to really know your business. Knowing your business can make all the difference. When you know your business well, you can set up systems and ways that will reduce the daily work for yourself, and, along with better business results, you will soon be able to achieve the freedom you probably longed for like most of us.

Far too often though, I see business owners stressing and leading lives in which they are always completely overwhelmed with work and anxiety, and they seem to be running around putting out fire after fire while never getting ahead. Meanwhile, their health is deteriorating and their personal relationships are crumbling.

Knowing your business can put you in a position where you can remove yourself from the daily equation and you can control the business by remote control. You can ultimately become a shareholder, freeing up your time for your hobbies, family, travel or indeed other business pursuits and ventures.

Having run several businesses on remote control as I call it, I am living proof of this being possible, and I am now teaching and helping others do the same. I get very inspired by the good results and huge improvements that I see people achieve when I have helped them. Oftentimes, my advice entails relatively small adjustments that instantaneously take their business to a whole new level. One of the businesses that I looked at recently took one simple idea I gave them and tripled their profits and revenue stream within a few weeks.

It is wonderful to have the extra time when you remove yourself from the business, but removing yourself from the business may not just be in order for you to avoid working so hard, because, hey, maybe you love what you are doing. I am certain, however, that you would love to be able to have the freedom to spend the time on being a more active part of your children's lives or have a more engaging and fulfilling life with your spouse.

With more freedom, energy and time, you can go and explore new business opportunities and ventures, or simply gain a better perspective on your own business if you only have that business, opening up even greater possibilities for you. Multiple streams of income can also aid you in getting rid of debt and building wealth, and whether these streams of income stem from within the same business or multiple businesses, I often find that you will more easily find these opportunities when you have removed yourself from dealing with every little operational part of the business, and have more energy and thought resources available to you.

Having more free time while retaining a business that affords you a great income also makes it even more possible for you to go and seek inspiration, knowledge, connections and possibly even more business, elsewhere. Go to seminars and learn there. Seminar topics and the right teachers can sharpen your skills and hone your skills to perform better in or on your business. At seminars you will find other like-minded people and often people who are very successful themselves. As an added benefit, you may often find new customers there too, as well as future collaborators or affiliates that can bring your business further or to that next level.

Join mastermind groups, even if you have to pay for them. Seek out top professionals who have skills, knowledge, success, connections and reach. They will help you along with your fellow mastermind partici-pants in expanding your mindset to the possibilities out there, and help you increase your ambitions and your results exponentially.

Ever heard the saying of your income level being an average of the top 5 people with whom you associate or hang out with? If you are serious about taking yourself and your business to the next level, then you need to be serious about masterminding and about the people you are around.

Communicating with other professionals can also help you in gaining a new perspective on your business, which can often be very highly desir-able - especially those people who have run their own business for quite some time. They tend to get stuck on one path; sometimes you just need to take a big step back and look at your business from above. In other words, you need to jump onboard a helicopter and fly above your busi-ness and get a better view. When you have assembled your new ideas, then consult your budget and see how you can implement them and what the effect will be.

Planning for success is essential – your budget is an essential part of that planning!

About Mikkel

Serial Entrepreneur, professional board member in Denmark, Sweden and the US, social media expert and consultant, small time investor and dreamer *extraordinaire.*

Mikkel Pitzner is a partner in unique marketing and trailer rental company Freetrailer, which currently operates throughout Denmark and Sweden with more countries to come. Mikkel is also a partner in Aksel & Ko, a company that finds that special gimmicks or solutions that corporations need for their marketing purposes.

Originally from Denmark where he used to run what turned into the fourth largest car rental company and a leasing company he led to double its size. Also, up until recently, he owned and operated the largest limousine service company in Denmark whose profits he managed to grow 3200% during the first year of ownership alone. Also, he successfully ran an import and distribution company of scuba diving equipment until that company was sold to a German distributor.

Mikkel is also a best-selling author and speaker, and teaches entrepreneurs how to create a business that will provide you with the lifestyle of your choice, while taking you off the treadmill of your job, so you can spend your time on things of your choosing.

He currently resides in Florida with his wife Olga and one-and-a-half-year-old son Gabriel He is building four new business ventures simultaneously, while helping a local manufacturer in a struggling and challenging economy.

CHAPTER 36

Branded, Specialty and Promotional Marketing Vehicles

By Paul Edgewater

Putting your company logo and messaging on your fleet (even if your fleet comprises of just one vehicle), is one of the most cost effective opportunities to promote your products and/or services. You might say that branded vehicles run in my DNA. My great-grandfather William Theodore, born 101 years before me in 1865, was apprenticed as a spice blender. He grew into a traveling salesman in south central New York State for Newell & Truesdell, purveyors of wholesale groceries and "Yankee Notions" in the last century. His service vehicle, a Model T Ford panel truck, was  emblazoned with the logo: "New & True." Where a lot of earlier branding seems "quaint" and outmoded now, "Wm T's" Ford Model T retains its dash and presents an unforgettable sight even today. The photo here is circa 1916.

Wouldn't you think that by now, almost a century later, everyone would have learned that this is one of the most cost-effective methods of advertising based on ROI ever devised? They haven't. Thousands and thousands of company vehicles traveling the highways are utterly blank or without a dash of branding of any kind. What a shame and what a wasted opportunity, especially when considering that mobile media advertising offers the lowest cost-per-impression of any major advertising medium.

Research by the American Trucking association, reveals that wrapped or branded vehicles get an average of 138 visual impressions per mile. That gives your brand, company or cause, first hand exposure to about 16 million potential customers a year—per vehicle. Additionally, a study by the ad agency, RYP & Becker Group, reveals some truly exciting data. 97% of survey respondents recalled the copy and creative of the wrapped vehicle. 98% thought the wrapped vehicles created a positive image for the advertiser. Finally, 96% thought vehicle graphics had far more impact than billboards. I hope you are convinced and are now planning on branding your fleet (even if it's just one vehicle, or your personal car), and if your fleet is already branded, let's take this opportunity as far as we can.

To stand out in this era of sensory overload, we must do something beyond the ordinary to survive and thrive in our modern business climate. Nowadays, no one is going to tell their friends about a truck with magnetic logos stuck on the doors. Logos on the side of your vehicles are a good start, but they're not going to be enough. There are many other ways to take vehicle branding further. Following are some options you may want to consider. Harvey MacKay, in his timeless tome, "*Swim With The Sharks Without Being Eaten Alive,*" makes the wise suggestion of putting your company logo on the roof of your vehicle (in addition to the sides and back). He wrote that almost 25 years ago, yet today, countless side-branded-only vehicles roll down streets and roads all over the world, with mute, blank roofs staring back at all those executives in high-rise offices (or any office above the 2nd or 3rd floor, for that matter). We can take a cue from some service vehicles like police cruisers and ambulances, as we'll often see messaging on their roofs.

Ambulances also put their messaging on the leading edge of their hoods—with the copy in reverse—so that we can read the messaging in our rearview mirrors when they are behind us. This reverse messaging on the hood is a great place to put your website address (check with local restrictions on this tactic, as some municipalities have archaic laws against reverse copy on the hood of any vehicles except ambulances). Putting your messaging on the back of your fleet is also crucial. It's worth noting, this is the best surface on your vehicles where you can have detailed information about your goods or services, as this is the only surface that can be viewed for a prolonged period of time by other motorists when your vehicles are on the move. Anyone following your vehicles can potentially follow them as long as they'd like. They don't have to pass you until they have read your messaging (so keep it really interesting).

To recap:

· Messaging on the doors (or anywhere on the side). Utilize logos and minimal copy here (7 words-max). Have your creative do most of the talking on these surfaces.

· Messaging on the roof or top surface of the hood/trunk. Make it big and bold here. Something that can be read from a high floor in a tall building. This means large fonts and few words (5 words max).

· Messaging on the leading edge of the hood in reverse (keep it simple; website only, for instance). Again, check your local ordinances.

· Messaging on the rear. Go into more detail here and keep it interesting, compelling and creative. Something akin to, "You're following the leader in (insert your product or service and note features and benefits). Call us today and we'll put you in front of your competition." Make sure your phone number, website, social media links and QR codes are prominently displayed here.

Let's examine a few different platforms/tactics:

WRAPPED VEHICLES

In recent years, advances in adhesive vinyls and large-scale printing have brought about a proliferation of wrapped vehicles. Wrapping the body-style-du jour, is a common tactic. You'll see it on the latest SUVs, Scions, Jukes, Cubes, Smart Cars, Fiat 500s and Minis, etc. A few years ago, the tactic was common on Beetles, PT Cruisers, HHRs, Hummers, etc. The tactic works very well, but sometimes wrapped vehicles are getting attention based not just on the graphics affixed to them, but also due to the novelty of the vehicle's body style.

We advise our clients to not fall into the trap of making a wrap decision based solely on the novelty of a body style (unless they have the budget to regularly replace their fleet, and/or if they are leasing their fleet). At best, once those hot new body styles become ubiquitous, they will lose half of their appeal. Some beauties age fast and may prematurely look 'long in the tooth.' This will give your company or message an out-of-touch image. Avoid this by making the wrap creative so that the wrap will stand on its own accord – even if you've only wrapped a Honda Accord! The wrap should be cool and compelling whether it's on Smart Car, or on a 1973 Dodge Tradesman 300 Van. This way, it won't look like last year's hat or hemline in three months.

Wraps are not cheap (the average investment is $2,000-$4,000 for a small-to-midsize car, factoring in creative time), so you don't want to keep wrapping vehicles just because the body style has lost its appeal, especially when you consider that modern vinyls can last up to 5 years. When deciding on a platform, put as much weight into the utility of the vehicle as well as its visual appeal. Remember, these vehicles are going to have to earn their keep by carrying out myriad tasks; looking great, conveying the proper message for your offer and carrying supplies and personnel to and from special events, etc. This is why platforms like Step Vans, cargo or full-size passenger vans are such a good choice. They are rarely restyled and thus look contemporary for years.

Think of the Red Bull campaign when it was using Suzuki X90s a few years back. Although it was the perfect platform for what they were doing at the time (wrapping the vehicle and placing a large Red Bull can on the trunk deck that doubled as a cooler to bring chilled Red Bull to special events), once Suzuki ceased production of the X90, that was that. Now they are using Minis, but the bodies had to be highly modified to accommodate the can and the cars have lost the distinctive Mini roofline. Forget that the X90 was a far superior platform from a utilitarian standpoint than the Mini. Red Bull is held hostage by the body style of their promotional fleet. They could make this campaign a lot more cost effective by not going with the body style-du-jour (as minis are already yesterday's news). If I ran the campaign, I would suggest a giant four-pack of Red Bull cans in the back of a compact pick up truck. That way, the cans could always be moved into a contemporary truck as styles change. Compact pickup trucks are inexpensive to purchase or lease and are utilitarian as well. Minis on the other hand, are not.

Instead of just logos, copy and/or photos on the vehicle, why not create an optical illusion? Most of us in the promotions industry have seen this practice. For instance, make the vehicle look like it's see-through with an exploded image on its side, or its rear end, revealing your products inside the vehicle, or put the image of a different kind of vehicle on the side of a larger vehicle? For example, affix the profile of a sports car or motorcycle, replete with rider, to the side of a van, so that the wheels line up with the host vehicle's wheels. That will not only cause myriad double-takes, but the spinning of the host vehicle's wheels will also give movement and momentum to the static image on the graphics. The visual needn't be just a gimmick. It can be an attention grabber and memory jogger. In an instant people holistically see your company name, number or website in that fleeting moment of time. Remember, you have to engage eyeballs and not let their gaze drift and wander and forget. On the road you have only seconds to achieve this as your vehicles speed past your target consumer. Note: you can place ads/graphics on your windows on the vehicles too. On these surfaces, a perforated vinyl is used that is see-through from the inside, but almost opaque from the outside. Legally, all windows can be covered except the front side windows and windshield.

To recap:

· Make the wrap stand on its on accord and do not base the appeal on the body style it's applied to.

· Choose a body style that has appeal, but put more emphasis on its utility and staying power. In other words, choose a body style that doesn't get restyled too often. Do your research here.

· Keep in mind, a wrap is expensive but can last up to 5 years. Pick a platform you can live with to maximize ROI.

3-DIMENSIONAL GRAPHICS

The Red Bull wrap example leads us to the next tactic: 3-dimensional graphics. The current Red Bull Minis are indeed wrapped vehicles, but they also incorporate a 3-dimensional element; the giant Red Bull can. This is not a new idea. Zippo cigarette lighters had a great 3-dimensional car back in the 1940's. It was a Chrysler made to look like two

flaming Zippos. As the car drove down the road, the message being communicated to the consumer was that a Zippo lighter can be lit (and will stay lit) in the wind; how clever and how appealing.

Monster.com had a fleet of Land Rover Discoveries with their roofs made to look like monsters in the late '90s/early 2000s. It was clever in two ways; one, the monster itself was an appealing icon, but by using a vehicle associated with being upwardly mobile, there was a subliminal message as well; find a job (or post a job) with Monster.com and you'll be successful enough to buy a Land Rover.

Another great example (and possibly the most famous branded vehicle) is the Weiner Mobile. Consider how iconic the Wiener Mobile is. We all know and love the Weiner Mobile. This fleet of vehicles attracts a crowd wherever they go, and when they park somewhere, the public converges upon it. If this isn't the Godfather of the 3-dimensional graphic (or promotional vehicles in general), I'm not sure what is. If this tactic didn't work, Oscar Meyer wouldn't still be driving them around. The first one hit the road in 1936! Your company or cause can be a pop icon too.

Some insect exterminators make a giant cockroach and put them on top of their fleet vehicles. It's whimsical, but it is also a call to action, because you'd never want those in your home - big or small! Ask yourself, what image or object defines your product, service or cause (e.g., a gavel for a law firm, a stethoscope for a physician, a tooth for a dentist, etc.). Now imagine it with wheels tooling through town. Intriguing, no?

ROLLING SHOWROOM VEHICLES

Another attractive platform is the interactive Showroom Vehicle. The rolling showroom or exhibit, where people are invited to walk through the vehicle when it is parked at a special event, is a great opportunity for total immersion for your target consumer. Our company designed and built such a vehicle for Starbucks a few years back called "Green Moments." Its purpose was to highlight Starbucks' commitment to the environment, while at the same time promoting a new green tea Frappuccino they had just released. The best platforms for this type of vehicle are class A motorhomes. They already have much of the equipment that you'll need built in: plumbing, electrical, lighting, etc. You may start from scratch with most other platforms.

WHAT WILL YOUR VEHICLE BE DOING?

From another point of view, think of all the missions and applications of the branded vehicle. Beyond being a moving billboard, what function does it serve your company or cause? Does it make deliveries? Is it a guerrilla marketing vehicle carrying staff and tchotchkes? Where will it be seen? Who is going to see it on its regular route? Can it take the scenic route where there are more vehicles on the road with eyeballs to grab? Does it need to get from point A to point B in a hurry? Can it be parked in front of your business and just sit there? One of the best vehicles my company has produced is for Cascal Fermented Soda.

 We built two Ford-based step vans. They can carry a pallet's worth of soda to an event (chilled in a giant refrigerator), 2 staff members, a fully-equipped kitchen, a serving window and more. Most importantly, they have over 900 square feet of advertising real estate flanking the sides, front and back. They are fully-equipped promotional vehicles that also function as delivery/support vehicles as well as rolling billboards. Step vans provide more bang for the buck than almost any other platform.

Now is a good time to bring up the operational use of 3-dimensional-graphiced-vehicles. They cannot be driven like we drive a regular automobile. Earlier I mentioned the Monster.com Land Rovers. Yes, they were interesting. Yes, they got a lot of attention. But you couldn't change lanes very quickly when driving them. With all the extra sprung body weight above the center of gravity, they tended to tip and roll over. These vehicles were not designed to win the Daytona 500 or Le Mans in their stock condition and the fiberglass 'monster' on the roof exacerbated this quality. Just remember, you can't be a hot dog when driving the Wiener Mobile. Getting into an accident with a branded vehicle can be a disaster - especially if someone gets hurt. That's free press that no one needs. Be careful!

Here's an awesome tactic. Think of the branded vehicle as a way for new or struggling stores located in towns to circumvent local laws against temporary and/or effective permanent signage. There are burgs that send out the Spanish Inquisition when you try to hang a banner in your window. They can tell you to take it down and levy a fine. But there are few, if any laws, even in those Orwellian towns, which govern whether or not you can temporarily park a vehicle in the parking lot, or a parking space in front of your store during business hours or longer.

I have even seen this done with cars that are obviously not in running condition. There is a pizza joint outside of Chicago that parked a really old VW Beetle in front of their store with their name on the roof. Technically, it's just a car parking there, not a regulated "sign", so the sign police don't have a case; very clever.

ROLLING BILLBOARD TRUCKS

This is a good opportunity to weigh the pros and cons on mobile billboard trucks, which are literally billboards on wheels for rent. They usually have daily, weekly and monthly rate packages. If you live or do business in a medium to large market, you have probably seen these. I have some pretty strong opinions against their use, but I will let the reader decide what the best use of their money is ultimately.

The pros:
- They do get a lot of attention—from the sides.
- They are also backlit, which is very effective.

The cons:
- These vehicles are often tall and narrow and have no branding opportunities on the front, back or top surfaces. A few companies have sprung up that are producing mobile billboard trucks on box truck platforms that utilize the back and front surfaces, as well as the sides with backlit signs. However, even though these 4-sided billboards are much better than the 2-sided variety, they still don't utilize the roof surface.
- You are often sharing these platforms with other clients who have also bought 'time' on the trucks, so your message isn't always visible (often the signs change up during their routes).
- They are very, VERY expensive to rent. When looking into the ROI of these platforms, most businesses decide against them.

In defense of the narrow models, the sides are huge - much bigger than the sides of box truck varieties or step vans, but it is this author's opinion that the trade-off in the size of the sides is worth it when using the box-variety platform, because the front and rear surfaces are utilized. Not only can people see your message coming, but, if for some reason they miss the sides, they can see it going. Both of these platforms are great if you have a very special event to advertise, or some other sort of one-off or infrequent occasion that needs some big exposure. If however, you plan on advertising on a regular basis, may I suggest you go a different route? These trucks are prohibitively expensive to rent (usually $500-$1,000 per day). Why not think outside of the box (truck) and purchase a used box truck and cover the front, sides and back with high quality vinyl banners, and hire a driver to cruise the neighborhoods that are your target demographic? Additionally, this is a vehicle which can serve multiple purposes for your business, and I can assure you that it won't cost you $8,000-$30,000 a month to operate it. There are advantages to the billboard-for-hire trucks out there to be sure, but before you spend your hard-earned money on them, consider what you could do yourself for a lot less money.

The message is clear; if you have a company vehicle which is not logo-ed, wrapped or 3-dimensionalized, what are you waiting for? This applies to the personal vehicle you drive to and from the office as well. On a daily basis, you could be driving right past the biggest client you could ever hope for, but they don't know you exist—yet! Why not reach the thousands of people you pass every day on the way to the office, while running errands or driving to, and parking at, special events? You and your employees are driving those vehicles anyway. Remember, you don't have to reinvent the wheel here, there are many great vendors in most major markets who can assist you in properly branding your vehicle(s) or fleet, including my own company, Busy Bee Promotions.

I'll close with a good analogy. Imagine watching the Super Bowl during a commercial break, but instead of seeing an advertisement, there is just a blank white screen staring back at you for 30 seconds. You may think to yourself, "who would pay <u>all that money</u> to show all of us viewers a <u>blank screen?</u>" Let me ask you this; how is owning a <u>blank company vehicle</u> any different?

About Paul

Best selling author Paul Edgewater, is CMO & co-founder of Chicago, IL-based, Busy Bee Promotions, Inc. Busy Bee opened its doors in 1998 and conducts an average of 400 events monthly coast-to-coast.

Paul has been featured in *The Wall Street Journal*, *USA Today*, *Promo Magazine*, and on FOX News, CNN, CNBC, MSNBC, FOX, ABC, NBC and CBS news affiliates promoting products and services for clients such as Coca-Cola, Starbucks Coffee, Verizon Wireless, Groupon, Whole Foods Market, AT&T and many, many more. His specialty is in maximizing his clients' exposure in and out of their respective market places by executing very unconventional, attention-getting tactics – including an acclaimed, free-20-second spot he garnered for Starbucks Coffee on Fox News by rattling off talking points while doing "360s" on a branded Segway Personal Transporter!

Paul is the author of *"The Book On Promotions - How The Free Market Will Save The World, One Tchotchke At A Time"* and *"Counter Attack - Business Strategies For Explosive Growth In The New Economy"* co-authored with world-renowned business leader, Brian Tracy (both available at: www.PaulEdgewater.com). He has more than 30 years of sales, marketing and promotions experience and is motivated by his intense love of the private sector and the free market system, and takes great pleasure in connecting his clients with new customers. In addition to his business pursuits, he is a weekend athlete with three marathons under his belt and also an accomplished singer, bass player, drummer and animal lover.

Paul lives steps off the Magnificent Mile in beautiful downtown Chicago and is available for speaking engagements and consultations.

For booking information or to contact Paul directly, visit: www.BusyBeePromotions.com or call Toll-Free 1-888-438-9995

CHAPTER 37

POWERFUL ETHICS = POWERFUL BUSINESS

By Leigh Steinberg

My client was, at that moment, the number one running back in the NFL. And, at that same moment, he was refusing to report for preseason training camp.

The reason? He wanted off his team. As his agent, I had already tentatively worked out a trade deal so this superstar player could join the organization of his choice. I explained to him that, while his exit plan was being finalized, he still needed to live up to his existing contract and show up. For whatever reason, he didn't trust his current team owner. He was afraid that if he did begin working out with the team, the owner would remember what he was giving up, back out of the deal, and keep this player stuck where he didn't want to be for the rest of the season.

Making matters worse was the circle of friends and family members with which this player surrounded himself. They were, to be blunt, sycophants, who only reinforced his paranoia and told him he was right to stay away. All they did was bolster whatever negativity he carried around with him. If he was standing on the balcony of a 60th floor hotel room and announced he was going to jump, they probably would have all told him, "Go ahead and jump! You're the man!"

Of course, I'm exaggerating, but the fact was that this was an incredibly difficult situation for me, both professionally and personally. My negotiations with the team regarding the trade had been in good faith and, as anyone who knows me is aware, I pride myself on high ethical conduct in all my dealings. These kinds of antics went against everything I believed in. I explained to the player that his reputation was on the line here; if he didn't show at camp, it would be a red flag to the rest of the NFL that he was difficult. He'd be regarded as damaged goods and could possibly make the team that was trading for him take a long second look; maybe they were offering too much, maybe he wasn't worth the possible trouble he might cause down the line.

Bottom line? If he wanted the trade to go through on our terms, he needed to go to camp and normalize the situation.

He still refused and did not show up. The trade did, in fact fall through, his team suspended him for a number of games and he ended up losing millions of dollars in revenue.

I raised a lot of eyebrows when, later, I ended up severing relations with the player, one of the major superstars of the NFL at the time. I knew, however, that the NFL largely functions on relationships, as do most businesses – and I had assured the owner that the player would report to camp as he was obligated to do. The short term commissions I would have earned were not as important as the long term integrity of my agency. I needed to send a signal that my word was my bond.

That way of doing business has allowed my agency to dominate the representation of NFL players for three decades. And it demonstrates my overriding philosophy – powerful ethics leads to powerful business.

PUTTING VALUES INTO ACTION

For me, the key in life is finding a way to take one's core values and find a career that reflects those values. When you're able to inject your values into your work, you tap into a passion and an energy level that is transcendent. It keeps you excited about what you do.

Now, a sports agent probably isn't the first profession that comes to mind when the topic of values comes up – and it really wasn't what I intended to be. I was a grad counselor in an undergrad dorm at UC Berkeley, working my way through law school, when the school moved the freshman football team into my dorm. That allowed me to build some pretty good relationships with those guys. I went on to graduate from law school in 1974 and traveled the world for a year before I came home to find a job.

That job found me, however, in the person of Steve Bartkowski, a star member of the football team that had lived in my dorm – and, in 1975, the very first player picked in the very first round of the NFL draft by the Atlanta Falcons. Just as I was choosing from various legal career options, Steve asked me to represent him in contract negotiations.

Yes, me. The guy who had yet to actually spend a day of his life practicing law.

This was obviously an amazing opportunity – even more of an opportunity than it would have been usually, because, at that time, the very short-lived World Football League was in a very heated competition with the NFL for players. That enabled me to create a bidding war between the Falcons and the WFL. The result? Steve received the largest rookie contract in NFL history, eclipsing both O.J. Simpson's and Joe Namath's, the two previous standard-bearers.

And by the way, the WFL went out of business later that year.

This initial experience culminated in Steve and myself flying into Atlanta to sign the contract with the Falcons. When we returned to the airport to fly back home to Los Angeles, we were shocked to find a massive crowd, like the kind you'd see at a major movie premiere, waiting for us. And the first thing we heard entering the airport was a nearby television reporter announcing, "We interrupt the Johnny Carson Show to bring you a news bulletin – Steve Bartkowski has just arrived at the airport and we'll be bringing you a live in-depth interview…"

Well. I looked at Steve like Dorothy looked at her little dog Toto in "The Wizard of Oz," and said, "Steve…I have a feeling we're not in California anymore…"

It was the first time I personally experienced the power of the incredible adulation and veneration top athletes received from everyday Americans. They were the ultimate celebrities in everyone's eyes. And I begin to visualize how that power could be used to promote positive values and meaningful change.

I was sold on being a sports agent. I felt that this career would give me the opportunity to fulfill the two admonitions that my father had given me in terms of how to live life. The first was to treasure relationships, especially within your family. The second was to try and make a meaningful difference in the world and help people who couldn't help themselves.

It was clear that athletes could serve as role models that represented the kind of principles that would be beneficial to this country and to the world. If they retraced their roots to their high school, college and professional communities, they could set up programs that would enhance their quality of life, stimulate fundamental positive values and, at the same time, become known for the quality of their character.

Professional athletes have the ability to cut through the perceptual screen that the public puts up when it comes to authority figures. People might tune out law enforcement figures, teachers, or political leaders, but they look up to and listen to athletes in a completely different way. That meant those athletes could cause a meaningful change in public attitudes by taking on a cause and giving it higher visibility and validity.

My clients ended up setting up over 150 scholarship funds. Others ended up repaying the college tuition that their football scholarships covered; quarterback Troy Aikman and baseball star Eric Karros did so with their alma mater UCLA, as did NFL players Edgerrin James with the University of Miami, Kerry Collins with Penn State and Steve Young with Brigham Young University.

Another NFL great, Warrick Dunn, set up the Warrick Dunn Foundation, which assisted single mothers with ownership of the first homes they would ever have – and brought on Home Depot to help outfit those homes. This program dramatically changed these women's lives. The late, great Derrick Thomas created "Third and Long," a foundation to help bring literacy to inner city kids in the home of the team where he played his entire career, the Kansas City Chiefs, and placekicker Rolf Benirschke began "Kicks for Critters," which has raised millions for the fund for endangered species at the San Diego Zoo.

UNDERSTANDING PRIORITIES AND VALUES

The clients I just discussed were all people whose generosity of spirit validated my choice of career. They tackled causes close to their own hearts and made a significant difference to many lives. As their agent, I encouraged that – because, again, I believe everyone should embrace their values and live them.

And that's why, in order to properly represent athletes in negotiations, I always made sure to understand their individual values and what was important to them. Rather than merely muddle through a surface conversation that might only have involved black-and-white issues such as money and the length of the contract, I asked questions and I *listened.*

This isn't as simple as it sounds. You need to ask piercing questions that motivate the person to peel back the layers of their surface responses, as you would with an onion, to get down to what they are really all about. Men especially are not used to sharing on that level. But if you don't enable them to articulate their priorities, so you don't waste time and energy on side issues that aren't nearly as important, you can't really represent them to the fullest.

This is true of any business negotiation – you must try to understand what the person on the other side of the table is really after. When you understand their greatest anxieties and fears, as well as their hopes and dreams, it allows you to construct win-win situations in your discussions.

With athletes, I would ask them to list their long term personal goals, such as economic security, geographical location, and family considerations, as well as professional ones, such as endorsements, public profile and the features of the kind of team they'd like to play on – the coaching style, the playing surface of the home field, and whether the team was a contender for the Super Bowl. Next, I would ask them to rank each of these various goals in order of importance.

Again, this is a process that anyone in business should use in planning his or her own career path. They should examine their own priorities in life and pursue them accordingly, in order of importance. In either activity, the first key is research – understanding the individual goals of whoever you're negotiating with or for, understanding the current business concerns and business climate and then, trying to see the world as the other person sees it. Finally, you must try to speak directly to the most critical priorities of the other person.

And fully comprehending the word "priorities" *is* a priority. Every single item can't be of equal importance in a negotiation. Some have to be more significant than others. And properly dealing with that order of significance is the difference between being able to make a deal and having to walk away from the table. As I used to tell my kids, the most important subject in school they could take was psychology – understanding human motivation and behavior, and being able to predict what they might do next, is always a function of interacting with other people.

Here's how it worked with another one of my clients, Tim McDonald. When he was going through the NFL free agency process, I asked him to list his priorities and values in the manner I just described. I knew multiple teams would be presenting multiple options and it would be easy to enter a situation where stress and confusion caused by these different choices might lead to Tim making a decision he wouldn't ultimately be happy with. It's always a pressure-packed situation and there comes a time when the human psyche just says, "Enough!" and pushes for any decision to bring some relief.

He made his list. And, obviously, money was a big factor. But his true goals were to get to a team that had a chance to make the Super Bowl, as well as live closer to his family in Fresno, California, where he was from. The team that was offering the most money was the Philadelphia Eagles; he also had a very viable offer from the Atlanta Falcons and a few other teams. But then the San Francisco 49s expressed interest. They were a winning team with a great organization, and, of course, they were the closest of all the NFL teams to Tim's home town.

Tim was able to separate the offers from the six or seven teams and realize that 49s' location and organization were more important to him than the actual money offer. He told me to get the best economic deal I could from San Francisco and make the deal. The 49s ended up winning the Super Bowl the very next season – and Tim showed his community spirit by donating $2000 to the Boys and Girls Clubs of the Bay Area every time his team won a victory.

SHORT TERM VS LONG TERM

Tim took a short term loss to ensure long term career fulfillment. We all face that situation in our professional lives, and too many times, immediate choices force us to compromise our principles and to trade significant problems further down the line for a quick pay-off. As a client once told me, "I can live with the fact that you may not return a phone call as quickly as I might like. I can live with the fact that you might not accomplish all my goals as quickly as you might like. But if you ever lie to me about the nature of what really happened during your negotiations, it destroys the trust that is the key to our relationship."

The person who is kind when he comes home to his family, but goes into the office everyday using the most horrible tactics to accomplish business goals ultimately destroys his most valuable relationships. Lying, attacking and overpromising are all strategies that may lead to some short term success, but will catch up with you at some point.

We've seen government officials ruined by scandal and we've seen huge corporations like Enron completely undone by greed. In contrast, being true to one's own core values builds a strong foundation for the future. A business person who pays attentions to ethical rules knows he can never be imperiled by some transgression he's committed in the past.

As my client who refused to show up at training camp found out for himself, an over-reliance on situational ethics actually burns the bridges in *front* of you. We all want to make it to the other side, where we can enjoy personal and professional fulfillment. Ethics and prioritizing our values gets us all to that destination in a way we can be proud of.

About Lee

The world's most famous sports agent, Leigh Steinberg pioneered the sports management industry. With an unrivaled history of record-setting contracts, Leigh has secured billions of dollars for his clients, and directed more than $600 million to various charities around the world.

He has represented many of the most successful athletes and coaches in football, basketball, baseball, hockey, boxing, golf, etc., including the number one pick in the NFL draft for an unprecedented eight times in conjunction with over 60 first round picks.

A sports business guru, author, and sought after speaker, Leigh has lectured on the business of sports entertainment around the world; he is routinely interviewed on national television and frequently quoted by major news organizations around the country.